Teaching English to Second Language Learners in Academic Contexts

Teaching English to Second Language Learners in Academic Contexts: Reading, Writing, Listening, and Speaking provides the fundamental knowledge that ESL and EFL teachers need to teach the four language skills. This foundational text, written by internationally renowned experts in the field, explains why skills-based teaching is at the heart of effective instruction in English for academic purposes (EAP) contexts. Each of the four main sections of the book helps readers understand how each skill—reading, writing, listening, and speaking—works and explains what research has to say about successful skill performance. Pedagogically focused chapters apply this information to principles for EAP curriculum design and to instructional activities and tasks adaptable in a wide range of language-learning contexts. Options for assessment and the role of digital technologies are considered for each skill, and essential information on integrated-skill instruction is provided. Moving from theory to practice, this teacher-friendly text is an essential resource for courses in TESOL programs, for in-service teacher-training seminars, and for practicing EAP teachers who want to upgrade their teaching abilities and knowledge bases.

Jonathan M. Newton is Associate Professor and Director of the MA TESOL program at Victoria University of Wellington, New Zealand.

Dana R. Ferris is Professor of Writing and Associate Director of ESL at the University of California, Davis, USA.

Christine C. M. Goh is Professor of Linguistics and Language Education at the National Institute of Education at Nanyang Technological University, Singapore.

William Grabe is Regents' Professor of Applied Linguistics at Northern Arizona University, USA.

Fredricka L. Stoller is Professor of English and Applied Linguistics at Northern Arizona University, USA.

Larry Vandergrift was Professor Emeritus from the Official Languages and Bilingualism Institute at the University of Ottawa, Canada.

ESL & Applied Linguistics Professional Series
Eli Hinkel, Series Editor

Visit **www.routledge.com/education** for additional information on titles in the ESL & Applied Linguistics Professional Series.

Teaching English to Second Language Learners in Academic Contexts

Reading, Writing, Listening, and Speaking

Jonathan M. Newton
Dana R. Ferris
Christine C. M. Goh
William Grabe
Fredricka L. Stoller and
Larry Vandergrift

Routledge
Taylor & Francis Group

NEW YORK AND LONDON

First published 2018
by Routledge
711 Third Avenue, New York, NY 10017

and by Routledge
2 Park Square, Milton Park, Abingdon, Oxon, OX14 4RN

Routledge is an imprint of the Taylor & Francis Group, an informa business

© 2018 Taylor & Francis

The right of Jonathan M. Newton, Dana R. Ferris, Christine C. M. Goh, William Grabe, Fredricka L. Stoller, and Larry Vandergrift to be identified as authors of this work has been asserted by them in accordance with sections 77 and 78 of the Copyright, Designs and Patents Act 1988.

Library of Congress Cataloging-in-Publication Data
Names: Newton, Jonathan M. author. | Ferris, Dana R. author. |
Goh, Christine Chuen Meng author.
Title: Teaching English to second language learners in academic
contexts : reading, writing, listening, and speaking / Jonathan M.
Newton, Dana R. Ferris, Christine C. M. Goh, [and two others].
Description: New York : Routledge, 2018. | Includes bibliographical
references and index.
Identifiers: LCCN 2017045380| ISBN 9781138647589
(hardback : alk. paper) | ISBN 9781138647602 (pbk. : alk. paper) |
ISBN 9781315626949 (ebook)
Subjects: LCSH: English language—Study and teaching—Foreign
speakers.
Classification: LCC PE1128.A2 N495 2018 | DDC 428.0071—dc23
LC record available at https://lccn.loc.gov/2017045380

ISBN: 978-1-138-64758-9 (hbk)
ISBN: 978-1-138-64760-2 (pbk)
ISBN: 978-1-315-62694-9 (ebk)

Typeset in Galliard
by Florence Production Ltd, Stoodleigh, Devon, UK

This volume was the brainchild of Larry Vandergrift (Professor, Official Languages and Bilingualism Institute, University of Ottawa). During the early stages of preparing the manuscript, Larry became seriously ill, and he died on November 1, 2015. With Larry's passing, we have lost a great scholar in the field of second language learning. His dedication, warmth and generosity touched the hearts and minds of researchers, teachers and graduate students all over the world, and inspired many to continue in his footsteps. As colleagues of Larry, we are proud to dedicate this volume to Larry's life and his memory.

Contents

**13 Speaking Instruction and Assessment: Activities and
Options**   **219**

**14 Language Skill Development and EAP:
A Reflection on Seven Key Themes**   **243**

Acknowledgements

We are grateful, first and foremost, to Larry Vandergrift for his leadership in the early stages of planning and writing this volume. We are also grateful to Naomi Silverman at Routledge who was a staunch supporter of Larry's vision for this book; Naomi provided invaluable guidance up until her retirement in early 2017, at which time her role was most ably taken up by Karen Alder. Our thanks also to Eli Hinkel, the series editor, for her support and expert advice.

We all acknowledge the pre-service and in-service teachers with whom we have interacted over the years. They have offered us valuable insights into the teaching of skills to students preparing for academic study in English.

Preface

We, the authors of this book, are all active in research on the language-skill development of English language learners; we are also committed to making this research relevant and useful for language teachers. Thus, we wrote this book to provide a one-stop guide—one that is theoretically principled, evidence based, and practical—to teaching the four skills of reading, writing, listening, and speaking in English for Academic Purposes (EAP) teaching contexts.

Who Is This Book for?

We wrote this book for teachers, including practising teachers who wish to refresh their professional knowledge and emerging teachers who are enrolled in teacher education programs. With its emphasis on the application of principles to actual curriculum design and skills instruction, the book is particularly relevant to TESOL methods courses in addition to pre- and in-service teachers who are interested in English for academic purposes.

With these teacher audiences in mind, we have done our best to write in a readable style, to avoid jargon, and to not overburden the text with citations. We have also provided a glossary of acronyms and abbreviations for terms that we use but that may not be familiar to all readers. Inevitably there will be instances when the reader may be motivated to gain a fuller understanding of a concept or pedagogical tool that we have introduced. For this purpose, we have provided a set of recommendations for further reading at the end of each chapter.

How Is the Book Organized?

The book begins with an opening chapter that explains why skills-based teaching is at the core of EAP instruction. In this chapter, we provide a rationale for addressing each skill separately in the book, but also illustrate how the four skills interact and interrelate in real-world contexts, including in EAP and mainstream classrooms. The first chapter also introduces four overarching assumptions that are viewed as fundamental for effective skills-based instruction in EAP contexts. These assumptions center on the importance of motivation, meaningful language use, language knowledge, and metacognitive awareness.

From these important introductory considerations explored in Chapter 1, the book is then divided into four main sections, each addressing one of the skills: reading, writing, listening, and speaking. Each section begins with a brief introduction to the particular skill, followed by three chapters. The first of these chapters describes how the skill "works" and explains what research has to say about successful skill performance. The second and third chapters are strongly pedagogically focused, addressing principles and practical steps for building a curriculum focused on each respective skill in the second chapter, and instructional activities and assessment options in the third chapter. To ensure the value of the book as a useful teacher-development tool, we have included short tasks for discussion, action, and reflection both within and at the end of each chapter.

The book concludes with a final chapter in which we explore themes that run through all four main sections and that provide a unified core of principles for teaching the four skills in programs with EAP aims. The goal of the volume, in its entirety, is to help EAP teachers, curriculum designers, and materials writers meet the skill development needs of their students and set their students up for academic success.

Larry Vandergrift's Leadership Role in the Conception of the Volume

In late 2013, Larry Vandergrift—a widely cited researcher in ESL listening and a strong advocate of making research relevant to second language teaching practice and practitioners—developed an idea for an EAP skills volume that would cover the four major language skills. His vision was for a volume that would provide both research and teaching-practice perspectives for each language skill, be authored by key researchers for each of the language skills, and be accessible for language teachers, curriculum designers, and materials developers who work with a wide range of EFL/ESL students. This volume, *Teaching English to Second Language Learners in Academic Contexts: Reading, Writing, Listening, and Speaking*, is the fulfillment of Larry's vision.

As each of us begun drafting our contributions for the volume, Larry became seriously ill. Despite his illness, Larry remained committed to the project and remained active in shaping the volume until his death on November 1, 2015. At this point, Christine Goh, who had previously published with Larry (Vandergrift & Goh, 2012) and who is a leading scholar with an international reputation for her research on listening in the language classroom, accepted an invitation to join the team of authors and complete the section on teaching listening skills.

As Larry's co-authors, we would like to acknowledge Larry as the driving force for the development of this book.

Glossary

CBI	content-based instruction
CLIL	Content and Language Integrated Instruction
CORI	Concept-Oriented Reading Instruction
DR–TA	Directed Reading–Thinking Activity
DSGO	discourse-specific graphic organizer
EAP	English for Academic Purposes
EIL	English as an International Language
EFL	English as a Foreign Language
ELT	English Language Teaching
ESL	English as a Second Language
ESP	English for Specific Purposes
IELTS	International English Language Testing System
L1	first language
L2	second language
NfM	Negotiation for Meaning
NNS	Non-Native Speaker
LRE	Language Related Episode
TBLT	Task-Based Language Teaching
TOEFL	Test of English as a Foreign Language
wpm	words per minute

1 Teaching Language Skills in EAP Contexts

Jonathan M. Newton, Fredricka L. Stoller,
William Grabe, Larry Vandergrift,
Christine C. M. Goh, and Dana R. Ferris

Skills-based teaching is at the core of EAP instruction. One of the key goals of EAP instruction is to prepare students to *use* English effectively in their academic studies, whether in managing heavy reading demands, writing varied academic genres, comprehending lectures, or participating in tutorials and group discussions. Our emphasis on language skills is not meant to diminish the importance of systematic instruction focused on building students' language knowledge, including vocabulary and grammar. Such language-focused instruction should continue throughout formal EAP classes and be integrated into skills-based EAP instruction. Ultimately, EAP programs should aim to help students develop the skills, strategies, and metacognitive awareness needed to achieve success in academic study (Alexander, Argent, & Spencer 2008; Charles & Pecorari, 2015; de Chazal, 2014).

Although we have chosen to address each of the four skills in a separate section in this volume, we are not suggesting that each skill is to be taught separately. Far from it. The skills inter-relate in many ways in language-class-room settings (and in mainstream academic classes); for example, speaking rarely occurs without listening, writing is typically connected to reading, and listening (to lectures, for instance) is usually linked to reading and writing. Even in classrooms where the skills are timetabled separately, the complex embedding of skills is usually inevitable, as when a listening comprehension activity requires students to read questions before listening and later answer the questions in writing. This kind of seamless integration of skills is also intrinsic to popular approaches to language teaching such as task-based language teaching (TBLT) and content-based instruction (CBI),[1] just as it is fundamental to using English for academic study.

Nevertheless, there are good reasons to explore the nature of each skill in its own right. First, the four skills continue to provide an organizing principle for many EAP curricula, as they do for published textbooks and high stakes international English proficiency tests such as IELTS and TOEFL. Second, to be an effective teacher of any of the four skills (taught in discrete-skill classes or in an integrated fashion) is best achieved with an understanding of the intricacies of the skills as well as expertize with skill-specific pedagogic principles and practices. For example, effective writing instruction is best accomplished when teachers (a) understand the writing process and (b) have an awareness of the various options for providing feedback on written work and the research evidence in support of these options. As another example, listening instruction is enhanced when teachers have expertize in structuring listening experiences so that students can systematically develop both bottom-up listening skills and top-down listening skills and strategies. For all four skills, teachers benefit from being familiar with skill-specific practices and understanding why certain activities or approaches are more effective than others for developing each particular skill. To this end, the guidance that we provide in this book is based on extensive research into the four skills and the effectiveness (or otherwise) of skill-specific pedagogic options.

Four Overarching Assumptions

Across the major sections in this volume are four overarching assumptions, which the reader should view as fundamental for effective skills-based instruction in EAP contexts. The first underlying assumption centers on the importance of students' positive motivation to achieve both short-term and long-term (language learning) goals. The other underlying assumptions relate to (a) the importance of meaningful language use, (b) the need to pay attention to the development of students' language knowledge (specifically vocabulary and grammar), and (c) the role and importance of students' meta-cognitive awareness in EAP contexts. In our explanation of each assumption in the sections that follow, readers will notice that we pay a little more attention to the first underlying assumption (motivation) than the others; we have done this in part because motivation is typically underrepresented in discussions of language skills instruction.

Promoting Motivation

The first underlying assumption that is relevant to all sections in this volume is the importance of students' positive *motivation* to achieve both short-term and long-term (language learning) goals. Understanding motivation in language-learning contexts requires a synthesis of psychology-based theories of motivation and language-learning research on motivation.

An effective synthesis of psychology-based theories of motivation highlights students' goals, values, and beliefs. These internally established factors translate into student behaviors through engagement, as measured by intensity of student effort, time on task, persistence in attaining outcomes, and amount of practice (Guthrie, Wigfield, & You, 2012; Schwanflugel & Knapp, 2017). The relationships among motivation, engagement, and achievement can be thought of in the following way: Motivation, facilitates engagement, which, in turn, facilitates achievement (Eccles & Wang, 2012). Motivation, in this framework, is multi-dimensional, based on several general motivation theories: Self-efficacy theory, expectancy-value theory, self-determination theory, and social motivation theory. These theories highlight student self-efficacy, values, intrinsic motivation, and peer values (Klauda & Guthrie, 2015).

Our understanding of motivation from a second language (L2) learning perspective requires that we consider other variables, which are not addressed in first-language (L1) psychology research. As an example, Dörnyei and Ushioda (2011) combine well-established psychology-based theories of motivation with a much wider range of issues particular to L2 learners, including varying levels of language proficiency, age, educational backgrounds, differing L1s and cultures, reasons for learning the L2, and family/societal expectations. The L2 learner not only has attitudes about and motivations toward learning and success, but also attitudes about L1 and L2 sociocultural contexts that impact motivation for learning as well as engagement and ultimate achievement.

Overall, research in educational psychology and L2 learning has affirmed the importance of motivation (and its complex nature). What is perhaps most important for the purposes of this book, and the teaching of the four skills, are the ways in which teachers can help build student motivation (and counter de-motivation) across EAP curricula. To build student motivation, language teachers, whatever skills they are teaching, should strive to do the following:

1. Create a learning environment that generates interest among students and that is relevant to their learning goals.
2. Talk with students about their goals for learning and relate their goals to course and curricula objectives.
3. Create a class environment that builds collaboration among students.
4. Provide many opportunities for different types of group and pair work during which students complete tasks, compare task outcomes, and reflect on what they did well and what they need to work on.
5. Provide students with plenty of opportunities for practice, along with useful feedback.
6. Give students choices with aspects of task assignments.
7. Match students' growing skills with increasing challenge in terms of learning.
8. Ensure that students carry out a good percentage of tasks successfully.
9. Give students the time needed to be successful.
10. Give students opportunities to provide you, the teacher, with feedback on how well they are learning and/or what challenges they are facing.

Structuring Lessons for Meaningful Language Use

The second of the overarching assumptions that run across this volume is that *meaningful language use* constitutes a core of skills-based instruction. This idea will not be a surprise to anyone familiar with contemporary communicative approaches to second language teaching and learning such as CBI and TBLT. The key point here for skill-based teaching is that the *uses* of language required in academic study should be addressed in the language classroom to prepare EAP students for future academic pursuits. In other words, academic skill development requires opportunities to practice meaning-focused target performance. This principle resonates with research on the transfer-appropriate processing (TAP) model of memory (Goldstein, 2015), which has shown that the way we process information determines the facets that we remember or get better at.

Developing Language Knowledge and Skills

The third assumption that pertains to language-skill instruction centers on language learners' need for opportunities to develop their *language knowledge*, which entails explicit attention to vocabulary and grammar. With regard to vocabulary, all EAP teachers, no matter the teaching context, should be committed to introducing and recycling vocabulary to promote not only vocabulary growth but also the strategies that students can use on their own to continue building their vocabulary (Nation, 2013). The number of words that are used in academic settings is large. Whatever the actual number is (there are debates about this), we know that language teachers in all class-rooms should attend to students' vocabulary learning needs.

Grammatical knowledge also contributes in important ways to reading and listening comprehension as well as effective speaking and writing. Early versions of communicative language teaching (CLT) emphasised learning through communication to the exclusion of opportunities for attending con-sciously to language form; such approaches have been shown to be ineffective in fostering balanced language development. Much debate in second language acquisition (SLA) theory and among English language teaching (ELT) professionals involves the question of just how explicit instruction on language forms can be best realized in practice. There is no simple answer. The nature of the forms (e.g., simple or complex grammatical rules), students' language proficiencies, the learning context, and students' purposes for studying language all inform teacher decision-making in this area (Doughty & Williams, 1998). In EAP contexts, generally, the goal is to provide students with plenty of guidance to increase their language knowledge alongside language skills development.

Raising Metacognitive Awareness

Fourth and finally is the assumption that skill development in EAP contexts can be enhanced through learner *metacognition*. Metacognition is our ability to think about our thinking and how we process information and manage learning. For the purposes of this volume, we are referring to the learning of language skills for academic purposes. The good news is that metacognition can be taught. An important outcome of raising students' metacognitive awareness is the ability for students to self-regulate learning; that is, they set goals for their learning and then monitor, regulate, and control their cognition and motivation (Pintrich, 2000). In language-learning contexts, self-regulated language learners have the ability to manage the language-learning process and the outcome(s) of specific language tasks to maximize learning. Self-regulated learners can also select, manage, and evaluate their own language development inside and outside the classroom. Students who are aware of the benefits of specific language-learning strategies may also consciously use these strategies to improve their overall ability to process and use the target language. Students who are conscious of the challenges that they face in their own language learning may also be motivated to find ways of addressing them.

Given the important role of metacognition in successful language learning, the pedagogical approaches and activities presented in this book will help students develop richer metacognitive knowledge about themselves as language learners in addition to the nature and demands of each of the four language skills. With teacher guidance, students will learn to plan, monitor, problem solve, and evaluate the effectiveness of their language use and the progress of their overall language development. When integrated with well-planned tasks, the building of students' metacognitive awareness can be a powerful tool for improving skill development and learner motivation.

These four overarching assumptions—namely motivation, meaningful language use, attention to students' language knowledge (vocabulary and grammar), and metacognitive awareness—represent basic foundations for our understanding of skills-based language teaching. In addition to these foundational ideas, the reader will notice a number of common themes explicitly addressed across the four sections of the volume. In the final chapter of the book, we offer our views on these important themes, common across language skill areas.

Further Reading

Alexander, O., Argent, S., & Spencer, J. (2008). *EAP essentials: A teacher's guide to principles and practice*. Reading, UK: Garnet Education.

Charles, M., & Pecorari, D. (2015). *Introducing English for academic purposes*. New York, NY: Routledge.

Dalton-Puffer, C. (2017). Same but different: Content and language integrated learning and content-based instruction. In M. A. Snow & D. M. Brinton (Eds.), *The content-based classroom: New perspectives on integrating language and content* (2nd ed., pp. 151–164). Ann Arbor, MI: University of Michigan Press.

de Chazal, E. (2014). *English for academic purposes*. Oxford: Oxford University Press.

Dörnyei, Z., & Ushioda, E. (2011). *Teaching and researching motivation* (2nd ed.). New York, NY: Routledge.

Doughty, C. J., & Williams, J. (1998). Pedagogical choices in focus on form. In C. J. Doughty & J. Williams (Eds.), *Focus on form in classroom second language acquisition* (pp. 197–261). Cambridge: Cambridge University Press.

Eccles, J., & Wang, M. (2012). Part I commentary: So what is student engagement anyway? In S. Christiansen, A. Reschly, & C. Wylie (Eds.), *Handbook of research on student engagement* (pp. 133–145). New York, NY: Springer Science.

Ericsson, A., & Pool, R. (2016). *Peak: Secrets from the new science of expertize.* Boston, MA: Houghton Mifflin Harcourt.

Goldstein, E. B. (2015). *Cognitive psychology: Connecting mind, research and everyday experience.* Stamford, CT: Cengage Learning.

Guthrie, J., Wigfield, A., & You, W. (2012). Instructional contexts for engagement and achievement in reading. In S. Christiansen, A. Reschly, & C. Wylie (Eds.), *Handbook of research on student engagement* (pp. 601–634). New York, NY: Springer Science.

Klauda, S., & Guthrie, J. (2015). Comparing relations of motivation, engagement, and achievement among struggling and advanced adolescent readers. *Reading & Writing, 28*(2), 239–269.

Nation, I. S. P. (2013). *Learning vocabulary in another language* (2nd ed.). New York, NY: Cambridge University Press.

Pintrich, P. R. (2000). The role of goal orientation in self-regulated learning. In M. Boekaerts, P. R. Pintrich, & M. Zeidner (Eds.), *Handbook of self-regulation* (Vol. 451, pp. 451–502). San Diego, CA: Academic Press.

Schwanenflugel, P., & Knapp, N. (2017). *The psychology of reading.* New York, NY: Guilford Press.

Notes

1   Also known as content and language integrated instruction (CLIL) in Europe (Dalton-Puffer, 2017).

Section 1

Introduction to Reading

William Grabe and Fredricka L. Stoller

In our three-chapter section on second-language reading for academic purposes, we have three simple goals:

- to describe, in an accessible way, what reading comprehension is, how it works, and how it varies in different contexts;
- to build upon our understanding of current research on reading and reading development with a set of 12 curricular principles that can guide effective reading instruction; and
- to introduce teaching techniques and assessment options—supported by research evidence, principles of reading curriculum design, and our collective teaching experiences—that can be incorporated into instruction as ways to engage students in becoming better readers.

We wrote these chapters believing that reading comprehension abilities in academic contexts, and the ability to use information learned from reading, are critical for student success in secondary and post-secondary settings (Anderson, 2015). This view of reading highlights the importance of understanding what skilled readers do so that we can build effective pathways for teaching reading and support the development of second-language students' reading abilities.

We have organized our first chapter (Chapter 2) around 11 key questions about reading comprehension. The answers to these "Frequently Asked Questions" explain fundamental ideas about the nature of skilled reading. Our second chapter (Chapter 3), building upon what we know about skilled reading and reading-skills development, provides guidelines that can be used by teachers, materials writers, and curriculum designers to shape effective reading instruction and efficient instructional design. Our third chapter (Chapter 4) is divided into three sections: (a) teaching techniques for improving students' reading abilities, (b) techniques for integrating reading and writing, and (c) issues related to reading assessment.

With regard to Chapters 3 and 4, we'd like to add a few additional comments. First, it is important to note that there are no curricular principles that apply equally across all student groups and instructional settings. Prioritizing certain curricular principles over others is the responsibility of teachers (as they get to know their students), curriculum designers, materials writers, and program administrators. Despite these caveats, the evidence-based principles that we introduce in Chapter 3 represent an excellent starting point for those reviewing, renewing, and/or developing second-language reading curricula.

Second, in Chapter 4, we describe good teaching and assessment ideas that put into practice the curricular guidelines in Chapter 3 and the research synthesis in Chapter 2. Most of these practical techniques can be adapted for students at different proficiency levels; ideas that seem appropriate for lower-level students, for example, may be exactly what students at more advanced levels need to practice (e.g., reading fluency). Space does not permit a full inventory of good teaching and assessment ideas for reading instruction. The in-text references and further readings listed at the end of the chapter can be referred to for additional ideas.

Third, and more generally, we understand that most teachers and curriculum designers work within program constraints and with mandated textbooks. Recognizing these constraints, there are still opportunities for teachers to make small changes in their ways of teaching to improve students' reading abilities. We encourage teachers to explore the ideas introduced in Chapters 3 and 4, perhaps testing them out with informal "experiments" (or action research) to determine their effectiveness.

Finally, we know that students in more advanced academic settings often seek simple solutions for reading mastery. We have a simple solution, but not a quick one. The bottom line is that students can only become more skilled readers in academic settings if they read, read a lot, and read for a variety of well-defined purposes.

2   How Reading Comprehension Works

William Grabe and Fredricka L. Stoller

Second- and foreign-language learners who are studying English for academic purposes need to develop and eventually master more advanced reading abilities. In academic settings (that is, in secondary and post-secondary contexts), reading serves as a primary means for conveying informational content to be learned. The information (and related vocabulary) that students learn from reading is typically needed for academic writing, speaking, and listening tasks. Rather than leaving reading-skill development to chance (as many teachers do because they are not trained to teach reading and/or they do not see it as their responsibility), teachers can do a lot to help students become better readers. Understanding reading comprehension, and all it entails, greatly assists novice and experienced teachers in becoming effective reading teachers.

The purpose of this chapter is to provide a clear explanation of reading comprehension, focusing on these various perspectives:

- how reading comprehension works;
- how it differs for first-language (L1) and second-language (L2) students;
- how it varies based on L2 students' language proficiency, the reading task, text difficulty, text types, and students' social and educational backgrounds;
- how it is learned.

Teachers can use this foundational knowledge to help build effective reading curricula (or improve reading curricula) and decide what teaching techniques to incorporate into their lessons (discussed in Chapters 3 and 4). The overriding goal of this chapter is to provide teachers with a better understanding of reading so that they can help their students become more skilled readers who can succeed in their studies and future employment.

Our explanation of reading comprehension begins from the perspective of the fluent L1 reader to show how reading comprehension works for good readers. The fluent L1 reader creates the benchmark for what the L2 student needs to work toward and the various challenges to be surmounted. The chapter is organized around a series of questions. Providing answers to these questions should build a coherent picture of reading comprehension. This overview culminates with evidence-based criteria around which to build instructional curricula for reading-skill development.

Who Reads and Who Needs to Read?

Being a good reader is important for educational and economic opportunities worldwide.[1] Although literacy skills (reading and writing) do not guarantee economic success, academic achievement, or social security, *not* having good literacy skills makes educational and economic lifetime goals difficult to achieve. Students with academic goals for secondary and post-secondary degrees certainly need to be good readers. In our three chapters on L2 reading development, we focus on the academically oriented L2 learner.

What Do We Read and Why Do We Read?

At a simple level, we can say that we read, in print and digital formats, for pleasure, study, work, and everyday activities. We read entertaining books

---

Task 2.1

Reflect on the print and digital reading that you regularly engage in. With what types of texts do you find reading easy and enjoyable? With what types of texts do you find reading challenging? What accounts for those challenges? What steps do you take to overcome the challenges that you face when reading?

Task 2.2

In what language(s) do you read? If you read in more than one language, what differences do you encounter when reading in one or the other? What do you think are the causes of these differences?

Task 2.3

Make a list of 8 things that you've read in the past 24 hours: Why did you read these "texts"?
Now, make a list of everything that you can remember looking at (reading) in the past 24 hours. How long is your list?

magazines, textbooks, professional materials, e-mails, web pages, text messages, and newspapers. We also read flyers, notes, announcements, cereal boxes, directions, ads, and dozens of other written messages throughout a day if we are good readers.

Good readers always read for a purpose. In one sense, *having a purpose for reading is the foundation for everything we do when we read.* We might read a novel in the evening to be entertained or to relax after a busy day. We read websites for quick access to information, possibly to remain current with global news. We read magazines and newspapers (in print or digitally) to become more informed on topics of interest. We read academic and/or professional materials to complete school/workplace tasks and to develop expertize in targeted areas. We read social media to stay connected with a wide group of people, including family and close friends. This list of purposeful reading activities could be expanded much further.

Academically, we read for a number of purposes, one being that we read to fulfill teacher expectations. More specifically, academic reading tasks entail reading to find answers to questions, to learn new ideas and related details, to develop expertize, to synthesize information from across a long text or multiple texts, to look for evidence for an argument or position, and to critique someone's ideas. Each purpose requires that we read in different ways. For example, when we read texts that are perceived to be important for a high-stakes academic task, we read with a higher level of attention, with more strategic awareness, and often at a slower pace. We judge our successes in understanding the texts that we read based on how deeply we need to extract ideas and information from the text to meet our reading goals (often referred to as setting a higher or lower "standard of coherence" for reading comprehension). Our reading behaviors change because of other factors too, including (but not limited to) text type, text difficulty, reading proficiency, motivation, and amount of prior practice with the text and/or task type. Certainly, reading more challenging texts, as we are likely to do in academic settings, engages our reading abilities in different ways from reading easy and enjoyable texts.

> **Quote:** "Common reading goals include reading to study; reading for entertainment; reading to search for information (scanning or skimming); reading to learn; reading to integrate information from multiple sources (e.g., multiple texts or text and graphics); reading to evaluate, critique, and use information; and reading for general comprehension."
>
> (van den Broek & Kendeou, 2015, p. 109)

What Is Reading Comprehension?

If reading varies somewhat depending on purpose, how can we talk about reading comprehension as a single idea? Certainly, we can talk about skimming a text (for the gist), reading for a writing task, reading carefully to retain details, reading critically to determine the value of information presented, and reading to understand main ideas (and some details). All of these reading goals require the same underlying cognitive skills, but with different levels of attention for specific sub-skills. For example, skimming a text to generate some quick idea about the information in the text may involve (a) just reading the first sentence of select paragraphs, (b) reading the first paragraph and then skipping to the concluding paragraph, or (c) reading the first paragraph, skipping some sentences, and slowing down to read the last two paragraphs more carefully. Reading to learn, which is quite distinct from skimming, usually occurs with more challenging academic texts; it involves more careful attention to details, slower reading rates, the interpretation of details in relation to background knowledge, and the use of combinations of reading strategies to understand challenging concepts. Unlike skimming and reading to learn, reading for main idea comprehension (the principal goal of fluent L1 readers in the course of a day) requires a combination of the following: (a) a reading rate of 250 to 300 words per minute (for fluent L1 readers); (b) consistent automatic processing of vocabulary and grammatical structures in the text; (c) processing of semantic information in each sentence; (d) the ability to read in this way for an extended period of time; and (e) fewer strategies—because the text is likely less challenging than a conceptually dense academic text. Reading for main idea comprehension is less demanding than some other reading-related tasks (e.g., reading to write a synthesis of multiple texts).

Despite the variability in how we read different texts for specific purposes, the basic mental machinery for reading comprehension is generally consistent. Thus, we can talk about reading comprehension as a singular activity. As an analogy, we can think of reading comprehension much like a car. We have fairly consistent expectations that cars have certain capabilities, but we make use of different features as we need them: We use the gas pedal to accelerate; we use turn signals when appropriate; we use windshield wipers when it is raining; we use lights when it is dark. But in all cases, the car can get us to our destination because of the features that all cars have in common.

So we can make a simple statement defining reading comprehension: *Reading comprehension is the ability to extract, interpret, and use information from a print or digital text.* This brief statement is accurate, but it does not tell us very much about what we actually do mentally when we read (or how we might use the information read). As mentioned earlier, when we read to understand a text, we always read for a purpose and with a more specific goal in mind. But we also do more.

What Skills and Abilities Support Reading Comprehension for Good Readers?

We use a wide range of cognitive skills and language knowledge resources when we engage in reading comprehension activities (Geva & Ramírez, 2015; Perfetti & Adlof, 2012). We can talk about these skills in terms of lower-level processing and higher-level processing. Let's consider the differences between these two types of processing, both required for efficient reading.

Lower-level processes typically require the following abilities/language resources:

- rapid and accurate word recognition (i.e., lexical access), especially for high-frequency words;
- a large recognition vocabulary;
- good syntactic knowledge of the language;
- good tacit awareness of text structure and organizational patterns, which vary by writer purpose and by written genre;
- formulation of main ideas from text processing;
- fluent and usually automatic extended text processing.

Among these various lower-level skills and language abilities, multiple studies of developing L2 readers have shown vocabulary knowledge and grammatical knowledge, in particular, to be very strong predictors of reading comprehension abilities.

Lower-level skills involve the processing of multiple types of linguistic knowledge (e.g., word forms, phrasal groupings, pronoun references, word ordering information, words with multiple meanings) and some strategic responses to text processing (e.g., rereading a sentence) when momentary comprehension challenges are experienced, for example, when encountering an odd structuring of a sentence, or a few unknown words that seem important. Lower-level processing, among skilled readers, generally becomes automatized as a result of consistent and extended practice. What *automaticity* means for good readers is the ability to carry out these processes without needing to make conscious decisions about them or reflect on them. (Note that lower-level skills does not mean easier, but rather, more likely to be automatized. Good readers actually cannot control lower-level skills, except when these lower-level processing skills do not work well for some reason.)

Higher-level processing of texts, on the other hand, is much more accessible to conscious awareness. Higher-level processes include the ability to:

- recognize and infer less obvious main ideas or textual connections;
- mentally summarize main ideas, synthesize information, and read critically;
- monitor comprehension and make repairs as needed;

- read challenging texts strategically (using multiple comprehension strategies in combination to improve understanding);
- apply text information to complex academic or professional tasks;
- use background knowledge (i.e., knowledge of the world, prior educational experiences, family and community knowledge, cultural knowledge) appropriately; and
- direct attention to specific text features that support comprehension or specific interpretations.

When good readers encounter texts that are challenging to comprehend, they are able to consciously consider what they are trying to do, attend to problems in processing, and reflect on whether they have been successful in solving comprehension difficulties (or not).

Both lower-level and higher-level processing are important for successful reading comprehension and they occur almost simultaneously when lower-level processes are automatized. These two major levels of processing require two fundamental instructional building blocks for reading skill development:

- getting a lot of practice reading (so that automaticity will develop over time) and;
- learning to be strategic (so that one can handle complex, challenging texts and tasks).

Both building blocks are needed for the development of advanced reading comprehension abilities.

> **Quote:** "As a reader proceeds through a text, each new input (e.g., sentence) triggers a new set of cognitive processes. Some of these processes are automatic; others are strategic, initiated by the reader to create coherence."
>
> (Helder, van den Broek, Van Leijenhorst, & Beker, 2013, p. 44)

These two major levels of processing, however, do not provide a complete picture of the skills needed for reading comprehension. Readers also make use of cognitive resources that go beyond linguistic knowledge bases and specific reading processes. They are the cognitive resources that we use more generally to navigate our way through everyday life (and academic life). They include:

- memory skills, especially working memory skills (which retain active information and integrate information and processes to construct comprehension);

- background knowledge and connections across knowledge bases;
- inferencing, using background knowledge, and connecting textual information;
- the ability to read for extended periods of time (which results from practice, persistence, and positive attitudes); and
- motivation to be a good reader and achieve task success.

Specifying the lower-level processes, higher-level processes, and cognitive resources needed to achieve reading comprehension is important for understanding reading comprehension. But our discussion, thus far, does not explain *how* we read for comprehension—what we are actually doing from moment to moment.

How Does Reading Comprehension Work?

Reading comprehension is truly a miraculous ability that most people gradually learn to control and use with the help of more knowledgeable others. The human brain has evolved genetically only for spoken language production and comprehension (speaking and listening). Thus, generations of readers have had to *learn* to process written language (words and structures); in fact, they have learned to process written language even faster than spoken language input by redirecting brain functions that are originally predisposed genetically for spoken language processing. We have also learned over time to store, activate, and process aspects of written language information in different parts of the brain (Dehaene, 2009). If we are not taught to read by some mentor or teacher, we will not become readers. Given these differences between spoken production/comprehension and reading, it is remarkable that so many people, with appropriate support, become such good readers.

Automatic Processing of Lower-Level Skills

In the process of learning how to read, we humans make good use of general cognitive abilities. As a result of gradually developing a large store of vocabulary for reading purposes, and engaging in thousands of hours of practice (during school years and before), we become able to automatically identify words, recognize word meanings, process information from grammatical structures, and access basic meaning ideas from clauses. It turns out that we humans are amazingly fast pattern recognizers and we are also extraordinary at tacitly learning statistical probabilities for what to expect when we read (Dehaene, 2009; Seidenberg, 2017).

As skilled readers, we recognize almost all the words that we see on a written or digital page. When reading, we move our eyes approximately nine letter spaces forward with each jump (saccade) of our eyes. This eye-movement process is consistent and automatized as well. Skilled readers recognize, in focused vision, over 80 percent of the content words in a text and about

50 percent of the short function words. We are so fast that we focus on 4 to 5 words per second for every second that we are reading fluently (with non-challenging texts). We stop at each word roughly on average for 240 milliseconds (about a quarter of a second). When we read 4 to 5 words per second, we read 240 to 300 words per minute (wpm). (How did we calculate this? 4–5 words per second × 60 seconds per minute = 240–300 wpm.) We actually only need one tenth of a second, on average, to recognize a newly focused word. The rest of the time is used to connect the word to growing clause information, to meaning idea units, and to growing text meaning as we link meaning idea units (Grabe, 2009). Although good readers themselves are not aware that all this is going on (because it happens automatically), hundreds of eye-tracking studies have consistently shown this picture of the automatic processing of texts; that is, the picture of how we read (Rayner, Pollatsek, Ashby, & Clifton Jr., 2012).

Figure 2.1 Higher-level processing activities that occur while reading

• monitoring comprehension • recognizing non-comprehension moments • making basic inferences that connect information across clauses and different parts of prior text • building and keeping active a set of main ideas for text meaning • connecting main ideas and text meaning to background knowledge as appropriate	• using strategies for repairing (mis)comprehension with more challenging texts • reassessing the level of understanding needed to attain reading goals (i.e., the "standard of coherence" desired) • determining if the information seems to fit prior knowledge • deciding if the information is interesting • deciding whether or not to continue reading

Higher-Level Processing of Texts

At the same time that we, as fluent readers, are engaged continually with the "relatively cost-free" automatic processing of lower-level linguistic information, we are also engaged in a number of higher-level processing activities (the other portion of the 240 milliseconds per word beyond automatic word recognition), as shown in Figure 2.1. Ultimately, it is the combination of lower-level processing and higher-level processing that leads to reading comprehension if the text, content, and task are not too difficult (Cain & Oakhill, 2012).

The Text Model of Comprehension and the Situation Model of Text Interpretation

When we read, we put together a set of main ideas from the text that are emphasized in various ways and that make sense with respect to our emerging expectations. As we read multiple paragraphs and multiple pages, we create two models of the information in our brains: A text model and a situation model (Kintsch, 2012). The *text model* is our mental construction of what we believe the *writer* is trying to convey in the text. While constructing a text model, we do not decide if the text information is wrong or right, we do not decide to agree or disagree with the author, and we do our best to understand the text as it is, that is, as the author intends. In sum, we try to generate an overall summary of the text's main ideas with relatively little reader bias. Roughly, good readers generate very similar text model summaries, depending, of course, on the type of text being read and the type of task being assigned (explained further below).

Most readers have had the experience of reading a text and thinking that they know what the author is saying, but they find that they may disagree with the author or with other readers. And they can think of one or more reasons for the disagreement. In these cases, the reader is first generating a text model and then almost simultaneously filtering it through their growing situation model, influenced by personal interpretation. The *situation model*, then, is generated by readers as they interpret the texts that they read. More specifically, the situation model that we produce results from our interpretation of text information in light of reading purpose, background knowledge, task difficulty, perceived importance of text information, evaluation of text information, attitude toward the text and the author, level of motivation to continue the task, and possibly other factors.

Readers develop both a text model and situation model (the latter based on personal interpretation) when they read, especially when reading academic texts with more challenging goals. Some examples might help demonstrate how and why reading requires these two levels of text comprehension. Differing text types highlight the differences between a text model of comprehension and a situation model of interpretation. Let's start by considering texts that privilege the *situation model of interpretation*. Poems are written to be interpreted; we could say that poems are written to tap our situation-model capabilities. Poems can be opaque (but moving); they can be limited in the information provided and force the reader to fill in some set of background information; poems invite the reader to interpret some level of meaning that is personal to the reader. There is no one way to summarize a poem that is agreed upon by a group of good readers, even if some aspects of the poem can generate a basic (and usually underspecified) text model. Though quite distinct from poems, political editorials and opinion pieces also privilege the situation model of interpretation. When reading them, we can be very critical and make evaluative interpretations (or not) depending on who the writer is, what the publication source is, who/what is discussed, and what stance is taken by the author. As readers of such texts, we are flooded with inferences about underlying messages, attitudes toward topic and author, and our goals for reading.

The need to generate a *text model of comprehension* is the primary goal for other types of texts (and tasks). In academic and professional environments, we are often asked to summarize information from a text, sometimes as a preliminary step to a critique of the text or other tasks. A much more extreme example of privileging a text model is with a procedural manual that provides directions for shutting down a nuclear reactor when it is overheating. It does not matter who is reading the manual. What is important is that the information is processed the exact same way by all readers, every time the manual is read. A manual for shutting down a nuclear reactor is not at all like a poem that is open to reader interpretation. In these instances, the situation model closely mirrors the text model.

General Cognitive Skills

Additional factors impact reading comprehension. For example, motivation for reading, in general, and motivation for completing specific reading-related tasks, more specifically, are important factors that influence reading comprehension. Working memory is an additional cognitive factor that plays a very important role in reading comprehension. A further, and somewhat obvious, factor in understanding reading comprehension centers on the limits of L2 proficiency and background knowledge that vary considerably among L2 readers (addressed later in this chapter).

In closing this section, we return to the idea of reading comprehension as a truly amazing ability. A particularly revealing way to think about the miracle of reading is to consider what a good reader does (or can do) in a two-second span of time while reading, as outlined in Figure 2.2.

It is important to remember that all of the items in Figure 2.2—beyond the first one—are, or may be, occurring more or less at the same time that the mind is identifying five new words and accessing their meanings each second. Even more remarkable is the fact that we can read for extended periods of time doing this kind of processing. Even more startling is that we often do this for enjoyment and can do this for an hour without stopping! The wonder is how we do not all get headaches after any five minutes of engaging in this type of cognitive processing. Most amazing of all, actually, is how many people become strong fluent readers in a second or even a third language.

How Does L2 Reading Differ from L1 Reading?

Up to this point in the chapter, we have made the general assumption that L1 and L2 reading abilities share many of the same skills, and that the reading construct is very similar in terms of underlying cognitive and linguistic compo-

Figure 2.2 What a good reader does (or can do) in only two seconds of reading

---

00:02	**In any two seconds, a good reader . . .**

1. focuses on and recognizes about 10 different words;
2. extracts from these words grammatical information (e.g., who is doing what to whom and how);
3. uses this grammar context and signaling to identify the right word meaning (because many content words have multiple meanings and change their meaning depending on whether they are used as verbs, nouns, adjectives, etc.);
4. forms phrase- and clause-level idea units to be assembled into a larger clause unit;
5. finds connections across new and prior phrase and clause units where information overlaps (to build a larger set of coherent meaning units and main ideas);
6. identifies main ideas that emerge from text and word signals or from consistently repeated ideas and information;
7. decides how a newly emerging main idea candidate fits in with the growing overall text meaning;
8. uses background knowledge, as appropriate, for greater comprehension;
9. monitors comprehension and recognizes instances of non-comprehension;
10. adjusts strategies for processing information as needed;
11. evaluates the information and its possible uses;
12. decides if the information is interesting, useful, and/or task relevant;
13. decides if s/he likes the information;
14. decides to continue reading or not.

---

nents. In most respects, this is a reasonable position to take. At the same time, any consideration of L2 reading abilities has to recognize the several ways in which L2 reading abilities and experiences differ from L1 reading abilities and experiences (Chen, Dronjic, & Helms-Park, 2016). Most of these differences (Figure 2.3) center, either directly or indirectly, on the linguistic resources that a reader can bring to bear on text comprehension.

A growing debate exists about the extent of the differences between L1 and L2 readers (Chen, Dronjic, & Helms-Park, 2016; Geva & Ramírez, 2015; Koda, 2016). Drawing on the arguments made by numerous key researchers, a number of statements can be made about these differences:

- First, beginning and intermediate L2 reading abilities are more distinct from L1 reading abilities than advanced L2 reading abilities are. As L2 readers become fluent and highly skilled in reading comprehension, the reading processes involved become more similar (though perhaps never the same).

- Second, the extent of the linguistic differences between the L1 and the L2 (e.g., the linguistic differences between Spanish and English vs. Chinese and English) will have an impact on L2 reading. The impact of L1/L2 differences diminishes with increasing L2 reading proficiency (but will not disappear).
- Third, higher-level processing skills will be potentially the same in both L1 and L2 contexts because they relate to comprehension skills more generally, and they are not strongly constrained by limited amounts of linguistic knowledge. Nonetheless, practice and instructional support are needed to help L2 learners use these higher-level skills with more challenging L2 texts.

Figure 2.3 Ways in which L2 reading abilities differ from L1 reading abilities

- L2 learners have a much smaller set of L2 linguistic knowledge resources (e.g., vocabulary, grammar, and discourse structure awareness) to draw upon as they are developing their L2 reading abilities.
- L2 students, overall, have much less experience with reading in the L2. They simply will have had much less practice in L2 reading. (And we know the important impact of continual practice.)
- L2 students experience L2 reading differently because they have experiences reading in two (or more) languages and because cognitive processing involves two language systems (e.g., accessing the bilingual lexicon, knowing what successful reading feels like in the L1 (or not), using a joint strategic processing system [Koda, 2016]).
- L2 learners may have developed somewhat distinct cognitive processing depending on the L1s they learned to read.
- L2 students experience a range of transfer effects from their L1 reading skills (including cognitive skills, strategies, goals, and expectations). Some transfer effects involve L1 interference; others support L2 reading processes (Dressler & Kamil, 2006).
- L2 learners rely on different combinations of general background knowledge when reading in the L2. Prior educational experiences, community culture, and life experiences will differ from student to student and between students as will their academic expectations of the L2 classroom.
- L2 students encounter distinct social and cultural assumptions in L2 texts that they may not be familiar with or find somewhat hard to accept.
- L2 learners often have different motivations for reading in the L2 (than will L1 readers), depending on their academic and life goals.

It is also worth pointing out that for L1 and L2 readers, the *underlying cognitive processes* involved are generally the same (e.g., working memory, speed of processing), but the linguistic limitations, limited experiences with reading practice, and the fact that two languages are simultaneously available create real L1–L2 differences. These differences remain until L2 linguistic resources and processing abilities have grown sufficiently strong and fluent. In fact, as L2 reading abilities improve in the areas specified in Figure 2.4, reading comprehension processes for L1 and L2 reading look increasingly similar, although not with exactly the same patterns and combinations of strengths for comprehension.

Figure 2.4 Areas in which improvements need to be made in the L2 for L1 and L2 reading comprehension processes to become more similar

---

- greater amounts of reading practice and exposure to L2 print;
- greater resource knowledge of the L2 and L2 sociocultural contexts;
- greater amounts of content knowledge in specific domains;
- greater fluency and automaticity in L2 reading skills;
- increased numbers of successes in L2 reading and the recognition of those successes.

Quote: "Patterns of brain activity in L2 processing appear to converge on L1 patterns with increased experience with a language and with higher proficiency levels."

(Dronjic & Bitan, 2016, p. 45)

Why Do L2 Reading Abilities Differ So Much from Person to Person?

One final piece of the puzzle remains about L1 and L2 reading differences. Among L1 readers in school settings, almost all learners become readers in the L1, even if not at the levels "expected" for their grade levels and ages. Among L2 students, we find much more widely varying outcomes with respect to learning success. That is to say, L2 learners vary widely in their levels of success in developing L2 reading comprehension abilities. There are many reasons for this variation. For example, L2 reading is often not critical for students' future academic or work success (because reading in the L2 is not an expectation). Sometimes L2 reading development is only driven by a need to pass a test or complete a course. Sometimes students are more or less motivated depending on their personal goals. Sometimes L2 reading is needed to achieve fairly narrow academic or professional goals. These reasons, and others, allow L2 students to stop L2 learning at various stages without any stigma of being labeled "a poor reader."

How Fluent Should L2 Readers Become?

The obvious answer to this question is *as fluent as possible*. Fluent reading is critical for L2 readers *who need to read a lot*, either for academic or professional purposes. In fact, one cannot be a strong L2 reader without being fluent. Unfortunately, L2 students generally read more slowly than comparable L1 students.

Becoming a fluent L2 reader requires a lot of practice and a lot of effort over time. A fluent reader is not only fast, but also accurate; without accuracy, comprehension suffers. L2 reading fluency, in fact, is somewhat complex. A fluent reader must have a very large recognition vocabulary, including auto-matized processing of just about all high-frequency words. In addition, a fluent reader must know how to adjust his/her reading rates in response to goals, text difficulties, and task requirements.

Assuming that fluency is an important goal as students become better L2 readers, some basic questions about reading fluency need to be asked: What is a good reading rate for L2 reading comprehension? How and why does reading fluency vary? The bottom line is that reading rates vary not only because of students' reading proficiency, but also because of different types of texts being read, different purposes for reading, and different levels of text difficulty. English L1 students read at about 200 wpm when they reach 8th grade (about 13 years old), and that rate is after a few thousand hours of reading practice and new vocabulary being learned continuously. (See Figure 3.3, in the next chapter, for a more detailed overview of fluency rates for L1 readers, when they are reading for different purposes.) Over time, and with extended practice, we might expect adolescent and adult L2 readers to read for general understanding at about 200 wpm, recognizing that there will be a lot of variability. As a final note, even fairly good L2 readers will read difficult texts much more slowly, just as L1 readers read difficult texts more slowly too.

How Does Reading Behavior Vary When the Goal Is Reading to Learn?

L2 students who need to read for academic purposes must learn to handle (with teacher scaffolding) more challenging, academic texts in order to carry out a range of academic learning tasks. This goal is at the heart of reading for academic purposes. In academic contexts, and for learning purposes, L2 students need to learn to:

*   understand and interpret information and ideas accurately;
*   summarize information from a text;

- synthesize information from multiple parts of a text or across texts;
- use background knowledge appropriately;
- critically evaluate materials and ideas from texts; and
- use text information for a range of academic tasks.

Often, these tasks and associated texts are fairly challenging and require intensively focused reading comprehension skills as well as a number of reading strategies that help students address text and content difficulties while they are reading. With a lot of practice, L2 students become strategic readers as they become more proficient in L2 reading for (and in) academic settings. In the process of becoming more strategic, L2 readers engage more effectively with challenging texts to learn new ideas and apply them. Becoming a strategic reader requires a lot of practice, not only by reading more challenging texts, but also by practicing and talking about the uses of combinations of strategies to resolve text comprehension difficulties.

How Does Digital Reading Vary from Print Reading?

As we move further into the 21st century, the role of digital literacy in the lives of readers has taken on greater importance. Beyond reading texts on computers, readers now find texts in many digital formats on websites and smart phones, and in blogs, tweets, text messages, and Facebook entries, to name just a few digital venues. The current debate (which will likely be ongoing) is whether or not digital media create texts and reading purposes that take us beyond the skills and strategies needed to comprehend print media. Points of view range from (a) digital media leading to radically different ways of reading and learning to read to (b) digital reading presenting some new challenges for readers, but the underlying reading skills are essentially the same. From our perspective, it is unlikely that digital reading skills will substitute in some way for fundamental reading abilities needed for print media.

Digital media now exist in environments that represent new contexts for reading and a wide range of new text types (Cho & Afflerbach, 2017; van den Broek & Kendeou, 2015). These new contexts and text types certainly create the need for new reading skills and strategies that learners must master. In digital contexts, students need to learn to navigate, effectively and efficiently, multiple websites while searching for information (e.g., understanding which keywords and descriptors to use for informational website searches). They need to work harder to focus on their goals for reading as they can become easily distracted by other pathways. They need to recognize (requiring more critical reading) (a) issues of bias and interpretation of information on different websites, (b) the (un)reliability of information, and (c) the sources of website information (e.g., commercial versus non-commercial). Learners also need to keep track of the array of digital materials accessed in the midst of moving from website to website, or across website links, and identify and recall where information comes from. Learners also need to be able to critically evaluate sources of information for relevance and usefulness. Finally, they need to find ways to evaluate and integrate multiple sets of information that may not fit well together or even be somewhat contradictory. These skill requirements are especially important for academic and professional uses of digital material.

Some of these skills and strategies are also important for working with multiple print texts for a series of tasks; thus, the print versus digital text dichotomy is not a clear-cut divide. Certainly, these issues put to the test any assumptions that working with digital texts will be easier for students or more helpful for learning purposes (Bauerlein, 2015; Kamil, 2015).

The problems that arise in discussions about the changing role of digital texts and online literacy in students' lives relate to the assumption that digital reading skills will be easier for learners because most younger people have grown up with digital access from an early age. However, reading to learn new information, and then use that information for academic and professional tasks, still requires the mastery of skills for reading comprehension discussed throughout this chapter. If anything, reading an array of digital materials, when used for academic purposes, creates new challenges that require additional instructional support as readers become more proficient. Moreover, searching through e-mails, tweets, Facebook entries, blogs, chats, text messages, and related texts does not generally develop the reading comprehension skills that students need for more advanced academic tasks with much longer texts.

Having pointed out these complexities for L2 learners, it is nonetheless true that the modern world requires facility with understanding an array of digital texts as well as print texts. As a consequence, digital texts should become an integral part of reading comprehension instruction. At the same time, despite efforts to champion new media, there is no clear research evidence that learning to read through digital media is in any way more effective as an instructional option than learning to read with print media. Moreover, reading instruction delivered through digital formats has not yet become a common subject of well-controlled research. At present, studies that do focus on instruction through digital formats have not yet reported any clear advantages for learners. We are likely to see more research in this area and only time will tell what implications emerge for reading instruction.

How Does Reading Comprehension Research Inform L2 Reading Pedagogy?

To conclude this chapter, we pose our last question about the connections between reading research findings and reading pedagogy. Overall, the combination of research on L1 and L2 reading abilities suggests important implications for L2 reading instruction, as itemized in Figure 2.5.

Figure 2.5 Implications from L1 and L2 reading research for L2 reading instruction

Reading comprehension requires the following skills and knowledge resources, to varying degrees depending on learners' L2 proficiency levels:

1. ability to decode graphic forms for efficient word recognition;
2. ability to access the meanings of a large number of words automatically;
3. ability to draw appropriate meaning from phrase- and clause-level grammatical information;
4. ability to combine clausal-level meanings to build a larger network of meaning relations (to comprehend the text);
5. ability to recognize discourse-level relationships and use this information to build and support comprehension;
6. ability to set goals for reading and adjust them as needed;
7. ability to use reading strategies with more difficult texts, for a range of academic reading tasks, and for the monitoring of comprehension in line with reading goals;
8. ability to use inferences of various types;
9. ability to draw on prior knowledge as appropriate;
10. ability to evaluate, integrate, and synthesize information from texts;
11. ability to maintain L2 reading comprehension processes fluently for an extended period of time;
12. motivation to persist in reading and to use text information appropriately in line with reader goals.

Each of the implications from research suggests opportunities for building a principled reading curriculum, taking into consideration students' proficiency levels, reading curriculum goals, and support for the translation of these research findings into effective instructional practices for L2 reading development (Grabe, 2009; Grabe & Stoller, 2011). Fortunately, a number of sound curricular principles, and a broad range of instructional teaching practices, do exist to provide the needed help. These principles and practices are discussed in the following two chapters.

Chapter Summary

This chapter introduces reading comprehension as a complex cognitive and contextually supported ability. At the same time, reading has been one of the most intensely researched areas, and now one of the best understood, among our complex cognitive abilities. Students learning to read texts for academic purposes combine lower-level skills (that are usually automatized) and higher-level skills (that support comprehension with challenging texts) in both L1 and L2 contexts. While L1 and L2 reading draw on similar cognitive and linguistic resources, there are clear differences in L1 and L2 reader comprehension abilities until L2 students develop advanced language resources and engage in extensive amounts of reading practice.

Discussion Questions and Tasks

1.   What do you now know about the skill of reading that you didn't know before reading this chapter? (Identify the three most important points.)
2.   Based on what you've read in this chapter, do you agree that the skill of reading is miraculous? If so, which aspects of reading seem most miraculous to you?
3.   Explain the differences between these terms in relation to reading. Then explain the importance of each for skilled reading.

   a.   lower-level processing and higher-level processing
   b.   a text model of comprehension and a situation model of interpretation

4.   Consider your own L2 reading abilities or those of your L2 students. What areas of reading deserve explicit attention to achieve improved L2 reading abilities?
5.   Identify an instructional setting in which you teach (or want to teach).

   a.   In which area(s), itemized in Figure 2.4, do the students in your target setting need to make the greatest gains? Explain.
   b.   Which implications from research itemized in Figure 2.5 seem most pertinent to students in your target setting? Explain.

Further Reading

Perfetti, C., & Adlof, S. M. (2012). Reading comprehension: A conceptual framework from word meaning to text meaning. In J. P. Sabatini, E. A. Albro, & T. O'Reilly (Eds.), *Measuring up: Advances in how to assess reading ability* (pp. 3–20). Lanham, MD: Rowman & Littlefield Education.

   This chapter provides one of the best brief conceptualizations of reading comprehension. The authors are leading researchers and they provide a readily accessible model of comprehension processes.

Seidenberg, M. (2017). *Reading at the speed of sight.* New York, NY: Basic Books.

   Seidenberg is one of the world's leading cognitive psychologists. In this book, he steps back from his research orientation and explains reading comprehension in a very accessible way for the interested general reader.

Spiro, R., DeSchryver, M., Hagerman, M., Morsink, P., & Thompson, P. (Eds.), (2015). *Reading at a crossroads? Disjunctures and continuities in current conceptions and practices.* New York, NY: Routledge.

   This edited volume provides multiples perspectives on the impact of digital text in reading comprehension. Many of the well-known authors offer differing perspectives, resulting in a complex picture of the importance of, and challenges associated with, digital reading.

Notes

1 See www.uis.unesco.org/literacy/ for global literacy-rate data. These UNESCO data are considered the standard for benchmarking progress internationally.

3 Building an Effective Reading Curriculum
Guiding Principles

William Grabe and Fredricka L. Stoller

In this chapter, we present a set of 12 guiding principles for second language (L2) reading curricula that are general enough, on the one hand, to be adaptable to a wide range of instructional contexts and specific enough, on the other hand, to keep us focused on reading-skills development for academic purposes. These principles build upon what we know about the skill of reading (as introduced in the previous chapter) and sound lesson-planning, teaching, and assessment in language-teaching settings. The principles, when translated into practice across a curriculum, aim to help students (a) improve their reading abilities and (b) become self-motivated, independent, and strategic readers who can handle reading demands in academic contexts (Anderson, 2015). These demands can include heavy reading loads, challenging texts, and the need to make effective use of textual information for other purposes (e.g., writing papers, giving oral presentations, studying for and taking exams).

The principles introduced here can guide classroom teachers, materials writers, assessment teams, and language-program administrators, in addition to those who are directly involved in curriculum design and renewal efforts. We believe that our principles are applicable, with varying emphases placed on each principle, to the range of L2 classroom contexts in which reading-skills development is addressed, including, but not limited to, the following:

- discrete-skill courses (with primary attention to reading);
- integrated-skills courses (in which reading is integrated with one or more other language skills, e.g., a reading–writing course);
- content-based courses (which make a dual, though not necessarily equal, commitment to language- and content-learning aims);
- extensive reading programs (with an emphasis on having students read large quantities of materials that are within students' linguistic competence); and
- courses that focus on English for academic purposes (EAP) and English for specific purposes (ESP).

In these varied instructional settings, curricula are oftentimes "defined by" the textbooks that are adopted for use. Our principles are applicable in textbook-driven settings, with some degree of textbook adaptation and supplementation. Whether curricula are textbook driven or not, the principles are pertinent *across* the curriculum (from beginning to advanced courses), as students become more proficient in English, as the texts that they are assigned to read become longer and more complex, as new written genres are incorporated into instruction, and as students spend more time reading-to-learn (rather than learning-to-read).

Our 12 curricular principles are not to be confused with the teaching techniques presented in the next chapter. The principles, however, can assist teachers in deciding which techniques to incorporate into instruction, taking into consideration students' needs, proficiency levels, and institutional constraints (e.g., instructional time and reading resources available, mandated textbooks, teacher responsibilities). Language programs that draw upon these principles for their reading curricula can expect a sound (evidence-based) approach to teaching reading, which can easily be defended if teachers are asked why they are proposing or implementing changes that differ from more traditional ways of teaching reading.

Principle #1: Asking Students to Read for Well-Defined Purposes, Rather than Simply Asking Students to Read (for No Purpose at All), Should Guide Reading and Re–Reading Tasks

In many L2 classrooms, students are simply assigned to "read" a textbook passage and answer post-reading comprehension questions "for the next class meeting." Such assignments are typically made without establishing any meaningful purpose for reading (except to comply with a teacher request). Even well-respected textbooks often direct students to simply "read this passage." Skilled readers, however, always read for a purpose. Well-defined purposes for reading influence the ways in which skilled readers approach texts; they also influence readers' expectations of the reading experience. Skilled readers might read quickly to search for information, to get the main idea of a passage, or to decide if the text is worth reading more carefully. In academic contexts, students might also read to evaluate, critique, or use information for other purposes (e.g., to write a summary, prepare for a debate). In other settings, readers may pick up a newspaper, magazine, or novel to simply read for general comprehension and enjoyment. Whatever our purposes for reading are, they greatly influence the ways in which we read (faster, slower, more carefully, more casually, with pencil or pen in hand) and our expectations.

Skilled readers often re-read important texts (for a second or third time), also for well-defined purposes. In fact, purposeful re-reading is a common strategy used by skilled readers to solve comprehension difficulties, identify important details, determine relationships among ideas, find evidence of an author's viewpoint, and, in school settings, review for a quiz or write a summary.

We should encourage our L2 students to read and reread for authentic purposes as one way to model and reinforce good reading habits. Specified purposes for reading vary; they depend on the nature of the text, students' familiarity with the topic, connections with other texts that students have read or will read, and ways in which students will use the information encountered (e.g., to write a summary, synthesize two or more texts, compare opposing viewpoints, explore connections between the text and personal experiences). Asking students to simply read, for no purpose at all, is counter-productive if we want students to develop the skills of a strong academic reader. Over time,we can encourage students to establish their own reading goals. Figure 3.1 juxtaposes reading assignments that provide students with a purpose for reading with those that do not specify any purpose at all. (See Figure 4.10 in the next chapter for a more complete list of authentic purposes for reading.)

Figure 3.1 Samples of purposeful reading and re-reading assignments: Do's and don'ts

Samples of Purposeful Reading and Re-reading Assignments: Do's and Don'ts	
Do's	Read pages 3–7 for tomorrow. While reading: • think about your own travel experiences. • compare your home town with the city described. • underline information that contradicts views introduced in the passage that we read last week. Re-read pages 3–7 and: • decide if you agree or disagree with the author. Be prepared to explain your decision in class. • decide if the problems and solutions discussed in the passage are similar to and/or different from those in your own situation. • select one or two of the recycling recommendations that would work best in your community.
Don'ts ⊘	Turn to page 3 and begin reading. Read (or re-read) pages 3–7 for tomorrow.

Principle #2: Reading a Lot and Reading Often Are Crucial for Reading-Skills Development

Becoming a good reader requires reading a lot and reading often. There are simply no short cuts (Grabe, 2009). Unfortunately, students, even in discrete-skill reading classes, typically read very little. And what students do read is often done at home (if it is done at all), very possibly using the least efficient reading strategies to complete the assignment. Reading classes are often more like conversation classes than actual reading classes. Why? Because rather than focusing on reading-skills development, class activities center around a quick *oral* review of post-reading comprehension questions (often without any reference back to the reading passage), vocabulary-building activities (that are not always connected to the passage that has been read), and "personalization" tasks that connect the topic of the assigned reading to students' personal lives, without holding students accountable for what they have read. In sum, there is sometimes more speaking and listening practice in reading classes than reading itself.

If reading improvement is to become a curricular priority, students need to be reading a lot and often, in class and out of class. Students should be reading a range of materials, including (a) materials that are within their grasp for reading enjoyment (as we would see in an extensive reading program) and (b) materials that are more challenging (but not frustrating) so that students can practice using reading strategies to achieve their comprehension goals and, at the same time, feel a sense of accomplishment. Reading a lot does not mean that students must be continuously reading brand new passages; it is also useful to ask students to re-read passages for new purposes (Principle #1).

Teachers should promote additional reading opportunities whenever and however they can (e.g., on classroom walls, on a web-based learning management system like BBlearn, on a course or program website with links to supplementary reading materials, with project posters in hallways, in an easily accessible class or program library, on bulletin board displays). The goal is to make accessible interesting, motivating, age- and content-appropriate reading materials, thereby creating a print-rich environment. The intention is for students to naturally gravitate toward the texts and read them because either they are curious and interested, or because their course assignments will be enhanced by additional source materials, but not simply because they are assigned to do so by the teacher.

Principle #3: Reading Requires the Coordination of Numerous Reading Abilities that Should Be Addressed Explicitly Across a Reading Curriculum

We learned, in the first chapter of this unit, that successful reading entails the coordination of numerous processes, subskills, strategies, cognitive resources, and ways of reading. Reading curricula, therefore, should address them all in a deliberate, consistent, and scaffolded manner. Translated into practice, this means, at a minimum, explicitly:

- teaching for main-idea comprehension;
- building students' discourse-structure awareness to support comprehension;
- providing opportunities for reading-fluency improvement;
- helping students expand their vocabulary and develop strategies for independent vocabulary learning;
- introducing reading strategies while students are reading for comprehension and providing meaningful practice opportunities for their use; and
- building students' motivation for reading.

Instruction in, and regular practice with, these essential elements of reading should be addressed across the curriculum, as part of an overall effort to (a) guide students in understanding texts better, (b) help students work with texts as resources, and (c) build students' motivation for developing these reading abilities.

Principle #4: Teaching (Rather than Testing) for Main-Idea Comprehension Should Be a Standard Component of Classroom Instruction

Teachers, without realizing it, typically devote more time to "testing" reading comprehension than teaching for comprehension (Anderson, 2014). When structuring a reading lesson mainly (or solely) around a review of post-reading comprehension questions, we are testing comprehension rather than taking advantage of opportunities to *teach* students *how* to comprehend. Teaching *for* reading comprehension entails, at a minimum, teaching students and engaging students in discussions of:

- when and why to preview, predict, and check predictions;
- how to identify main ideas;
- how to make use of background knowledge;
- how, why, and when to use context clues to understand unfamiliar words, and, when context clues are not present, how to use other textual resources to comprehend new lexical items;
- how to use visual imagery to assist with comprehension; and
- when and for what purposes to reread.

Explicit attention to such essential elements of skilled reading, when combined with class discussions about the steps taken to make sense of the texts that students are reading, is certainly more important in the long term than simply reviewing post-reading comprehension questions and moving on (e.g., to the next textbook chapter). The classroom discussions that we are advocating provide valuable opportunities for students to talk—to one another and the whole class—about *how* to understand the texts that they read. During such discussions, students might highlight the importance of certain text features (e.g., bolded section headings, end-of-reading summary, illustrations) and key vocabulary, as well as the range of strategies used and their purposes for using them before, during, and after reading. Such discussions require an investment of classroom time; they should become part of the normal reading-classroom routine rather than something extra if and only if time permits.

Principle #5: Training Strategic Readers Is More Effective than Teaching Reading Strategies One at a Time

Skilled readers are, by definition, strategic. Strategic readers know *which* strategies to use—in addition to *when*, *how*, and *why* to use them—to overcome comprehension difficulties and achieve comprehension goals. Reading curricula that are committed to training strategic readers, rather than teaching strategies one at a time, are better positioned to help students develop skilled reading abilities.

Consider the differences between teaching individual reading strategies and training strategic readers. The former is perpetuated by textbooks that introduce one reading strategy at a time, often within a decontextualized lesson segment. With this common approach, students might be introduced to previewing (in chapter 1), predicting and checking predictions (in chapter 2), connecting the text to background knowledge (in chapter 3), creating mental images (in chapter 4), inferencing (in chapter 5), and so forth. With this standard instructional approach, students are rarely asked to use such strategies while actually reading for comprehension. Nor are they guided in using multiple strategies in combination, which is what skilled readers do.

When training strategic readers, on the other hand, teachers:

- provide explicit introductions to reading strategies used to achieve text comprehension;
- incorporate multiple opportunities for guided practice in strategy use while students are actually reading for comprehension;
- guide class discussions about strategy use (focusing on which strategies are used, when, how, why); and
- recycle strategies (in new combinations) with new passages.

A commitment to strategic-reader training is likely to result in more skilled and confident readers. When strategic reading is regularly addressed across the curriculum, as the texts that students read become longer and more complex, students, over time, develop the habits of strategic (and independent) readers. Appendix A provides an inventory of strategies commonly used by skilled readers. (See Ferris, Chapter 6, this volume, for a related discussion about developing strategic writers.)

Task 3.1

Think about your own reading habits. Which of the strategies in Appendix A do you use regularly when reading challenging, academic texts?

Principle #6: Making a Commitment to Vocabulary Teaching and Learning Is Foundational to Students' Reading Success

It should come as no surprise that vocabulary knowledge is closely related to reading abilities and reading comprehension. In fact, vocabulary and reading have a symbiotic relationship. That is, vocabulary growth leads to improved reading comprehension and, at the same time, amount of reading leads to vocabulary growth. Students' vocabulary growth benefits from an across-the-curriculum commitment to reading in addition to explicit attention to vocabulary building, vocabulary recycling, and vocabulary-learning strategies.

As students develop more advanced language abilities, they read more complex informational texts and new textual genres with the expectation that their attention will shift from learning-to-read to reading-to-learn. When students are exposed to new content areas, they inevitably encounter new vocabulary that is important for comprehension (Schmitt, Jiang, & Grabe, 2011). One of the challenges that teachers face is that they cannot possibly teach all the words that students need to know. Thus, introducing students to strategies for independent vocabulary learning is important. At the same time, teachers can contribute to students' vocabulary growth by judiciously selecting the lexical items that they teach and recycle. One systematic way for teachers to select vocabulary for explicit attention is by categorizing lexical items likely to be unfamiliar to students into four categories, as shown in Figure 3.2. Lexical items falling into the ++ (plus–plus) category are excellent "candidates" for explicit instruction. Words categorized as −− (minus–minus) do not merit instructional time. Teachers must decide how much time, if any, to devote to words categorized as +− (plus–minus) and −+ (minus–plus). Teachers can also make use of corpus tools (e.g., www.lextutor.ca, www.academicvocabulary.info) to inform meaningful vocabulary instruction.

Principle #7: Reading Fluently—at Word and Passage Levels—Is Essential for Efficient Reading Comprehension Abilities

Fluency in reading, central to efficient reading abilities, is both a contributor to and a product of comprehension (Klauda & Guthrie, 2008). Fluent reading involves automaticity (recognizing words and phrases without effort), rate (reading quickly), accuracy (reading accurately), prosody (reading with

Figure 3.2 Systematic way for teachers to identify lexical items worthy of explicit attention

Evaluation Criteria for Vocabulary Likely to Be Unfamiliar to Students		Lexical Items Worthy of Explicit Instruction
Word/Phrase Critical for Text Comprehension	Word/Phrase Useful Beyond the Text Being Read	
+	+	High Priority Plus–Plus (+ +)
+	–	Plus–Minus (+ –)
–	+	Minus–Plus (– +)
–	–	No Priority Minus–Minus (– –)

appropriate word groupings), and reading with comprehension. Another way to think about reading fluency is to consider what fluent first-language (L1) readers can do:

> Fluent L1 readers can recognize almost every word they encounter in a text automatically. Fluent L1 readers can read a passage aloud at a rapid steady rate with good comprehension and with little hesitancy due to the basic syntax or the words they encounter. Fluent L1 readers read most texts at between 250–300 words per minute. Finally, fluent L1 readers can read for extended periods of time without difficulty or effort.
>
> (Grabe, 2009, p. 289)

This description of the fluent L1 reader does not come close to describing most L2 students' reading fluency. In fact, our L2 students are often the first to tell us that they read too slowly, that reading is frustrating, and that they have trouble comprehending (and remembering) what they are reading. Students with academic aspirations, especially in advanced academic contexts, need to develop their reading fluency so that they can comprehend the large amounts of reading that will be assigned.

Reading fluency, however, does not develop "overnight." A commitment to reading-fluency development is needed across the curriculum (through to advanced levels of instruction, with learners of all ages). Making such a commitment recognizes the incremental process that, with time, moves students toward the reading fluency needed in academic contexts. In addition to the reading fluency activities introduced in the next chapter (e.g., purposeful rereading, repeated reading, and oral paired rereading), we must remember

Figure 3.3 Fluent L1 reader rates when reading for different purposes
(from Carver, 1992)

Reading Rate (words per minute, wpm)	Purpose for Reading
600 wpm	Scanning
450 wpm	Skimming
300 wpm	Reading with understanding
200 wpm	Reading to learn
138 wpm	Reading to memorize

that students develop fluency first and foremost by reading a lot and often (Principle #2).

Although it is noted above that fluent L1 readers read most texts at between 250–300 words per minute, this is, in actuality, an oversimplification of a much more complex reality. In fact, skilled readers read at different rates, depending on their purpose(s) for reading (Principle #1). Fluent L1 reading rates, commonly referenced, are presented in Figure 3.3. What these various reading rates suggest is that reading curricula need to regularly engage students in reading for different purposes, accompanied by a variety of fluency-building activities.

> **Quote:** "Effective instruction in academic language must take the development of (reading) fluency as one of its goals."
>
> (Nagy & Townsend, 2012, p. 102)

Principle #8: Building Students' Motivation to Read Is Essential

Teachers know that student motivation plays an important role in language learning, including reading-skills development. Students' attitudes toward reading are typically linked to previous experiences with reading (in and out of the classroom) and their perceptions about the usefulness of reading. These days, students actually read quite a bit (on their cell phones, on social media), but they rarely view it as "reading" (Geva & Ramírez, 2015).

Research has consistently shown that positive motivation and positive attitudes toward reading lead to improved reading comprehension and greater amounts of extended reading (which, of course, has other benefits, including the development of reading fluency and vocabulary growth). Students who self-identify as readers and who enjoy reading are more likely to develop into skilled, autonomous readers (McCardle, Chhabra, & Kapinus, 2008). This is due, in part, to students' sense of self-efficacy, their willingness to read, and their openness to reading instruction and related activities.

The good news is that teachers, and the materials that they integrate into instruction, can have a positive impact on students' motivation to read (Komiyama, 2009). Research has shown that students become motivated when they:

- have some choices (of texts and tasks);
- read texts (print and digital) of topical interest;
- experience reading success;
- work within a supportive group of peers; and
- understand the purpose(s) for the reading-skills development activities that teachers incorporate into instruction.

Reading curricula should make a commitment to building students' motivation for reading with these easy-to-implement teaching practices.

> **Quote:** Teachers "should consider ways to motivate students and, perhaps more importantly, help students take responsibility for their own motivation."
>
> (Anderson, 2015, p. 105)

Principle #9: Connecting Reading to Writing Prepares Students for the Realities of Most Academic Contexts

In academic settings, tasks that require the integration of reading and writing are commonplace. In fact, the ability to integrate reading and writing is critical for academic success (Grabe & Zhang, 2013; Hedgcock & Ferris, 2009). Using textual resources to complete academic writing tasks is challenging for students and requires a lot of practice. When making a curricular commitment to reading–writing integration, students can be guided in numerous tasks, including summarizing, synthesizing information from multiple sources, and responding critically to textual input. Students can also practice taking notes while reading, and using their notes for authentic purposes (e.g., writing a paper, studying for an exam, preparing an oral presentation). Reading curricula, especially at the point when students are reading informational texts, should connect reading and writing; this can be accomplished by:

- focusing explicit attention on reading comprehension with the texts that students will use in read-to-write tasks;
- reinforcing the importance of being responsible for text information (rather than relying on personal opinions);

- addressing paraphrasing and citation conventions;
- raising students' awareness of the expectations of different read-to-write tasks; and
- guiding students in developing their writing skills (as a natural outcome of skill integration).

Grabe and Zhang (2013) recommend initiating reading–writing integration early in language-program curricula and providing opportunities for a lot of iterative practice. [See Ferris, Chapter 6, this volume, for a writing perspective on reading-writing relationships.]

Principle #10: Assessing Students' Reading Progress Is an Essential Part of Teaching, Curriculum Development, and Student Learning

Earlier (in our discussion of Principle 4), we stated that the teaching, rather than the testing, of main-idea comprehension should be central to what we do in our reading classes. Nonetheless, in reading curricula, there is an important place for assessment, which, for practical purposes, can be divided into three types: Proficiency, achievement, and formative assessment. The first type of assessment (not addressed in this chapter) typically involves standardized tests; the results of such tests are used to sort students by proficiency levels. The second type of assessment, achievement tests, aims to determine how well students have learned skills or content that has been taught in a course or curriculum. These tests are given to students at the end of instructional units, at the end of a course, and/or at set points in the curriculum. We will call these measures "assessments *of* learning." Formative assessment, the third type of assessment discussed here, measures students' day-to-day (or weekly) improvements. We refer to this type of assessment, if used with the intention of helping students to learn, as "assessments *for* learning" (Wiliam, 2011; Wiliam & Leahy, 2015). Both assessments *of* learning and *for* learning can be carried out through formal testing formats and through various informal measures; both are important indicators of the effectiveness of a reading curriculum.

The major difference between the concepts of assessment *of* learning and assessment *for* learning centers on how indicators of student performance are used. In assessment *of* learning, teachers gather evidence, from both formal and informal measures of student performance, to decide how well students seem to be learning and how well the curriculum is working. The concept of assessment *for* learning, on the other hand, is one that all teachers should embrace as part of their ongoing efforts to improve students' learning. Assessment *for* learning focuses on students' performance "at the moment," most commonly through informal measures of progress. This form of assessment should result in teacher feedback that helps students:

- become aware of their learning progress;
- engage in self-assessment (i.e., self-reflection) to improve learning outcomes; and
- work with the teacher and peers to improve their performance.

This way of thinking about assessment is different from common conceptions of assessment, but it is fundamental to student learning and, in this case, reading development.

> **Quote:** "The teacher's job is . . . to engineer effective learning environments for students. The key features of effective learning environments are that they create student engagement and allow teachers, learners, and their peers to ensure that learning is proceeding in the intended direction. The only way we can do this is through assessment. That is why assessment is, indeed, the bridge between teaching and learning."
>
> (Wiliam, 2011, p. 50)

Principle #11: Selecting and Adapting Texts Should Be Driven by Students' Proficiency Levels, Current and Future Reading Needs, and Interests

What teachers ask students to read, and how teachers use those reading materials, can greatly influence students' progress in reading-skills development (in addition to students' motivation for reading). In ideal circumstances, text selection is guided by identifying reading materials that complement students' L2 proficiency levels, ages, maturity levels, and interests and that can be read independently or with scaffolded instruction. Yet in most settings, textbooks are selected by others for teacher use. In these cases, teachers can build upon those textbooks to promote reading improvement. For example, if the mandated textbook does not include any fluency-development activities, teachers can design them around textbook reading passages and add them to their lessons. If the textbook does not address reading strategies explicitly, teachers can adjust their lessons to do so. If the textbook does not include read-to-write tasks that hold students accountable for reading-passage content (Principle #9), teachers can devise such tasks themselves. Similarly, if a textbook chapter (or unit) includes only one reading passage on a particular topic, teachers can locate related readings (e.g., on the Internet, in magazines). With supplementary readings, topic-related vocabulary is recycled and content learning is likely to be more successful, thereby simulating academic contexts where students commonly read related texts to build their content knowledge. Even teachers with little extra time to modify their reading lessons can augment their textbooks in small but principled ways to more fully promote reading-skills development (Stoller, Anderson, Grabe, & Komiyama, 2013).

Reading curricula that combine easy and challenging reading passages permit teachers to address students' varied reading needs. Easy reading materials (e.g., level-appropriate graded readers) can be read for enjoyment, without frustration, and with opportunities for reading success. In extensive reading programs,[1] students are encouraged to read large quantities of material (often self-selected) that are within their grasp. More challenging reading materials are also needed for students with academic reading goals. Appropriately challenging (but not frustrating) texts lend themselves to scaffolded instruction, which can be supported by teacher-created "reading guides." Scaffolded instruction and reading guides can engage students in actively and purposefully using the strategies that skilled readers would use to understand the text (e.g., previewing, making predictions, reading to confirm or modify predictions, filling in a graphic organizer to view relationships among parts of the text, inferring, re-reading, taking notes, summarizing). Reading materials that are too challenging (i.e., at the frustration level because of, e.g., too many unknown words, grammatical complexity, or poorly signaled organization) are instructionally ineffective. Such materials quickly de-motivate students and de-motivated students do not enjoy reading, do not read much, and, therefore, do not (and cannot) improve their reading abilities.

> **Quote:** "Rarely in language education do we find a teaching approach [specifically *extensive reading*] that is so universally hailed as beneficial, important, and necessary . . . yet is so underutilized and even ignored in curricula, course/lesson design, and materials development."
> (Hedgcock & Ferris, 2009, p. 208)

In addition to integrating easy and appropriately challenging texts into instruction, students benefit from reading texts of different types, including:

- prose and non-prose (charts, diagrams, tables);
- fiction and non-fiction (informational texts), the latter being extremely important in academic contexts;
- texts with different types of discourse organization (e.g., description, comparison-contrast, problem-solution, chronology); and
- print and digital texts.

With regard to the suggestion that we include digital texts in our curricula, it is common knowledge that digital media have become a part of our students' everyday lives. Yet, reading digital texts for academic purposes, rather than for social purposes, is accompanied by its own special challenges.

Students need to learn how to navigate their ways through the non-linearity of digital texts (caused, in part, by the countless links encountered, many of which may be irrelevant to the target of academic inquiry) and determine the trustworthiness of the digital text/site (Coiro, 2015). Students also benefit from reading texts that lend themselves naturally to reading for different authentic purposes (Principle #1), which could include texts that are suitable for, as examples, (a) reading for main ideas and details and/or (b) re-reading to draw inferences, respond critically, evaluate text information, or connect to other texts.

Principle #12: Structuring Lessons around a Pre-Reading, During-Reading, and Post-Reading Framework Should Guide Class Planning

Reading lessons, interpreted broadly, should be structured around pre-, during-, and post-reading stages that permit students to be exposed to and practice the range of reading subskills and strategies used by skilled readers at different points in the reading process (Hedgcock & Ferris, 2009). The amount of class time devoted to each stage of the reading lesson is highly variable, depending on instructional goals, students' reading proficiencies, length of class meetings, and the texts assigned. A single lesson might include all three reading stages, though the text would have to be quite short and/or the class session quite long to do so. Probably more typical would be a span of numerous class sessions during which we would see pre-, during-, and post-reading activities.

Each stage of the reading lesson, as shown in Appendix B, serves a distinct set of instructional purposes. Equally important is the fact that each stage provides opportunities to introduce and have students practice stage- and text-appropriate reading strategies. Of the three stages, it is the during-reading stage that is most often neglected in published textbook materials. Adapting textbook materials to incorporate during-reading strategies (and authentic purposes for reading) can truly enhance a reading curriculum.

Chapter Summary

In this chapter, we have introduced 12 principles that can inform the development and/or refinement of L2 reading curricula. The 12 principles are listed below in summary form in Figure 3.4.

Although presented individually, in actuality, the 12 principles support one another and work together to help students become more motivated, skilled, and strategic. For example, when we ask students to read a lot (Principle 2), we are providing students with practice in the various subskills and strategies inherent in skilled reading (Principles 3 and 5), stimulating vocabulary growth (Principle 6), and promoting fluency development (Principle 7). When we plan our lessons around a pre–during–post format (Principle 12), it is easier

Figure 3.4 Principles that should permeate curricula committed to reading-skills development

Principle #1: Asking students to read for well-defined purposes, rather than simply asking students to read (for no purpose at all), should guide reading and re-reading tasks.

Principle #2: Reading a lot and reading often are crucial for reading-skills development.

Principle #3: Reading requires the coordination of numerous reading abilities that should be addressed explicitly across a reading curriculum.

Principle #4: Teaching (rather than testing) for main-idea comprehension should be a standard component of classroom instruction.

Principle #5: Training strategic readers is more effective than teaching reading strategies one at a time.

Principle #6: Making a commitment to vocabulary teaching and learning is foundational to students' reading success.

Principle #7: Reading fluently—at word and passage levels—is essential for efficient reading comprehension abilities.

Principle #8: Building students' motivation to read is essential.

Principle #9: Connecting reading to writing prepares students for the realities of most academic contexts.

Principle #10: Assessing students' reading progress is an essential part of teaching, curriculum development, and student learning.

Principle #11: Selecting and adapting texts should be driven by students' proficiency levels, current and future reading needs, and students' interests.

Principle #12: Structuring lessons around a pre-reading, during-reading, and post-reading framework should guide class planning.

for us to teach (rather than test) reading (Principle 4), train students to use appropriate lesson-stage and text-specific strategies to achieve their reading goals (Principle 5), integrate read-to-write tasks into instruction (Principle 9), and engage in assessments *of* and *for* learning (Principle 10). When we select and adapt texts with students' varied reading and academic needs in mind (Principle 11), we are able to provide students with opportunities for extensive reading (Principle 2), which leads to reading enjoyment, reading successes, and increased motivation (Principle 8). We are also able to guide students in reading and re-reading for different purposes (Principle 1), practicing the range of skills needed for effective reading (Principle 3), and using reading strategies appropriate to pre-, during, and post-reading stages

(Principles 5 and 12). As these few examples illustrate, the curricular principles showcased in this chapter work in concert to address students' reading-skills development.

At the same time, we all realize that there cannot possibly be a one-size-fits-all formula for effective reading curricula, given the diversity of our students, resources, programs, locations, and goals. It would be unrealistic to devote equal time to all 12 principles at every curricular level. Thus, reading teachers, curriculum designers, and language program administrators must strive to find the proper balance among the 12 principles to meet students' evolving abilities across the curriculum. Emphases among the principles should shift as students move from beginning reading proficiency levels to more advanced reading abilities. The aim is to prioritize the principles that will benefit students the most as they become more-skilled readers.

Discussion Questions and Tasks

1. Consider your own experiences learning to read in an L2 classroom. Of the 12 principles introduced in this chapter, which principles do you wish had figured more prominently in your reading-skill development experience? Why?

2. Choose an ESL/EFL textbook that makes some commitment to reading-skill development. Evaluate 2–3 textbook chapters. What kind of commitment does the textbook make to the 12 principles introduced in this chapter? If you were to teach with the textbook, how might you supplement it to give students a fuller, more principled reading-skills development experience? Be prepared to link each of your ideas to one or more of the principles introduced in this chapter.

3. Briefly describe a target group of language learners (in a particular L2 location, at a particular proficiency level) with present and/or future academic reading needs. With these students in mind, identify and rank order the top 5 curricular principles introduced in this chapter (with #1 being the most critical principle). Be prepared to defend your rankings.

4. Interview a language teacher or language-program administrator. Find out the degree to which and how each of the principles introduced in this chapter are addressed in the program in which he/she teaches/works. After the interview, consider 3–5 changes that could be made in the reading curriculum to make a stronger commitment to reading-skills development. For each change, identify the principle(s) underlying it.

5. Imagine that you teach in an instructional setting that does not make a strong enough commitment (or any real commitment) to reading-skills development. What 4–5 ideas might you propose in order to address such shortcomings? For each suggestion, identify the principles that offer the best support for your ideas.

Further Reading

Anderson, N. J. (2015). Academic reading expectations and challenges. In N. W. Evans, N. J. Anderson, & W. G. Eggington (Eds.), *ESL readers and writers in higher education: Understanding challenges, providing support* (pp. 95–109). New York, NY: Routledge.

The author reports the results of a survey of university faculty about amount of reading, reading expectations, and reading challenges faced by students in five academic disciplines. Implications for English for academic purposes curricula are explained.

Grabe, W., & Stoller, F. (2011). *Teaching and researching reading* (2nd. ed.). New York, NY: Routledge.

The authors explain the complex nature of reading, compare L1 and L2 reading, offer pedagogical suggestions, explain the value of action research, and outline 29 adaptable action research projects that teachers can conduct to better understand their reading classrooms.

Grabe, W., & Zhang, C. (2013). Reading and writing together: A critical component of English for academic purposes teaching and learning. *TESOL Journal, 4*(1), 9–24.

The authors focus on the value of integrating reading and writing instruction for L2 learners in English for academic purposes programs.

Notes

1   See http://erfoundation.org/wordpress/ for information on the Extensive Reading Foundation; http://erfoundation.org/wordpress/graded-readers/graded-reader-list/ for lists of graded readers and links to graded-reader publishers; http://moodlereader.org/ for 1,000s of graded-reader quizzes, which can be used to monitor and assess students' extensive reading.

Appendix A

Figure 3.5 Common reading strategies (adapted from Grabe & Stoller, 2011)

Global Reading Strategies[1]	Monitoring Reading Strategies
Planning and forming goals for reading**	Monitoring main idea comprehension*
Reading selectively according to goals	Identifying reading difficulties
Previewing*	Taking steps to repair faulty comprehension (e.g., rereading, looking forward or backward, checking illustrations, pausing and posing questions, pausing to subvocalize main idea, considering prior knowledge)
Forming predictions**	
Checking (confirming, rejecting, or modifying) predictions	
Posing questions*	Judging how well objectives are met
Answering questions*	Rereading**
Connecting text to background knowledge*	Reflecting on what has been learned from the text
Identifying important information/ main ideas	**Support Reading Strategies**
Paying attention to text structure*	Using the dictionary
Using discourse markers to see discourse relationships	Taking notes**
	Paraphrasing**
Connecting one part of the text to another	Translating (mentally)**
	Underlining or highlighting
Making inferences	Using graphic organizers*
Creating mental images*	Synthesizing*
Guessing meaning from context	
Summarizing*	[1] Three broad categories adapted from Mokhtari & Sheorey (2008).
Critiquing the author, the text, feelings about the text	* Empirically validated reading strategies. ** Indirectly supported reading strategies used in validated multiple-strategy instruction.

Appendix B

Figure 3.6 Major goals for and reading strategies used at different stages of the pre–during–post framework (adapted from Grabe & Stoller, 2011)

Lesson-plan stage	Major goals for, and reading strategies used at, different stages of the pre–during–post framework

Pre-reading	➢ Guide students in
	   • establishing a purpose and goal(s) for reading
	   • connecting text to background knowledge
	
	➢ Provide information needed for comprehension (e.g., vocabulary, background)
	➢ Set up students' expectations
	➢ Stimulate interest
	➢ Build student confidence and motivation
	➢ Model and guide students in practicing other strategies appropriate for this stage of reading, including
	   • previewing, predicting, posing questions, identifying main ideas
	   • paying attention to text structure, creating mental images

During-reading	➢ Guide students in
	   • reading according to previously established purpose and goals
	   • comprehending the text (e.g., with graphic organizers that students fill in)
	   • constructing meaning, monitoring comprehension, and taking steps to repair faulty comprehension
	   • connecting what is read to what is known
	
	➢ Support ongoing summarization
	➢ Model and guide students in practicing other strategies appropriate for this stage of reading including
	   • confirming, rejecting, or modifying predictions made during the pre-reading stage
	   • taking notes, underlining, highlighting, writing margin notes
	   • inferencing, guessing meaning from context (where possible)

Post-reading	➢ Guide students in
	   • re-reading to check comprehension
	   • exploring how text organization supports comprehension
	   • summarizing, synthesizing, evaluating, elaborating, integrating, extending, and applying text information

- critiquing the author and aspects of the text (e.g., writing, content)
- recognizing comprehension successes

➤ Model and guide students in practicing other strategies appropriate for this stage of reading including
- re-reading for well-established purposes
- reflecting on what has been learned, judging how well objectives have been met
- using text information (and notes, underlining, and highlighting completed while reading) for other purposes

4 Reading Instruction and Assessment
Activities and Options

William Grabe and Fredricka L. Stoller

In this chapter, we introduce instructional activities and assessment options that teachers can adapt for classrooms with reading-skills development goals. The activities and assessment options included represent extensions of what we know about skilled reading (introduced in chapter 2) and principles for reading curricula (presented in chapter 3). We have organized the chapter around three major sections, with the first section devoted to teaching techniques for improving students' reading abilities. In the second section, we explore techniques for integrating reading and writing. Finally, in the third section, we identify techniques for assessments *of* learning and assessments *for* learning (concepts introduced in the previous chapter, as part of Principle 10). Our sample activities, built upon readings in second language (L2) reading textbooks, illustrate how easily supplementary reading-skills development activities can be created with the passages that students are assigned to read in their L2 classes.

Realistically, teachers will not adapt every idea presented here for immediate use. Teachers should identify those teaching practices that complement the goals of their current classes and consider the adaptation of others in future classes. For teachers who are working in settings with minimal flexibility, we advocate small, principled changes to teaching practices because they are better than no changes at all (Stoller, Anderson, Grabe, & Komiyama, 2013).

Instructional Activities that Improve Students' Reading Abilities

In this section, we introduce teaching techniques that can improve L2 students' reading abilities; the techniques focus on promoting word and phrase recognition efficiency, building students' recognition vocabulary, raising students' discourse structure awareness, training strategic readers, improving students' reading fluency, increasing students' motivation for reading, and teaching for (rather than testing) reading comprehension.

Promote Rapid Word and Phrase Decoding

Skilled readers decode words and phrases automatically. L2 students might enter our classes with reasonable control over basic word and phrase recognition, yet they benefit from word and phrase recognition practice with the new lexical items encountered as they progress in their language studies. Three activities that promote word and phrase recognition speed and accuracy, and that support reading fluency, are described below. The general format of these tasks can be used across the curriculum; what will change, of course, are the key vocabulary items incorporated into the tasks.

Word and Phrase Recognition Exercises

Few L2 reading textbooks include word and phrase recognition exercises. Fortunately, teachers can easily create them with vocabulary from the texts that students are reading. Because relatively little class time is needed for task completion, it is recommended that teachers create 2–3 recognition exercises for each reading textbook chapter. Common recognition-exercise formats are shown in Figures 4.1 and 4.2 (see also Crawford, 2005; Stoller, 2012). Students generally enjoy recognition exercises that are completed in a beat-the-clock fashion, with record-keeping charts for tracking progress.

Timed Semantic Connection Exercises

Another way to provide practice in quick lexical access is by means of semantic connection exercises (Figure 4.3), made up entirely of words that students are familiar with (and that are important for comprehension of a particular passage). Under timed conditions, students consider the key word (on the left) and multiple choices (to the right), and select the one word (or phrase)

Figure 4.1 Common word recognition exercise format (with key phrases from Savage, 2010)

Key Word					
1. *bacteria*	branches	bottles	bactéria	backfire	hysteria
2. *toxin*	token	taken	towns	toxin	tonic
3. *plastic*	placate	plaster	plateau	pacific	plastic
. . .	Number correct: ___ / 20				
	Time: ___ seconds				

Figure 4.2 Common phrase recognition exercise format (with key vocabulary from Savage, 2010)

Key Word				
1. *piece of plastic*	pieces of plastic	piece of plastic	parts of plastic	pieces of plywood
2. *as large as*	as thick as	as lovely as	as light as	as large as
3. *a natural process*	a national process	a nocturnal process	a natural process	a natural product
. . .				
Number correct: ___ / 20 Time: ___ seconds				

Figure 4.3 Sample timed semantic connection exercise (with key vocabulary from Savage, 2010)

Key Word					
1. *toxins*	currents	seawater	disposable	satellites	bacteria
2. *harmful*	helpful	dangerous	surface	however	therefore
3. *(to) solve*	a problem	the route	the race	an expert	the surface
. . .					
Number correct: ___ / 20 Time: ___ seconds					

that is (a) topically related to the key word (as in item #1), (b) similar in meaning (as in item #2), or (c) a common collocate of the key word (as in item #3).

Lexical Access Fluency Exercises

More advanced L2 students benefit from lexical access fluency exercises too (Figure 4.4). As a variation on the timed semantic connection task (Figure 4.3), these exercises require students to match key words or phrases (bolded, on the left) with their definitions or synonyms (to the right) under timed conditions. Students progress through three sets of the same key vocabulary items and definitions/synonyms, though the items on the right are scrambled in each set, with less time allotted for the completion of each set (e.g., 60, 50, 40 seconds). These exercises require little class time and one three-part set could easily be created for passages assigned to students to read.

Figure 4.4 Sample lexical access fluency task (with vocabulary from Savage, 2010)

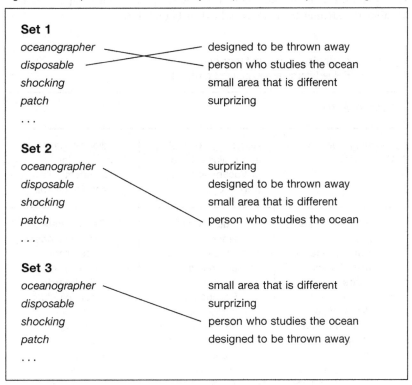

Set 1

oceanographer — designed to be thrown away
disposable — person who studies the ocean
shocking   small area that is different
patch   surprizing
. . .

Set 2

oceanographer   surprizing
disposable   designed to be thrown away
shocking   small area that is different
patch   person who studies the ocean
. . .

Set 3

oceanographer   small area that is different
disposable   surprizing
shocking   person who studies the ocean
patch   designed to be thrown away
. . .

Other activities that promote efficient word and phrase decoding include flashcard use, oral paired rereading (explained later in the chapter), and extensive reading with easier materials.

Help Students Build a Large Recognition Vocabulary

Skilled reading requires a large recognition vocabulary. Teachers can make a commitment to L2 students' vocabulary growth in many ways (Zimmerman, 2009). Because few textbooks offer ideal conditions for sustained vocabulary development, teachers can supplement their textbooks to provide students with the multiple and varied exposures to vocabulary that are needed for vocabulary learning. Teachers can create *print-rich classroom environments* (see Principle 2 in the previous chapter); judiciously select vocabulary for *explicit instruction* (see Principle 6, Figure 3.2, in the previous chapter); deliberately (and frequently) *recycle* vocabulary in meaningful contexts; and provide students with opportunities to *practice* using new and recycled vocabulary.

Vocabulary-building techniques, such as those listed in Figure 4.5, are more effective than simply (and solely) asking students to memorize words (and be tested on them). In the sections that follow, we elaborate upon the four vocabulary teaching techniques bolded in Figure 4.5.

Figure 4.5 Vocabulary teaching techniques
(Bolded items are explained further below)

Techniques for . . .		
Teaching New Vocabulary	Recycling Vocabulary and Building Layers of Vocabulary Knowledge	Building Student Motivation for Independent Vocabulary Learning

• Bring in or draw pictures
• **Build concept-of-definition maps**
• Consult (learner) dictionaries
• Explain with a story or anecdote
• Guide students in word analysis
• Juxtapose new vocabulary with antonyms & synonyms
• Provide easy-to-understand definitions
• Translate
• Use graphic displays that show new word in relation to known words
	• **Build "word walls"**
	• Create matching and ranking activities
	• Engage students in discussions and writing tasks that encourage the use of key vocabulary
	• Teach collocations and connotations
	• Teach word families
	• **Use a word splash to engage students in vocabulary sorting**
		• Teach strategies for independent vocabulary learning using
		  – **flashcards**
		  – context clues (when present)
		  – visuals
		  – vocabulary notebooks
		  – word-part knowledge

Concept-of-Definition Maps

New key words can be introduced and connected to what students already know by creating concept-of-definition maps with the class (Figures 4.6 and 4.7). With this approach, students view new lexical items from four vantage points, providing students with multiple perspectives for building their understanding of the word.

Figure 4.6 Generic concept-of-definition map

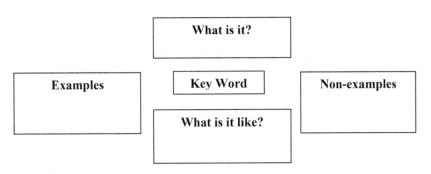

Figure 4.7 Concept-of-definition map (for a keyword in Savage, 2010)

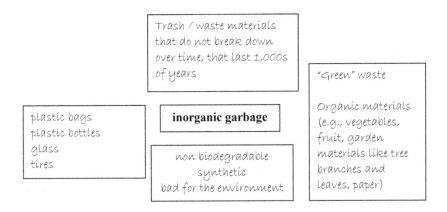

Word Splash and Sorting Activities

Word splashes, which randomly display lexical items on the board, lend themselves to sorting activities in addition to useful discussions of key-word associations, thereby providing opportunities for recycling and building layers of knowledge. Word splashes, developed by the teacher or developed jointly with students who nominate entries, are accompanied by discussions of word meanings, as a pre-reading task. Alternatively, a larger set of words can be provided by the teacher and nominated by students as part of a post-reading activity. After a word splash is created, the teacher asks students to cluster related words from the word splash and label each group of words with an overarching category label. By means of such a task, vocabulary words are recycled; students engage in active discussions about words, concepts, and their relationships; and students make meaningful connections among words. The outcome of a word splash–to–categorization task could be a semantic map that displays (a) main and secondary ideas from one or more reading passages and (b) their relationships (Figure 4.8).

Figure 4.8 Semantic map resulting from a word splash-to-categorization task (to accompany the Ocean of Plastic passage in Savage, 2010)

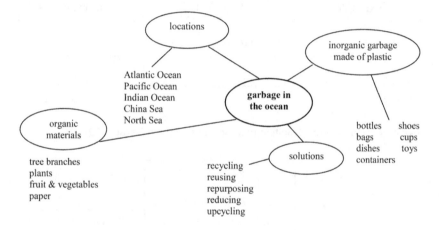

Word Wall and Related Tasks

Key vocabulary from core readings can be placed on a classroom wall or bulletin board, when feasible, possibly accompanied by a picture and/or definition (Eyraud, Giles, Koenig, & Stoller, 2000). Of course, the simple display of words (selected by the teacher and/or students) does not guarantee vocabulary learning. Actively engaging students in tasks that involve the meaningful use of words on the wall helps students learn the new vocabulary; teachers can ask students to move words around on the wall to create meaningful word clusters (e.g., words that belong to a particular content area, words from the same parts of speech, words with positive or negative connotations, collocations). Teachers can also assign tasks that promote the meaningful use of word-wall items with, for example, summary and synthesis tasks, speed writes, and word-ranking activities.

Flashcards for Independent Vocabulary Building

Students can create (on their own or with an online program like Quizlet. com) and use flashcards for vocabulary learning. Flashcards typically include the key term and its definition(s), and may also include the term's part of speech, pronunciation, translation, synonyms or antonyms, collocations, a brief example, the original sentence in which the term was encountered, or possibly students' own sentences. Students can use flashcards to review terms and to teach or "quiz" their classmates. Flashcards can also be used as springboards for learners' active engagement with the terms when, for example, writing a summary, composing a letter to a friend about a reading passage, journaling, or role playing.

Raise Students' Discourse-Structure Awareness

Good readers recognize the organization of textual information and the signals that provide cues to this organization (e.g., words that signal rhetorical patterns or topic shifts, transition phrases, headings, paragraphing) as one way to achieve comprehension. Instruction that aims to raise L2 students' discourse-structure awareness engages students in regular discussions of how texts are organized and how discourse structure is signaled (Jiang & Grabe, 2007, 2009). Discourse-specific graphic organizers (DSGOs; Grabe & Stoller, 2011, pp. 231–232; Jiang, 2012), which clearly reflect text-specific organizational patterns (e.g., comparison–contrast, problem solution, chronological order, process), serve as exemplary tools for raising students' discourse–structure awareness (Appendix). Common tasks for exploring discourse–structure at different stages of a reading lesson, are explained in the following sections.

Pre-reading Tasks for Building Discourse–Structure Awareness

At pre-reading stages, teachers can guide students in examining text headings (and subheadings) and then predicting what each section is about. The goal is for students, over time, to take these steps independently without being directed to do so. Students can also be asked to preview pre-selected text sections and highlight key words that signal discourse structure (e.g., first, second, third; on the one hand, on the other hand; therefore). Similarly, students can examine pre-determined paragraphs and decide their function in the text (e.g., to introduce a problem, propose a solution, make a comparison, explain a step in a process). These activities not only raise students' discourse awareness but they also model skilled-reader strategic awareness.

During-Reading Tasks for Raising Discourse–Structure Awareness

While students are reading, they can be guided by their teacher to discover text organization features. Depending on the nature of the text being read (in terms of organizational structure), teachers can ask students to do the following *while* reading:

1. Complete an outline of the text. As part of post-reading discussion, students can explain what makes each section identifiable as a separate unit.
2. Complete a DSGO (e.g., a timeline for a passage that is organized chronologically; a flow-chart for a passage that explains a process). As part of post-reading discussion, students can explain how the information placed in the graphic organizer was signaled in the text. (See Appendix for examples of partially completed timeline/chronology, problem–solution, description, and comparison–contrast DSGOs.)
3. Underline lexical clues that indicate major organizational patterns (e.g., cause–effect, comparison–contrast, problem–solution).
4. Highlight transition words and phrases that signal new sections (e.g., "And finally" to signal not only continuation but also the last in a series; "conversely" to signal a contrast). As part of post-reading discussion, students can report what they think the phrases and words signal.
5. Jot down a brief main-idea label for each paragraph (or sets of paragraphs) in the margin. As part of post-reading discussion, students can compare labels and explore the function of different paragraphs.

Post-Reading Tasks for Building Discourse–Structure Awareness

Discourse–structure awareness can be developed further in post-reading discussions and rereading tasks. Many of the while-reading activities just noted can be converted into post-reading tasks. Students can also be asked to reread a text to match main ideas and supporting information across two columns. Also effective are tasks that require students to reorganize scrambled paragraphs or sentences to reassemble a text or create a good summary.

Train Strategic Readers

Good readers read for well-defined purposes; they typically employ multiple strategies to achieve their reading-comprehension goals (e.g., previewing, making predictions, confirming or revising predictions, inferencing; see Appendix A in Chapter 3 for a more complete list). When good readers' default strategies—used without much conscious attention—do not lead to successful comprehension (which might happen when good readers encounter a challenging text, a new genre, and/or new content), a more conscious problem-solving mode of attention is activated. At this point, good readers draw upon a larger set of strategies, which they use in different combinations, to achieve their comprehension goals. In such circumstances, the reader may decide to reread the text (or parts of it), reconsider initial predictions, reexamine discourse markers, and/or try to unravel a complex phrase.

Quote: "Skilled readers have a large toolbox of strategic processes from which they can recruit to build coherence . . . Strategies are learned, implicitly or explicitly, and with practice become increasingly automated. Over the course of reading a text, the combination of automatic and strategic processes result in a landscape of activations [that lead to reading comprehension]."

(Van den Broek, 2012, p. 42)

Helping L2 readers become more strategic should be central to comprehension instruction. An emphasis on training strategic readers, rather than teaching individual strategies, is the ideal. Some essentials for strategic-reader training include the following:

- The teacher makes sure students read (and reread) in and out of class for well-defined purposes (Figure 4.9).
- The teacher introduces new strategies (in useful combinations) during lessons when students are engaged in reading for comprehension; as part of the lesson, the teacher guides students in a discussion of *how*, *when*, and *why* to use the new strategies to achieve reading comprehension goals.

Figure 4.9 Various authentic purposes for reading and rereading

Meaningful Purposes for Reading and Rereading		
Reading	Rereading	
• Read quickly to identify main idea(s) (skim) • Read quickly to search for simple information (scan) • Read for enjoyment • Read to learn • Read to integrate information with another information source • Read to write • Read to critique/evaluate • Read for general comprehension	• Reread to consolidate understanding • Reread to confirm the main idea, answers to post-reading questions, inferences • Reread to locate details, discourse markers • Reread to fill in a graphic organizer • Reread to apply, compare, clarify, explore relationships among ideas, extend knowledge	• Reread to prepare for a follow-up activity (e.g., a summary, synthesis, quiz, oral presentation, jigsaw activity • Reread to determine author stance, bias, position • Reread to find points of agreement or disagreement with another information source

- The teacher adds the "name" of each newly introduced strategy (e.g., Preview, Predict, Check Predictions) to a "permanent" display on a classroom bulletin board (or wall), or on a class website, for easy student consultation during class discussions.
- The teacher gives students opportunities to practice strategies (when they serve the purpose of helping students achieve their comprehension goals) and to discuss their use as part of pair work and whole-class discussion while working on comprehension activities.
- The teacher addresses strategies unique to Internet inquiry, including evaluating the trustworthiness of the site; staying on task according to reading purpose and resisting the temptation to pursue off-topic hyperlinks; handling the non-linear path of online reading (Cho & Afflerbach, 2017; Dobler & Eagleton, 2015).
- The teacher verbalizes combinations of strategies (planned out ahead of time) while reading a passage aloud to the class (Figure 4.10).

Figure 4.10 Sample teacher think-aloud to model strategic reading, used with a reading passage about ocean pollution (in Savage, 2010).

The teacher think-aloud is italicized; the excerpt of the textbook reading passage is in regular font. Superscripts indicate the strategies (in Appendix A, Chapter 3) being modeled: [1]previewing; [2]connecting text to background knowledge; [3]posing questions; [4]previewing; [5]connecting text to background knowledge; [6]forming predictions; [7]posing questions, monitoring comprehension; [8]using the dictionary; [9]summarizing; [10]inferencing; [11]posing questions; [12]inferencing; [13]posing questions; [14]forming predictions:

An Ocean of Plastic

(The title, An Ocean of Plastic.[1] Hmm. I know what plastic is,[2] but what is "an ocean of plastic"?[3] Oh, the map under the title shows the Pacific Ocean.[4] I'll read ahead.) A big part of the Pacific Ocean is choking on a huge sea of plastic garbage. *(Well, we know that the Pacific Ocean is really large,[5] so maybe there is a lot of plastic in the ocean.[6] I wonder what choking means[7]; I'll look it up later in my dictionary, if I can't figure it out on my own.[8])* Some scientists think it's as large as the United States, but almost no one noticed it until 1997. *(OK, this says that there is a LOT of plastic in the ocean, as big as the U.S.[9] That's terrible.[10] Why didn't anyone know about this earlier?[11])* Then an adventurer named Charles Moore made a shocking discovery, and scientists learned the ugly truth. *("Ugly truth" sounds bad.[12] I wonder what problems the ocean of plastic has created.[13] I imagine that the author will tell us.[14])*

Additional approaches for incorporating strategic-reader training into reading lessons are described in the following sections.

Guided Strategic Reading

Drawing from the Directed Reading–Thinking Activity (DR–TA) approach (Blachowicz & Ogle, 2008), teachers guide students in (a) relating background knowledge to the text, (b) determining goals for reading, and (c) engaging in a series of prediction and summarizing tasks at set pause points. The prediction cycle asks students to do the following:

- make predictions about what they think is coming next;
- read to confirm or refute their predictions;
- discuss predictions (in pairs and groups) and then with the whole class, and reformulate them using text information; and
- summarize what they have read before moving onto the next text segment.

Questions commonly asked to guide such discussions (with adaptations for different student proficiency levels and text types) include the following:

1. What do you predict will happen?
2. What are your reasons for these predictions?
3. What do you think now? How accurate were your predictions?
4. What made you change your mind?
5. Can you find information in the text to support or challenge your predictions?
6. What is the main idea of this section? (Write down a main idea sentence or phrase; then share with a classmate.)
7. What do you think will happen (or be covered) next?

When students have difficulties adjusting their predictions as they proceed through the text (possibly because they are unable to make good inferences or connect text segments), the teacher can ask students to reread particular segments to find information that will improve their predictions.

There are two keys to the successful adaptation of the DR–TA approach. First, the teacher must determine *how much* text should be read between pauses, during which students revisit, evaluate, and adjust their predictions. The teacher needs to be sure that "there is enough information [in the text segments read] for the students to check likely predictions, and also enough new information for further predictions to be made" (Blachowicz & Ogle, 2008, p. 140). The second key to successful DR–TA implementation is the realization that prediction is only authentic when the whole class is reading material for the first time. Pausing at page breaks or at the end of an identifiable section might lessen students' temptation to read ahead.

Identification and Discussion of Challenging Parts of a Text

L2 students' academic success depends, in part, on their ability to comprehend challenging texts. Teachers can ask students to identify a challenging text segment and then guide them in identifying the sources of difficulty (Figure 4.11) and strategies for overcoming the challenges. Instead of skipping over difficult segments, and focusing on what students understand, students bene-fit from working through difficult passages as a class; during such lessons, students discuss in groups and as a class the process of making sense of the challenging passage and the strategies that can help.

Figure 4.11 Possible sources of text difficulty (adapted from Grabe & Stoller, 2011, p. 261)

• Absence of concrete examples • Assumed background knowledge • Conceptual complexity • Confusing formatting • Density of text information • Grammatical complexity	• Lack of clarity in the writing • Length of sentences • Length of text • Poorly signalled organization • Unfamiliar content • Unfamiliar vocabulary or new meanings

Improve Students' Reading Fluency

Reading fluency is a critical component of effective and successful reading. When word and passage reading fluency practice is incorporated regularly (not just when there is some extra time) across reading curricula, students improve not only their fluency but also their reading comprehension. Explicit attention to passage-reading fluency can be developed with regular opportunities for (a) purposeful rereading, (b) repeated reading, and (c) oral paired rereading. Some of the activities that we suggest below entail reading aloud; these instructional activities are helpful, but should not be viewed as substitutes for silent reading. (For other fluency-building activities, refer back to the word decoding and vocabulary building sections above. See also Grabe & Stoller, 2011.) Note that the activities introduced here are commonly associated with instruction for students with lower-level proficiencies. Yet, fluency tasks, used with more challenging passages, are equally valuable for more advanced students who have even more pressing needs to become fluent L2 readers.

Rereading

L2 students are rarely asked to reread texts for new purposes, despite the fact that the rereading of familiar texts represents (a) one of the best ways to build reading fluency and (b) a common practice among skilled readers who reread to consolidate content learning and prepare for read-to-write tasks, among other purposes for rereading. It is suggested that teachers assign purposeful rereading tasks (refer back to Figure 4.9), before the class moves onto a new chapter or a new reading passage. Rereading helps students' reading fluency and also leads to vocabulary recycling, critical thinking, and the consolidation of content learning.

Repeated Reading

Repeated reading, not to be confused with rereading, is another classroom option for building students' fluency and reading abilities (Cohen, 2011). With *unassisted* repeated reading, students read short passages or text segments multiple times—silently and/or aloud on their own (in class and at home)—until they reach a set reading rate. With *assisted* repeated reading, students read passages multiple times, silently and/or aloud, along with a recording of the passage (on a CD or online) or with the teacher and/or a classmate. When establishing a repeated-reading routine, teachers should:

1. keep passages to between 70–200 words;
2. assign texts that students have *already* read or heard, or that will be *easy* for students' reading levels;
3. limit reading of the same passage to 3–4 times;
4. encourage students to read aloud with reasonable accuracy and intelligibly[1];
5. ask students to time their reading (from start to finish) and record the time spent reading on a record chart or read for a set number of seconds (e.g., 60, 90, or 120 seconds), even though, in the latter case, they may not finish the whole passage;
6. assign new texts when students have reached an improved rate, and/or when they improve their rate three times in a row with a single passage.

Oral Paired Reading

Oral paired reading is another reading fluency option. Students work in pairs with passages that they have *already* read; in this way, students can focus on reading more fluently, instead of having to focus on meaning and unfamiliar words. The routine is simple: Student A reads the passage aloud for a designated period of time (e.g., 30–60 seconds) as quickly and as accurately as possible, with appropriate phrasing. While Student A reads aloud, Student B reads along silently and assists Student A if necessary. At the end of the designated time period, Student A marks the end point of his/her read aloud. Then Students A and B switch roles. Student B reads the exact same passage as Student A, starting at the beginning. After the same designated time period, Student B marks the end point of his/her read aloud. The students then repeat the procedure for a second round, rereading the same exact text from the beginning. The goal of this reading activity is to advance further in the text in the second round. The number of words gained on the second reading is then recorded. After students become familiar with these general procedures and expectations, students typically look forward to these oral paired reading activities because they are goal-oriented, enjoyable, and contribute to fluency development.

Motivate Students to Read

Frustrating reading experiences, not uncommon among L2 students, can demotivate students, "a truly unfortunate consequence considering the importance of reading for most of our students" (Komiyama, 2009, p. 32). Students benefit from multiple types of motivational support:

1. Teachers share their reading interests with students by talking about what they are reading, why it is interesting, and what other types of reading they engage in. The teacher-as-role-model serves as a powerful motivator.
2. Students are encouraged to share what they are reading and why they find it interesting.
3. Teachers identify students' interests and then look for related readings to bring to class.
4. Teachers promote cohesiveness among learners, with pair and group work, to build a sense of community and to make it easier for students to support each other with challenging reading tasks.
5. Teachers set up students for success by selecting *texts* that are accessible to students (with scaffolded instruction, when necessary) and by devizing reading *tasks* that students are capable of completing. The texts and tasks should involve just enough challenge to require some effort.
6. Teachers devize attention-catching introductions to major texts and associated tasks to build student interest. They can do so by, for example, posing provocative questions, connecting the text to students' lives and/or academic interests, and examining visuals (in the text or supplementary ones) that might catch students' attention.
7. Teachers link course materials to students' prior knowledge, experiences, and academic interests.
8. Teachers give students some choice in reading materials (and related tasks).
9. Teachers help students build their knowledge about reading topics by bringing in supplementary passages (and other content resources) that connect to textbook content.
10. Teachers guide students in discovering what they have actually learned *from* reading so that students gain an appreciation for reading.

In line with item #10 above, there are benefits to making a curricular commitment to language- and content-learning aims, as discussed below.

Content-Based Approaches that Make a Dual Commitment to Language- and Content-Learning

Helping students appreciate what can be learned from reading can be achieved with content-based approaches to language teaching, including Content-Based Instruction (CBI) and Content and Language Integrated Learning (CLIL). Such approaches make a dual commitment to language and content learning (Snow & Brinton, 2017); they naturally lead to opportunities for extended reading, motivational learning experiences, strategic responses to increasingly complex tasks, greater choices in reading materials, and increased challenges to match students' growing skills. Content-based approaches naturally lend themselves to the recycling of important reading skills, the rereading of texts, and realistic tasks for interpreting, integrating, and evaluating information from multiple texts. Such tasks mirror the types of tasks that students will encounter in academic settings.

Concept-Oriented Reading Instruction (CORI)[2] is an instructional approach with content- and language-learning objectives (Swan, 2003); it is guided by instructional principles for stimulating student interest and motivation to read. The approach is organized around four stages:

1. immersion into a main theme, with a specific question that guides inquiry;
2. wide reading and information gathering on the theme across multiple information sources;
3. reading strategy instruction to assist with comprehension; and
4. project work that results in a tangible outcome that demonstrates what students have learned.

CORI activities lead to content learning in addition to reading-skills development, vocabulary building, fluency practice, enhanced discourse-structure awareness, and strategy training, the latter accompanied by consistent teacher modeling, scaffolding, and student discussions.

Teach for Comprehension

The ability to understand a text underlies all reading tasks; yet it is not a simple ability. Comprehension requires a reasonable knowledge of basic grammar, an ability to identify main ideas in the text, an awareness of discourse structure, and strategic processing. Reading comprehension instruction should direct some attention to grammar, particularly at beginning and low-intermediate levels. In certain cases, teaching a key grammar point will support students' reading comprehension. However, most EAP reading instruction occurs beyond beginning levels, and it is not necessary for a reading course to review grammar extensively. Certainly, a reading course is not the place in which to embed a grammatical syllabus. At the same time, it is important not to ignore grammatical knowledge as a resource for more advanced reading comprehension abilities (Nation, 2009).

Teaching for main-idea comprehension, rather than testing it, should be at the core of reading instruction (Anderson, 2009). Main-idea comprehension can be taught through, at a minimum, classroom discussions and attention to comprehension monitoring.

Classroom Discussion

Main-idea comprehension abilities can be developed through class conversations during which students identify and explore main ideas in the texts that they are reading. During those discussions, students are guided to note connections across parts of the text, between two or more texts, or between the text and their own background knowledge. Class conversations centered on main-idea comprehension may start with post-reading comprehension questions, but they are followed by requests for further elaboration, during which students answer:

- *why* questions (which oblige students to explain *why* their answers are appropriate, thereby leading to an exploration of main ideas, text recall, inferencing, and coherence building, that is, making connections across parts of the text);
- *where* questions (which require students to return to the text, reread, and point out *where* the text supports their answers); and
- *how* questions (which encourage discussions of *how* to understand the text better and the reading strategies used to do so).

Asking students to summarize what they have read, or some segment of a longer text, also provides them with helpful practice in identifying main ideas, articulating these ideas clearly (orally or in writing), and establishing links across main ideas and supporting details. To assist students in summarizing, teachers can start out by asking students to fill in a partially completed summary, outline, or discourse-specific graphic organizer (mentioned above). Students can also work in pairs or groups to craft effective summaries.

Comprehension Monitoring

Comprehension monitoring, entailing a combination of reading strategies, involves much more than the recognition of main ideas and the identification and untangling of difficulties experienced while reading. Monitoring can help students recognize when they (and their classmates) are not comprehending more challenging texts, or when they are not comprehending well enough to successfully fulfill their purpose(s) for reading. Strategies identified as playing a major role in comprehension monitoring are listed in Figure 4.12 (see also Appendix A in Chapter 3). Teachers can support reading comprehension development (and monitoring) by modeling these strategies, discussing them, guiding students in using them, and leading students in discussions about

Figure 4.12 Comprehension monitoring strategies used by skilled readers (from Grabe, 2009)

• Having a reason for reading and being aware of it • Recognizing text structure • Identifying important and main-idea information • Relating the text to background knowledge	• Recognizing the relevance of the text to reading goal(s) • Recognizing and attending to reading difficulties • Reading carefully • Rereading as appropriate • Clarifying misunderstandings

when the students used the strategies, *what* purpose(s) they served, and *how* they helped.

Instructional Activities that Integrate Reading and Writing

In academic environments, students are typically required to read-to-learn and read-to-write, the latter requiring the integration of reading and writing. Teachers of reading should work toward integrating reading and writing, whenever possible, to prepare students for read-to-write academic tasks. Teachers can do so by asking students to engage in reading-based writing tasks (Figure 4.13), sometimes referred to as *text-responsible writing tasks*.

When assigning reading-based writing tasks, such as those listed in Figure 4.13, teachers should hold students accountable for information in the texts that they are reading. As part of read-to-write instruction, teachers should address explicitly the writing skills (and vocabulary) required for effective paraphrasing and the all-important issues related to plagiarism and attribution.

Figure 4.13 Reading-based writing tasks (adapted from Grabe & Zhang, 2013)

• Taking notes while reading and/or filling in an outline (prepared by the teacher) while reading • Summarizing main ideas in a text • Paraphrasing complex sentences that are important for main-idea comprehension • Synthesizing information from two or more texts • Comparing viewpoints introduced in one or more texts and producing a critical synthesis • Answering short-answer or essay questions about one or more texts • Researching further a topic introduced in the textbook and writing a "research paper" or literature review • Summarizing and then critiquing a text

When making a commitment to read-to-write instruction, teachers can also introduce students to the reading and writing of varied genres, using texts as models for students' subsequent writing. A read–analyze and write approach (Stoller & Robinson, 2016) can bring several key ideas to students' conscious attention: text organization, rhetorical patterns characteristic of the genre, vocabulary choice, and genre-specific writing conventions. Like reading, which requires a lot of practice, students' read-to-write abilities require teacher scaffolding and many opportunities for practice and teacher feedback. [See Ferris, Chapter 6, this volume, for more on reading–writing relationships.]

Assessments *of* and *for* Learning

Assessments of reading comprehension are often associated with post-reading comprehension questions, included in textbooks and/or written by teachers. While such questions serve some evaluative purposes, they are limited in scope. They typically do not tell teachers much about students' improvements in word and phrase decoding, levels of vocabulary knowledge, discourse structure awareness, strategy use, reading fluency, and motivation to read. Post-reading comprehension questions are also sometimes answered correctly or incorrectly for reasons that may not best reflect what students have learned. Post-reading questions might be better used as opportunities for teaching (rather than testing) main idea comprehension.

As advocated in chapter 3, both assessments *of* and *for* learning have important roles to play in the reading classroom (and curriculum):

- Assessments *of* learning aim to determine how well students have learned (or are learning) the skills, subskills, and content taught (and practiced) in a course.
- Assessments *for* learning measure students' incremental (day-to-day, weekly) improvements and provide opportunities for teacher feedback and student reflection on their own learning. Assessment *for* learning should take place during every class session, as teachers observe students' engagement, motivation, and class performance on reading-related tasks in pre-, during-, and post-reading class segments.

Assessments *of* and *for* learning can be carried out through formal testing formats (Figure 4.14) and informal measures (Figure 4.15), although informal assessments are most often associated with assessment *for* learning.

Informal classroom-based assessments (and modified teacher practices that provide more effective learning opportunities, Figure 4.16) provide a much wider range of feedback for teachers and learners. The combination of informal assessments and modified teaching practices can lead to explicit feedback from the teacher, student discussions of and reflections on their own performance in non-threatening contexts, and opportunities for students to signal when they need help (see also Wiliam & Leahy, 2015).

Figure 4.14 Examples of formal reading assessment formats
(adapted from Grabe, 2009)

• Cloze passage formats • Fill-in-the blank items • Graphic organizer completion • Matching tasks • Multiple choice items	• Sentence completion items • Short written responses • Skimming items • Summary writing • True/false questions

Figure 4.15 Examples of informal reading assessment formats
(adapted from Grabe, 2009)

• Teacher documentation of uses of texts (e.g., for varied reading purposes, for read-to-write tasks, for fluency practice, with discourse-specific graphic organizers) • Teacher observations of students' in-class performance (e.g., reading, participation in discussions, read-alouds, motivation) • Teacher-compiled performance inventories	• Student records of reading engagement (# of pages read, # of books read, simple book reports, rate charts, reading journals) • teacher–student conferences (to discuss students' reading progress, goals, interests, preferences, choices, strategy use, challenges)

Figure 4.16 Examples of assessment *for* learning teacher practices
(adapted from Grabe, 2009)

• Teacher waits 3–5 seconds after asking a question, without answering the question when students are silent and without calling on a stronger student for the answer • Teacher moves from more traditional question-and-answer sequences about reading passages to questions that initiate discussions among students about their understanding of the text	• Teacher deals with wrong answers or performance difficulties in ways that engage students in finding good answers and achieving task success. Teacher provides feedback to encourage student learning • Teacher asks *why* questions and *why* follow-up questions to generate discussions about students' answers

Chapter Summary

A single chapter on teaching techniques and assessment, in the context of teaching L2 reading, cannot be comprehensive. Nonetheless, what we have tried to do here is introduce reading teachers, material writers, and curriculum designers to practical and adaptable techniques for enhancing L2 reading instruction, particularly for students with academic aspirations. We have sought to link the teaching and assessment ideas presented in this chapter with:

*   what we know about reading abilities and implications from reading research, which suggest *what* we should teach (chapter 2); and
*   L2 principles for curricular design, which suggest *how* to shape reading instruction (Chapter 3).

   We have also sought to emphasize the positive power of assessment rather than the anxiety-provoking side. We believe that an assessment *for* learning orientation can make a big difference in reading instruction and students' reading improvement. And, as we close, we want to remind teachers of the one other key to reading development that has always been true: L2 students, like all students, only learn to read by reading, and by reading a lot.

Discussion Questions and Tasks

1.   Think about the reading classes that you've either taught or taken as a student. Which of the activities described in this chapter have been a part of your language teaching and/or language learning experience? Of those activities that you have *not* experienced (as a teacher or student), which do you think are most valuable for reading-skills improvement? Explain.
2.   Select an ESL/EFL reading textbook. Survey the reading-skills development activities included in Chapters Three and Four. How well does the textbook address students' reading needs in the following areas: (a) word and phrases decoding, (b) vocabulary building, (c) discourse-structure awareness, (d) strategic reading, (e) reading fluency, (f) reading motivation, (g) main-idea comprehension, and (h) read-to-write integration. Use a 1–4 scale (1=poor; 4=strong) to assess the textbook in areas (a)–(h).
3.   Based on your textbook survey (in item #2 above), which one or two activities introduced in this chapter could be used to supplement the textbook and improve reading instruction?
4.   Briefly describe a classroom setting (location, students' English proficiency, students' reading needs). Which practical teaching ideas in this chapter would be most useful for these students? Why?
5.   What are the major differences between assessment *of* and *for* learning as introduced in the previous chapter and elaborated upon in this chapter? How might a stronger commitment to assessment *for* learning benefit students with pressing reading needs?

Further Reading

Jiang, X., & Grabe, W. (2009). Building reading abilities with graphic organizers. In R. Cohen (Ed.), *Explorations in second language reading* (pp. 25–42). Alexandria, VA: TESOL.

In this book chapter, the authors provide a step-by-step description of how to build discourse-specific graphic organizers to promote students' discourse-level awareness.

Stoller, F. L., Anderson, N., Grabe, W., & Komiyama, R. (2013). Instructional enhancements to improve students' reading abilities. *English Teaching Forum*, *51*(1), 2–11, 33.

The authors describe five types of modest instructional enhancements that teachers, who do not have a lot of extra teaching time, can integrate into their classes to help students become better, more confident readers.

Wiliam, D., & Leahy, S. (2015). *Embedding formative assessment: Practical techniques for K–12 classrooms.* West Palm Beach, FL: Learning Sciences International.

This volume describes specific ways for teachers to provide explicit, supportive feedback to students on their comprehension performance; it also describes techniques that students can use to signal comprehension difficulties.

Notes

1 Pronunciation should not be considered a key issue for repeated reading unless the word is pronounced so poorly that it could be confused with a different word.
2 See www.cori.umd.edu for extensive CORI-related materials, including descriptions of CORI projects and links to pertinent publications.

Appendix

Figure 4.17 Four discourse-specific graphic organizers (DSGOs) developed for
a four-paragraph reading passage with four patterns of organization
(adapted from DSGOs created by J. Xiangying, West Virginia
University, for "Telescopes: Tools for Examining the Heavens"
in Mikulecky & Jeffries, 2007)

1. Timeline/Chronology: Invention of telescopes (paragraphs 1 and 2)		
Early 1600s	—	• Children put two glass lenses together while playing with them in a Dutch optical shop; the owner of the shop looked through the lenses and noticed their magnifying effect. • Soon after that, he invented a device called a "looker."
1608	—	• The shop owner failed to sell the "looker." (1) _____
1610	—	(2) _____
1611, April	—	• Galileo showed his device to guests at a banquet and one of the guests named the device "telescope."
1700s	—	(3) _____

2. Problem–Solution: Problem with Galileo's telescope & Newton's solution (Paragraph 2)		
Problem(s)		Solution(s)
Problems with Galileo's telescope (4) _____ (5) _____ • This sometimes interfered with viewing.	➡	Newton's solution • Isaac Newton designed a new type of telescope that used a curved mirror. (6) _____ • The new type of telescope is called a "reflector."

3. Description: Today's world's largest optical telescopes (paragraph 3)		
Telescopes	Location	Key characteristics
(7) _____	Yerkes Observatory, Williams Bay, Wisconsin	Has lenses that are 40 inches across
World's largest reflecting telescope	Caucasus Mountains	(8) _____
World's second largest reflecting telescope	(9) _____	Has a 200-inch lens
Keck Telescope	On a mountain in Hawaii	Uses the combined light that falls on 36 mirrors, each 5.9 feet in diameter

4. Comparison–Contrast: Radio and optical telescopes (paragraph 4)		
	Radio telescope	Optical telescope
Comparison	• Both allow astronomers to collect data from outer space. (10) _____	
Contrast	• Collects radio waves (11) _____ • Uses radio receivers to record radio waves from distant objects in space	• Collects light waves • Uses lenses or mirror 12) _____

Section 2

Introduction to Writing

Dana R. Ferris

Developing college-level writing skills is challenging for all postsecondary students, regardless of their particular language backgrounds. In many contexts worldwide, secondary students are exposed primarily to rigid forms of writing designed primarily for passing examinations. They arrive in college or university with a limited view of what writing entails and what it can accomplish. As they move beyond first-year writing courses (if applicable) into general education and specialized major coursework, and, for some, into postgraduate or professional school contexts, the demands become even more complex, sophisticated, and specialized.

Postsecondary students who are writing in a second or subsequent language —i.e., not the primary language spoken in their homes as young children— encounter additional challenges that many monolingual students do not. These challenges may include:

- *a lack of fluency,* or the ability to write (and read) extensively in the second language (L2);
- *a lack of accuracy and complexity,* or the linguistic tools of vocabulary and grammar with which to express their ideas clearly, precisely, and effectively;

- *a lack of cultural knowledge*, which may hinder their ability to understand and write about content and to express their ideas in discourse formats that readers expect;
- and, due to these various knowledge and experience gaps, *a lack of confidence* that may lead to poor writing and learning strategies.

This section addresses what we know about writing in a second language and how it may be different from writing in L1. It also addresses individual and group differences across L2 populations. With these issues in mind, it then moves to practical suggestions for planning courses and curriculum for L2 writers (Chapter 6) and for classroom instruction (Chapter 7), including ideas about feedback to writers and writing assessment. Though future teachers who intend to focus their attention specifically on the teaching of L2 writing/composition may wish to read even further (see the "Further Reading" section at the end of each chapter), this section should provide a foundation for further exploration and a baseline for new L2 writing teachers.

5 Writing in a Second Language

Dana R. Ferris

Successful writing in academic and professional settings requires a complex range of skills and knowledge bases. Writers must have at least an adequate grasp of the content about which they are writing. They must understand the rhetorical situation, including the purpose for writing, and knowledge and expectations of their audience of readers. They need to appreciate the constraints and boundaries that accompany genres, tasks, and text types: A personal narrative is not structured like a history research paper or a science laboratory report or a business case study. Further, writers need advanced control of the linguistic features (vocabulary, spelling, grammar, cohesive ties) and extralinguistic features (punctuation, capitalization, formatting) appropriate for the content, genre, and target audience for their text. Finally, writers need effective strategies for managing their writing tasks; such processes tend to become more ingrained with experience, but writing instruction can facilitate the timely, successful development of writing strategies (or "strategic writers").

Student writers and their instructors, therefore, have a substantial task before them, and the challenges of developing and improving academic literacy are amplified when some or all of the students are writing in their L2. In this chapter, we will examine the following questions:

- What is unique/different about writing in L2 compared to writing in L1?
- What implications might these differences raise for postsecondary writing instruction?
- What are the characteristics of L2 writers, and what is salient about the larger contexts in which they develop their writing abilities?

This chapter also lays the foundation for the two subsequent ones, which address in turn curricular approaches for L2 writing course design and classroom approaches for L2 writing instruction.

How is L2 Writing Different From L1 Writing?

Before we outline specific areas of difference, some definitions and generalizations are in order. First, what do we mean by a "L2 writer"? For the purposes of this discussion, we will define "L2 writer" as follows:

> *Second language (L2) writers are students coming from homes where the primary language was not English.*

Depending upon the context, these student writers may include:

- English as a Foreign Language (EFL) students learning English as a L2 in their home countries
- International students primarily educated in their home countries who have come to the L2 context to pursue a postsecondary degree
- Late-arriving resident immigrants to a new country with partial education in the L2 context
- Early-arriving resident immigrants with all/most of their education in the L2 context
- Children of first-generation immigrants born and entirely educated in the L2 context

(Evans, Anderson, & Eggington, 2015; Ferris, 2009; Ferris & Hedgcock, 2014; Roberge, Losey, & Wald, 2015)

Although, as we will discuss later in this chapter, there is tremendous variability across and within these L2 writer subgroups, several generalizations tend to be accurate. First, L2 writers, even at the postsecondary level, are in the simultaneous process of acquiring both academic (college-level) literacy skills *and* are still in the long-term, ongoing process of second language acquisition. Compared with monolingual English speakers writing in their L1, the challenges of academic writing development are magnified and more complex. Second, many or most of these student writers, because of their backgrounds, will have had relatively less exposure to the patterns of the L2 through oral/aural interactions and through written text than will their monolingual peers. Amount of exposure is important because it builds both explicit and unconscious knowledge of the forms and patterns of language. (See Chapter 2 in the "Reading" section for more discussion of this point.) Finally, because of the nature of L2 instruction in many contexts, students may have spent their time learning rules and individual linguistic items (vocabulary, sounds) rather than building fluency by reading or writing extensively in the L2. Thus, the demands of college-level courses—to read hundreds of pages or write lengthy papers—may be new and overwhelming to them. Despite variation in how these differences manifest themselves in individuals and groups of students, these generalizations about L2 writers in college/university settings tend to be fairly reliable. In the next section, we turn to some more specific distinctions between L1 and L2 writers.

Task 5.1

Have you ever done academic (school) work in your second (or other) language? If so, make a list of what was most challenging for you, focusing especially on *writing* in a second language. Was it generating ideas in a L2? Text organization? Vocabulary? Grammar? What strategies did you use to address those challenges?

If you have never done substantial writing in a L2, use your imagination and/or your experience with writing in L1 to answer these questions. If possible, discuss your ideas with a classmate(s) who has experience with writing in a L2 and compare your experiences.

L2 Writers Know More Than One Language

Differences Across Writing Systems

While the above subheading may seem somewhat redundant given the "L2" label, it has several possible implications that are worth exploring. First, depending upon the writer's L1—and literacy development in that L1—the student may have learned to read and write under a completely different system of writing than what they encounter in the L2 (Birch, 2007; Ferris & Hedgcock, 2014). For example, students whose primary language was Chinese may have learned to read using the *logographic* writing system, in which a written symbol (or *character* or *sinogram*) represents a meaning (or what we in English would refer to as morphemes or words). Reading and writing in English as a L2, they have to work with an *alphabetic* system, in which individual symbols (letters) represent sounds, not entire units of a meaning. In contrast, a Spanish L1 speaker will also have become literate using an alphabetic system that is *transparent* (specific symbols have a consistent 1:1 relationship with sounds) and must adjust to the *opaque* alphabetic system that exists in English (meaning that sound/symbol correspondences are not as reliable as they are in transparent systems, so a reader has to memorize or adjust to different sound/spelling correspondences across a range of lexical items).

While differences between L1 and L2 writing systems may be more of an issue in L2 reading than in L2 writing, they still can cause specific challenges for L2 writers. Beyond the basics for beginners—new learners of English as a L2 will need to learn the alphabet and its range of sound-symbol relationships, and other basic writing conventions such as capital letters and punctuation—differences in writing systems may inhibit learners' L2 vocabulary development because they might use strategies for analyzing new words that work well for their L1 system but not the L2 system. Limited or imprecise vocabulary development can in turn inhibit effective L2 written expression.

Accurate spelling may also be an issue for some learners who are not accustomed to attending to such details in the L1; while spell-check and online dictionaries may mitigate some of those problems, they will not catch all of them. In any case, while teachers can't do much about their students' backgrounds with regard to L1 writing systems, awareness of the differences may help them target skills (e.g., for vocabulary analysis and editing for meaning and spelling) to which some of their students may need more attention.

The Role of the L1 when Writing in L2

An important characteristic of L2 writers, particularly if they are also literate and experienced in writing in their L1s, is that they have (at least) two languages to think about when they are writing in L2. There has been extensive research on the role of the L1 in L2 writing, and it has uncovered both benefits and disadvantages for student writers (Kobayashi & Rinnert, 1992). The first thing to understand is that use of the L1 in L2 writing is *inevitable*—it is just a natural cognitive process that cannot be forbidden or advised away by teachers or wished away by the L2 writers themselves (Manchón, Roca de Larios, & Murphy, 2007). The L1 can be valuable to writers in the idea-generation stage of writing—when they are grappling with the task and topic—especially if the content is something that they first encountered while learning or reading in L1 (Wang & Wen, 2002). Similarly, the L1 can be valuable when the L2 writer is drafting ideas and searching for a particular topic-specific lexical item (Murphy & Roca de Larios, 2010). The writer can use the L1 term as a placeholder and find the appropriate L2 equivalent later in the revision process.

However, L1 use in L2 writing can also be counterproductive under certain circumstances. Specifically, if the writer composes in L1 and then tries to translate the text into L2 (through their own abilities and/or by using an electronic translator), it can lead to grammatical errors, unidiomatic, strange-sounding prose, and, at its worst, incomprehensible texts (Wang, 2003). Student writers should be carefully apprised of the drawbacks of writing in L1 and then translating. In sum, teachers of L2 writers should be aware of the possible advantages and problems that may arise from L1 use and discuss useful strategies explicitly with their student writers.

L2 Writers Have Varying Experiences and Backgrounds

The most fundamental difference between L1 and L2 student writers is their knowledge and use of two or more languages when writing in L2. However, another strong distinction is that L2 writers typically have cultural and educational experiences that differ from those of their L1/monolingual peers. As with the previous point, this range of backgrounds should not necessarily be viewed by teachers as a problem; on the contrary, multilingual and multi-cultural student writers, whether they are in mixed L1/L2 classes or in L2-only classes, can bring depth and complexity that enriches the writing classroom. That said, there are specific ways in which differing student experiences can add challenges to writing instruction.

Schema Theory and Cultural/Content Knowledge for Writing Tasks

A *schema* refers to a mental framework that organizes an individual's prior knowledge and experience, and it may also include emotions and attitudes (Ferris & Hedgcock, 2014; Rumelhart, 1980). For example, if someone living in the U.S. goes to an unfamiliar indoor shopping mall, that person's prior knowledge of malls might lead him or her to expect a food court, small specialty stores for shoes, accessories, electronics, and skin-care products, large department stores, and so forth. She or he might also feel anticipation (if prior mall trips have been fun) or anxiety (if malls seem overstimulating). These expectations and reactions are not based upon this new mall but rather on prior knowledge about and experiences with malls.

Schema theory is especially relevant when discussing reading and listening comprehension for L2 learners (see Chapters 2–4 and 11–13), but students' prior knowledge affects L2 writing development in specific ways. First, their understanding of the topic and/or content of a writing task (including required sources) will be influenced by their cultural backgrounds. For instance, if the class reads the short literary work "The Story of An Hour" by Kate Chopin (1894), students' processing of the story will be affected by their own cultural beliefs and values regarding marriage and especially a woman's role in marriage.

Beyond cultural/content schema, L2 writers may be affected by their *formal schema*, which refers to knowledge about ways in which text types or genres are structured. Taking Chopin's short story referenced above, for example, the narrative is tightly structured and somewhat cryptic in its plot details. The understanding of what's happening to whom could be confusing if students are not helped with mapping the characters and plot lines. Formal schema as a construct becomes especially relevant when discussing academic genres such as persuasive/expository essays, research papers, summaries, and so forth. Extensive research in the tradition of *contrastive or intercultural rhetoric* has established that strategies for structuring texts and presenting arguments vary cross-culturally (Connor, 2011; Kaplan, 1966) and that such differences can cause L2 writers' texts to appear out-of-focus or rhetorically ineffective, even if they are grammatically and lexically precise (Eggington, 2015). For instance, in U.S. academic settings, student writers are encouraged to present arguments *deductively*, by clearly stating their purpose/viewpoint at the outset and then proceeding to argue for/support their proposition.

In other rhetorical traditions, however, writers tend to be more indirect and inductive in their approach, laying out the various arguments as they go along and only stating an opinion toward the end of the text, if at all (Eggington, 2015; Hinds, 1987).

With these issues in mind, teachers of L2 writers will want to carefully consider students' prior knowledge of the content or topic being addressed in class, providing resources and scaffolding as needed to fill in any gaps or bridge cultural differences. They also may wish to consider explicit genre instruction, with helpful models, so that L2 writers can analyze effective text structures for the task at hand. We will discuss genre-focused writing instruction further in Chapter 6, but at this point it is useful to mention that differing cultural and rhetorical knowledge bases may be a clear distinction between L1 students (or teachers) and L2 writers.

L2 Writers Are Still Acquiring the L2

A final distinction between L1 and L2 writers is that L2 students, for the most part, have differing levels of mastery over L2 structures needed for writing in academic settings. As noted by Ferris and Hedgcock (2014):

> Successful writing, by definition, includes and requires the effective deployment of a range of linguistic and extralinguistic features, including vocabulary, syntax, punctuation, capitalization . . . Such decision-making goes far beyond simply avoiding errors . . .
>
> (p. 310)

Effective selection of linguistic features for written communication also includes an understanding of rhetorical grammar (how syntactic choices, such as the use of active and passive voice, rhetorical questions, etc., can convey messages), genre and audience awareness and how they affect language choices, and the need for lexical precision and variation to create a clear and engaging style.

It should be obvious that advanced control of the L2 at the word and sentence level is a threshold skill for writing in that language. There is also extensive evidence that L2 writers at the post-secondary level do not bring the same linguistic repertoires to writing tasks that their L1 peers do: Many have less developed vocabularies, are less able and willing to use complex syntax, and are more limited in their use of cohesive devices such as transitions, pronouns, and synonyms (Hinkel, 2002; Leki, Cumming, & Silva, 2008; Silva, 1993). Teachers thus need to be conscious both of helping L2 writers become aware of error patterns and strategies for remediating them and of facilitating L2 writers' ongoing second language acquisition through encouraging vocabulary and grammar analysis with source texts and effective application of linguistic knowledge to their own writing (Ferris, 2011, 2015b, 2016; Hinkel, 2016; see also Chapters 2–4 & 6–7).

Contexts and Characteristics of L2 Writing and Writers

Contexts of L2 Writing

In postsecondary contexts, L2 writers may be found in a variety of programs and classes. The goals and characteristics of the programs will influence the types of experiences that the student writers and their instructors will have. Though what follows are necessarily generalizations, they will help those new to the field understand the landscape.

Foreign Language (FL) Contexts

FL instruction occurs in countries or regions where the L2 is not a primary or official language. Students taking L2 classes in such settings may be doing so to fulfill degree requirements or for future academic or professional goals (e.g., to study or work in an English-speaking environment).

It is relatively rare to find specialized academic writing instruction in FL settings like the composition courses and programs that exist in the U.S. (Reichelt, 2011; Thaiss, Bräuer, Carlino, Ganobcsik-Williams, & Sinha, 2012). Prior to post-secondary work, students may have only encountered L2 writing as a way to practice language forms, to discuss required works of literature, or to prepare formulaic responses to college entrance examinations. They may not be highly motivated to spend much time on or revise their L2 writing if they don't see instrumental purposes for engaging with it. Instructors teaching English writing in FL contexts may find that both students and administrators may expect a grammar-heavy test-preparation curriculum and resist U.S. instructional paradigms such as process writing (see Chapter 6). Also, because students may not have many opportunities outside the English class to build their L2 language and literacy skills, teachers will need to be creative and intentional in providing such opportunities, such as through extensive reading assignments (see Chapters 3–4) and journal writing assignments to build fluency and confidence through low-stakes writing tasks.

Second Language (SL) Contexts

L2 writers in SL contexts either live permanently in the L2 environment (resident students) or have chosen to come from their home countries to pursue a degree (international/visa students). Although, as will be discussed below, there are some key distinctions between resident and international L2 students, they share in common that they are studying English at an English-medium institution and have an immediate need to function well in the L2, including writing effectively for academic purposes. They also likely have more ongoing, everyday opportunities to be exposed to the L2 (in their other classes and in the surrounding environment) than do students in FL settings, and this factor facilitates their ongoing second language acquisition.

Two-Year or Community College Programs

One important post-secondary context for L2 students in a SL context is the open-access community or two-year college.[1] Students who need to build their language or other academic skills to pursue a four-year degree or other vocational goals may take ESL (English as a Second Language) and/or developmental writing courses. Often such programs are relatively affordable and classes are plentiful and available at a range of proficiency levels. There are two characteristics of community college programs (and their students) that are relevant for teachers to consider. First, because of the "open-access" nature of the institution, students may have a very wide range of abilities and backgrounds. It can be challenging for teachers to learn how to meet a diverse set of needs within the same classroom. Second, because community college students also may have other responsibilities, such as families and jobs, the class population can be transitory, making it important for teachers to be flexible and willing to make adjustments as time goes on and the composition of the class changes. Teachers may also find that some students are tired, overwhelmed by other responsibilities, and discouraged about their progress. However, community college students are often motivated and eager to learn and move forward with their education, and teachers will likely find that working with them can be very satisfying.

Intensive English Programs at Four-Year Institutions

Many four-year colleges and universities host *Intensive English Programs* (IEPs), which help L2 students develop their language skills before fully matriculating into college-level work. In some instances, students may be admitted to the institution conditionally until they complete required language courses. In other settings, students come only for the IEP, without any assurance or expectation that they will ever be admitted to the host campus. IEPs may be funded through the main campus budget or may be financially a separate entity with its own budget contingent on student enrollments.

Most IEPs offer courses in a variety of skills (listening, speaking, reading, writing, pronunciation, grammar, vocabulary) at a range of levels (from near beginner to almost college level). Depending upon the nature of the individual IEP, the experiences of students and their instructors can vary widely. Some IEPs are of high quality, upholding rigorous standards for curriculum and assessment, and instructors receive contracts with fair pay and benefits. Others are more focused on their profit margins and keeping their "customers" (the students) happy, so teachers are not encouraged to assign homework or grade stringently. In these latter types, teachers are often not paid well and have little job security beyond the current teaching session. As for writing instruction in particular, in the more business-oriented models, it can be difficult to make steady progress with student writing because teachers are expected to engage students rather than challenge them, and L2 writing development is hard work that students do not typically consider "fun." At the more integrated, academic IEPs, excellent state-of-the-art teaching may be the norm. However, coordination and articulation with other campus units, such as the English/composition/writing programs may be difficult, and student transitions from the IEP to other courses may not always go smoothly (see Atkinson & Ramanathan, 1995).

Undergraduate Writing Programs in Four-Year Schools

In the U.S., most colleges and universities have some form of a first-year writing requirement, and many also have a developmental (remedial/basic) writing course(s) for students who do not meet minimum writing proficiency levels upon admission. Such programs are typically offered through an English or writing department; some institutions have separate ESL programs that offer parallel programs for L2 students. There is great variation across different programs as to how L2 writers are served in these programs. In some, L2 students are provided with "sheltered" (ESL-only) writing courses, with trained L2 writing teachers, at the developmental level and sometimes at the first-year composition level. In others, they are simply mainstreamed with other students, with the assumption being that having been admitted to the institution, they need no further specialized language support.

As college and university student populations have become increasingly diverse, institutions are struggling with their assumptions about student preparedness. As noted in a recent publication by Andrade, Evans, and Hartshorn (2015), some schools will aggressively recruit and admit international students because of the tuition money they can bring, but in some cases, without maintaining appropriate admissions standards—matriculating students whose L2 proficiency isn't adequate—or without taking responsibility for supporting the students once they have arrived with language/writing courses, advising, and tutoring (the "sink or swim" approach).

Writing Centers

One approach taken by both composition and disciplinary faculty is to refer L2 students who need extra help to the campus writing center, usually a centralized resource staffed by tutors who will do one-to-one and/or small group consultations with student writers. In many contexts, these are staffed by peer tutors (other undergraduates) who are trained and supervised by writing center staff. Writing centers can be an excellent resource for L2 writers as they move through their undergraduate studies. However, in some contexts, the tutors are not specifically trained to work with L2 writers, and/or the stated philosophy of the center itself is somewhat counterproductive to the needs of L2 students. For example, writing centers often train their tutors in nondirective approaches to consultations, and this may be frustrating and culturally confusing to some L2 students, who expect an explanation rather than Socratic questioning. Many writing centers also have strict prohibitions against "editing" student papers in tutorial sessions, but in practice, this may mean that L2 writers cannot receive in-depth, contextualized assistance with language questions that may be the most pressing for them (see Leki, 2009).

L2 Writers: Subgroup Characteristics

At the beginning of this chapter, we provided a broad definition of "L2 writers" and characteristics that most/all of them may share. In this final section, we look more closely at the characteristics of different subgroups of L2 students and specifically how those may interact with their academic literacy needs. Again, the descriptions below are generalizations, but they provide an overview of writer characteristics.

International (Visa) Students

International students come from their home countries to the college or university for the purpose of attaining a degree (or pursuing short-term English study at an IEP). They usually have been entirely educated and are literate in their L1; however, there is a small but growing group of students who arrive as visa students during their secondary years to acclimate and work on their English skills before continuing to college (see Institute of International Education's annual *Open Doors* report for current statistics in the U.S.). Most international university students have some English proficiency, having studied the language in school in their home countries and attained at least minimally acceptable standardized test scores to gain admission. Depending upon their L2 education, however, their experience with writing in English may be limited or narrow in scope.

Many international students have strong formal grammar knowledge but have not learned effective strategies for applying their knowledge consistently to their own writing. They may also find required university-level reading tasks overwhelming, which in turn can limit their ability to successfully manage source-based writing assignments (Hirvela, 2016). Finally, their experience with U.S. composition-type writing classrooms may be limited or nonexistent, and they may need support with classroom activities such as working in groups to compose texts or do peer reviews (see Chapter 7), using technology effectively for writing, and participating in whole-class discussions led by the teacher.

Immigrant Students

By immigrant students, we refer here to "late arrivals" (Ferris, 2009)—students who immigrated to the L2 environment as older children or secondary students, say age 10 or above—rather than "early arrivals" (Generation 1.5 students), discussed below. These students, unlike most international students, are not newcomers and have assimilated at least somewhat to the culture and to the L2 educational system. They tend to be orally proficient in the L2 and can function well in large group and small group discussions. However, having had their K-12 education in their home country interrupted, they may have the dual disadvantage of underdeveloped L1 literacy and a relatively late start in acquiring the L2. Their language and literacy development may also have been influenced by the types of English language programs available to them in school after their arrival.

College-level L2 writers from this late-arriving immigrant group may be able to write more fluently in English than international student newcomers, and they may be more able to grapple with culturally specific content and educational practices. However, they may struggle due to underdeveloped reading skills and a productive vocabulary that is more conversational than academic. As to grammar and sentence patterns, they may have some intuitions about what "sounds right" (or wrong) but less formal knowledge about grammar than international students who took English classes in school in their home countries.

Generation 1.5 Students

This early-arriving (Ferris, 2009) group consists of students whose parents are first-generation immigrants and who were either born in the L2 environment or arrived at an early age, often before beginning school (Harklau, Losey, & Siegal, 1999; Rumbaut & Ima, 1988). As Roberge (2009) put it, they have "life experiences that span two or more countries, cultures, and languages" and "a self-perception of in-between-ness" (p. 5). They still fit the "L2 writer" definition given at the beginning of this chapter because their early years were spent in homes where English was not the primary language.[2] This primary language background, in turn, may have influenced their educational pathways when they began and proceeded through primary and secondary school.

Some Generation 1.5 students, having been raised and fully educated in the L2 setting, are self-sufficient in the L2 by the time they reach college age and don't need any form of L2 support. Others may have gaps in their language knowledge and writing skills and need specialized instruction just as the international and immigrant groups do. Complicating matters for this group is that they may not self-identify at all as "L2 students" and may be distressed or offended when tracked into developmental L2 writing courses with classmates who are new arrivals from other countries (Chiang & Schmida, 1999; Ortmeier-Hooper, 2008). This tends to be more a matter of perception and attitude than of pedagogy—the same pedagogical strategies can work well for mixed groups of L2 writers (Matsuda, 2008)—but it is a variable of which writing instructors need to be aware.

Instructors may find this overview of different subgroups of L2 writers useful as a starting point, but, as discussed further in Chapter 6, they will want to learn more about their own students' specific language and L2 literacy backgrounds before planning instruction for any or all of these groups of students.

Chapter Summary

In this chapter, we have reviewed general differences between writing in L2 versus writing in L1, and we have looked at educational contexts and subgroups of L2 writers. How can this knowledge help teachers of L2 writers, whether they encounter these students in IEPs, sheltered L2 composition classes, writing centers, or mainstream writing classes that include L2 students? Some implications are listed briefly below, with further practical applications to be discussed in more depth in the next two chapters.

1. **Differences across writing systems:** In some settings, if learners are relatively new to English language study, teachers should be prepared to review the mechanics of English writing (the alphabet, capitalization, sentence formatting, etc.). They should also be aware that for some students, learning new vocabulary and spelling patterns may be more challenging than for other students, depending upon the writing system(s) of their L1(s).

2. **Cultural and schematic differences:** Teachers of L2 writers will need to consider whether the content of writing tasks and source materials will be accessible to their students, and, where there are gaps, how they will help students to attain the background knowledge they will need to complete assignments successfully.

3. **Rhetorical differences:** Teachers should prepare students to analyze target genres for the reading and writing tasks they will undertake, understanding that text structure and argument patterns may vary cross-culturally, so what students may encounter in English may be different from what they have read (and possibly produced) in their L1s.

4. **Linguistic differences:** Teachers will need to help students continue with second language acquisition, particularly by teaching them strategies for applying new grammar and vocabulary knowledge to their own writing.

5. **Instructional contexts:** Teachers coming into new teaching situations will need to understand programmatic and student expectations for the learning situation and institutional resources and/or barriers that may facilitate or impede their students' success. While teachers may not be able to change the larger environment much if at all, they can help their students be prepared for it.

6. **L2 student subgroups:** Teachers should take time at the beginning of each new term to understand the characteristics and language/literacy backgrounds of the students in their classes and adapt instruction, feedback, and assessment accordingly for each group of students.

As you can see, writing in a second language is a complex undertaking, and teaching L2 writers involves more than just a syllabus, textbook, and lesson plan. In the following chapters, we will provide additional detail and suggestions about how to plan and provide instruction and support for L2 writers across a range of instructional settings.

Discussion Questions and Tasks

1. Of the various teaching contexts discussed in this chapter, which have you experienced or observed? How do you think teaching "academic writing in English" would vary across contexts (FL, IEP, community college, etc.)? What might a teacher need to adapt in various settings? What characteristics would stay the same across educational contexts?

2. The last section of the chapter focused on three specific subgroups of L2 student writers: international, immigrant, and Generation 1.5 writers. Do you think it is possible to teach two or all three of those groups in the same L2 writing class? If so, how might a teacher make such a class run smoothly? What might be problematic or challenging, and how could those problems/challenges be mitigated by careful instructional planning? If not, why not? What learner characteristics make you conclude that the group(s) should have their own separate classes?

3. Look at the six-point list of "implications" right at the end of the chapter. Which of these were new ideas to you? What would you need to know/learn more about to address these suggestions successfully as a L2 writing teacher?

4. To apply the ideas in this chapter, identify a L2 writer who is currently taking a writing class (or a class that includes writing) in any postsecondary context. Using the ideas from this chapter, design a questionnaire and/or interview questions, and interview him or her, finding out about the writer's background and experiences with L2 writing. Compare the writer's responses to the generalizations made in this chapter. If possible, obtain a sample of the student's writing and talk to the student about how the writer approached the writing task. Present your findings as a small case study, either in an oral presentation or a short paper.

Further Reading

Evans, N.W., Anderson, N.J., & Eggington, W.G. (Eds.) (2015). *ESL readers and writers in higher education: Understanding challenges, providing support.* New York, NY: Routledge.

This recently published collection provides a wide range of research insights and practical suggestions for universities, colleges, and writing/language programs working with international students at their institutions.

Ferris, D.R. & Hedgcock, J.S. (2014). *Teaching L2 composition: Purpose, process, and practice* (3rd Ed.). New York, NY: Routledge.

This book is a comprehensive manual on teaching courses for L2 writers. As a full-length work on the topic of teaching L2 writers, it goes into more depth and provides more detailed resources and suggestions than is possible in this four-skills volume.

Harklau, L., Losey, K., & Siegal, M. (Eds.) (1999). *Generation 1.5 meets college composition*. Mahwah, NJ: Erlbaum.

This landmark collection was the first full-length volume focused on Generation 1.5 writers in the U.S. It provides an excellent introduction to this fascinating population of L2 writers.

Matsuda, P., Cox, M., Jordan, J., & Ortmeier-Hooper, C. (Eds.) (2010). *Second-language writing in the composition classroom: A critical sourcebook*. Boston, MA: Bedford St. Martin's.

This edited collection is aimed particularly at teachers of L2 writers in mainstream composition settings, but its wide range of excellent papers will provide an excellent introduction to teaching L2 writing for any reader.

Notes

1 In the U.S., community (or "junior) colleges, subsidized by state governments, can be springboards for transferring to a four-year college or university and/or can lead to their own terminal degrees (Associate of Arts) or technical/vocational certification or licensing. Whether for academic or financial reasons, many multilingual students in the U.S. begin their postsecondary work at such institutions, and teachers in those contexts need to be aware of the student characteristics discussed in this section.

2 There are also, particularly in linguistically diverse regions such as California, students who grew up in bilingual homes—their parents' L1 plus English were regularly used. Demographically, they fit best under the Generation 1.5 label.

6 Building a Writing Curriculum and Developing Strategic Writers

Dana R. Ferris

As discussed in Chapter 5, writing in a second language is a complex endeavor, and contexts for writing and student writer characteristics can, and do, vary widely. With these practical realities in mind, it is impossible to discuss writing curriculum or syllabus design with a "one-size-fits-all" mentality. Rather, in this chapter, we will focus on three major themes, which should give individual instructors ideas to consider as they approach specific teaching situations. First, we will review the general curricular approaches, both historical and current, that have shaped L1 composition and the teaching of L2 writing over the past half-century. Second, we will present adaptable principles/ processes for teachers to follow in designing courses for L2 writers. Third, we will focus specifically on the curricular goal of developing *strategic writers* who will be equipped to manage their own learning and writing processes beyond their language/writing classes.

Approaches to Teaching L1 and L2 Composition

There have been several useful historical overviews of L2 writing instruction over the years (Ferris & Hedgcock, 2014; Matsuda, 2003; Raimes, 1991; Silva, 1990) that have focused on the stages that the teaching of L2 writing has passed through. These stages are reviewed briefly here and are adapted from the above-listed sources. Readers will notice that there are no end dates given for these stages. That is because elements of all of them remain active, to some extent, in classroom materials (textbooks, websites) and in the teaching of writing at the present time.

➢ *Focus on form* (sentence, paragraph, and essay level): 1966–. There are two historical approaches subsumed under this heading, the so-called "controlled/guided composition" model, and the "current-traditional" model. In the former, it was assumed that writing instruction should consist of tightly controlled language exercises so that students could practice specific grammatical forms (e.g., changing a paragraph written in first person to third person or from past tense to present tense) and produce "correct," well-structured sentences and paragraphs. In the latter, the control was extended from the sentence level to paragraph and essay-length writing, as students were taught to work within set structures (e.g., paragraphs with topic sentences, five-paragraph essays) to produce recognizable "modes of discourse" (e.g., process, narration, description, comparison and contrast, persuasion).

➢ *Focus on the writer.* 1976–. Heavily influenced by developments in L1 composition, the *process approach*, with subdivisions of *expressivism* and *cognitivism*, was introduced to L2 writing conversations by influential scholars (Krashen, 1984; Raimes, 1985; Zamel, 1982). In the process model, the focus was not on producing pristine sentences, paragraphs, and essays but rather on what individual writers can learn from going through the stages of writing. The elements of a process approach include multiple drafting, feedback between drafts, invention or prewriting activities, and guided opportunities for revision/editing after initial drafts have been composed.

➢ *Focus on the content.* 1986–. One of the immediate strong criticisms of the process approach when it was introduced into L2 writing was that it focused too heavily on students' own experiences, preferences, and feelings and left them unprepared for the real-world realities of timed written examinations and writing in the disciplines or professions (see Eskey, 1983; Horowitz, 1986). In response, the English for Academic Purposes (EAP) movement, under the larger umbrella of English for Specific Purposes (ESP), focused intensively on identifying the structures (text organization and language forms) needed to write in various disciplines. In this model, courses on (for example) "writing for science" or "writing for business" emphasize helping students grapple with and write about discipline-specific content.

➢ *Focus on the context.* 1986–. Several practical concerns were raised about the EAP approach to teaching L2 writers (see, e.g., Spack, 1988). One involved who the instructors should be: Can disciplinary content really be taught effectively by English instructors, and if not, can faculty in the disciplines effectively teach about writing/language issues? A broader issue involved the disciplines themselves: Every discipline has a range of genres and subgenres for written communication, some highly specialized. In response to these concerns, specialists in *genre pedagogy* advocated a *socioliterate* approach (Johns, 1997, 1999) to L2 writing instruction. In a socioliterate approach, rather than being explicitly taught the forms of a particular discipline, students instead are trained to be *genre researchers* (see Tardy, 2009) in their classes and workplaces—to understand the expectations of a specific target audience or context and learn to shape their own writing to become part of that discourse community (Swales, 1990).

It is also worth noting that not only are all four of these historical approaches still active in L2 writing instruction, but also that they are not mutually exclusive.

For example, EAP and genre-focused writing courses may use elements of the process approach. There are benefits and drawbacks to all of them, and a flexible stance and/or combination of approaches will probably serve students and teachers best.

Current Trends in L1 Composition

Beyond the four overlapping paradigms briefly described above, there are several other trends that currently influence the teaching of writing in L1 contexts and that often also affect L2 writing approaches (Ferris & Hedgcock, 2014; Tate, Taggart, Schick, & Hessler, 2013). They include collaborative pedagogy, critical pedagogy, service learning or community-engaged pedagogy, and multimodal/new media-focused pedagogy. Finally, "writing studies" approaches such as Writing about Writing and Teaching for Transfer (Downs & Wardle, 2007; Yancey, Robertson, & Taczak, 2014), focusing on "threshold concepts" about writing that students need to master in introductory courses (Adler-Kassner & Wardle, 2015), have become extremely important in current composition/rhetoric circles.

Task 6.1

Think about your own experiences as a writing student and/or teacher or tutor. Looking back at the historical overview in the previous section of how L1/L2 composition have been taught, make a list of which approaches were most present/salient in your own background in composition. Then list the ones you did *not* experience (or experienced to a lesser degree). For each, write a sentence about whether you think the approach worked well for you or did not, and why you think so. Then indicate whether you think the same would be true for L2 students you have taught or might teach in the future.

Space does not permit us to do justice to all of these different instructional paradigms here, but several themes can be extracted from this brief review that are significant for the following sections on course design:

1. **Process is important:** Whereas the classic "expressivist" approach to teaching writing as process (Zamel, 1982) may have only limited utility in most academic contexts, the main elements of the instructional model—allowing students to learn from writing multiple drafts and receiving feedback, helping students to generate ideas and plan their writing, guiding students through the stages of revision and editing after

they have initially generated texts—are extremely valuable, very beneficial to building confidence in L2 writers, and should be integral to the design of any L2 writing course.

2. **Rhetorical and genre awareness are important:** Teaching artificial "modes" of paragraph or essay development does students a disservice. Not only is this approach rigid and boring, but it also gives students the false impression that any writing task can be completed by following a formula. It is far more important to give students the tools to research and analyze the different rhetorical situations and genre expectations they will encounter.

3. **Reflection, or metacognition, is important:** Though reflective teaching as a construct is not unique to or new with the Writing about Writing/ Teaching for Transfer models, these currently popular approaches have done a good job of highlighting the value of metacognition in student learning and transfer. Reflective writing tasks, such as goal-setting at the beginning of a course, self-evaluation of progress made at the end of it, and real-time analysis of what the student has learned from completing a specific writing task, help students learn about writing rather than just completing assignments.

4. **A narrow(er) content focus may be appropriate:** One of the valuable aspects of the EAP/ESP approach to writing instruction is that it allows students to gain some in-course expertise on a specific topic or discipline, which helps them write more authoritatively and confidently on their subjects and to learn and use key vocabulary and syntactic structures. A content/theme-based writing syllabus may be a more effective way of designing L2 writing courses than forcing students to master new content and vocabulary for every writing assignment (see also Chapter 4).

5. **Collaborative activities in writing classes have both practical and cognitive benefits:** Advances in technology have led to an increased focus on collaborative or shared writing tasks in academic and professional settings. For example, affordances such as Google Docs and "track changes" (in Microsoft Word®) have made it much easier for students and co-workers to co-author or co-edit documents. Students in L2 writing classes need to be prepared for both the technological and social aspects of collaborative assignments. L2 writing instructors should not stay away from peer group work even if they worry students may be uncomfortable with it; rather, they should be preparing their students for what has become an increasingly interactive world for student and professional writers.

6. **Technology is changing everything about writing (and writing instruction):** In some settings, writing instruction is delivered entirely or partially (hybrid models) in online formats. In others, it is delivered in smart or computer lab classrooms. Even in face-to-face instruction in traditional classrooms, assignments are often delivered, collected, graded or commented upon, and returned through the campus learning manage-

ment system (such as Blackboard®, Canvas®, Moodle®, and so forth). Rapidly improving technology allows teachers (and peers) to respond to student writing electronically, either through written comments or audio- or video-recorded feedback—or to conduct virtual real-time conferences about student writing more conveniently. In their syllabus design, therefore, instructors need to think carefully about how they will utilize technology to meet the goals of a particular writing course and plan for helping students to feel comfortable with the specific applications with which they will work.

With these general models of writing/composition instruction in mind and the lessons we can learn from them, taken together, we can move to principles and processes for curriculum and syllabus design for L2 writing courses.

Steps for L2 Writing Course Design

Thoughtful, principled course design is a critical component of effective L2 writing courses. Of course, this statement is true of *any* teaching, but writing/ composition course syllabi are typically more complex to create than those of other class types. Planning courses well takes time, and it is fair to note that instructors may not always have adequate time for such planning, depending upon the nature of their employment. In some settings, for example, teachers may not be given their exact class assignment until a day or two before a term begins because scheduling may be based upon last-minute enrollment and/or placement testing considerations. That said, where possible, the course planning process should include the considerations and steps outlined in Figure 6.1 and discussed in more detail below.

Figure 6.1 The process of L2 writing course design

1. Investigate the teaching context.
2. Find out about the students.
3. Articulate course goals.
4. *Outline major assignment/teaching units.*
5. Select content/source materials.
6. *Plan for language development.*
7. *Write a course calendar.*

Many of these steps are general to any type of teaching, not just the teaching of L2 writing, so in the interest of preserving space, we will further discuss only the three specific items bolded in Figure 6.1 (#4 and #6–7 on the list).

Outlining Major Assignments and Teaching Units

Most composition classes are (or should be) structured around major assignments involving multiple drafts and intermediate steps needed to complete those assignments. Though there may be small, lower-stakes assignments completed during these major paper cycles (e.g., responses to reading, articulating a topic statement, outlining a draft, writing a revision memo between drafts), these major units will structure the time line for the course. Teachers should consider here both the content of the course and the specific types of writing (and reading) experiences they want students to encounter before the course is over. Figure 6.2 shows a simple example (taken from a first-year composition course) of how a sequence of assignments both addressed course content (rhetorical/genre awareness) and built specific writing skills. This was a theme-based course on the topic of generational differences.

There are infinite possibilities about how to select content and possible writing assignments. The key principle here is that such units of content/writing tasks should structure the big picture of the syllabus. Outlining them at this stage of the course design process helps a teacher with the steps that follow (see Figure 6.1).

Planning for Language Development

As discussed in Chapter 5, helping students continue to develop facility in analyzing and applying new vocabulary and grammar should be an important element of a L2 writing class. However, in reality, such activities can be difficult to incorporate and especially to integrate authentically with other reading and writing tasks without careful planning on the teacher's part. In designing the course, the teacher may want to consider several questions and options:

- Is there room in the syllabus and grading scheme for language learning/development assignments, such as a vocabulary journal or grammar self-study? Could such activities be a graded project, occasional homework, or for extra credit?
- Will the teacher provide any in-class grammar and/or vocabulary instruction? If so, how frequently will it occur, and how long will such activities take in a typical lesson plan?
- Will peer- and self-editing activities to focus on language accuracy and effectiveness (in later stages of the writing process) be part of in-class work or assigned homework? How will those fit into the course calendar?
- Will students have regular opportunities to analyze, record, and reflect upon their most frequent patterns of language error and their progress in reducing error (see Chapter 7; see also Ferris, 2016)?

All of these "language development" possibilities will take time and will need to be accounted for in the larger course design process. As noted in

Figure 6.2 Overview of major teaching units in a L2 writing course syllabus

Unit	Writing Tasks	Other Goals
1: Diagnostic	In-class essay; self-ID as Gen Y or Z; contrast self w/general characteristics	Diagnostic writing sample; error analysis; introducing theme/terms
2: Major Assignment 1	Discovery draft (personal narrative about generational differences); two summary and response tasks (from longer readings 3–4); final paper tying reading to personal experience	Narrative writing; summary and response writing; reading strategies (previewing, annotation, interpreting charts, graphic organizers); vocabulary (idioms and academic); grammar (verb tenses in narrative; reporting verbs in summary; stating opinions)
3: Midterm	Argumentative essay on parenting styles across generations (debrief but no revision)	Timed writing strategies; writing arguments
4: Major Assignment 2	Staged research assignment on generational differences in learning/education: finding sources, observation & interview, researched open letter on subtopic related to generations and school	Research skills (library, observation, interview); paraphrasing, evaluating sources, reporting on data collection, passive voice, vocabulary; open letter genre
5: Final	Argumentative essay on workplace differences across generations	See midterm; also applying knowledge and vocabulary from earlier papers

Ferris and Hedgcock (2014, pp. 343–344), there are at least four stages in a writing class syllabus where language focus activities can be natural and integrated with other course priorities:

1. **As part of an intensive reading sequence:** Studying language choices of the author(s) of a text the class is discussing together.
2. **As preparation for a writing assignment:** Focusing on specific content vocabulary and/or grammatical structures that might be useful in completing that particular task type (e.g., how to use past and present tenses when telling a story or when summarizing content from a source).
3. **Toward the end of a writing assignment sequence:** Providing brief in-class instruction on a particular language issue (e.g., the punctuation and syntax around direct quotations) before students begin a peer- or self-editing workshop on near-final drafts of an assignment.
4. **After an assignment has been graded and returned:** Giving a "common errors" lesson based on examples from the students' just-returned papers. This allows the teacher to address patterns or issues that may be problematic for most of the class more efficiently than giving detailed individual feedback on every student paper.

An instructor may not know, during the syllabus planning process, exactly what language features should be focused upon for a particular class. If that is the case, it is possible to anticipate these natural points in the syllabus and simply list "Language Focus: TBD" on the syllabus as a placeholder. Finally, the instructor may want to include some self-diagnosis and goal-setting about language priorities near the beginning of the course and reflective self-evaluation about progress toward these goals at the end of the term.

Writing a Course Calendar

Having made decisions about amounts and types of reading and writing tasks and about how language issues will be addressed, an instructor planning a course is now ready to plot everything out onto a course calendar. (In practice, these various steps tend to be carried out simultaneously and are iterative. For example, the calendar "reality check" step might cause the teacher to trim down the number of assignments or required readings.) There are several practical issues to keep in mind when calendaring specifically for a L2 writing course. First, in a process-oriented model, the teacher must allow adequate time for students to draft and revise papers and to obtain feedback, whether that is in class from peers, in one-to-one conferences with the teacher, or via written instructor feedback (see Chapter 7). All of these options take class and/or turnaround time, and that must be realistically considered. Second, the instructor will want to look carefully at how much work is being assigned between classes. If, for example, students are expected to read two texts, complete written homework, and revise a paper draft all for one class period, that is probably too much to expect, considering students' other responsibilities.

Once a teacher has gone through the above steps and created a substantial course calendar that applies all of the previous decisions made, s/he will find that day-to-day lesson preparation is relatively simple because the whole course has been systematically and thoughtfully planned from start to finish. Such course planning also allows instructors to convey clearly and convincingly to students that the course is purposeful, not haphazard, and that they are headed together in a productive direction. This builds student confidence and rapport between the class and the instructor from the very first day, and this direction can be reinforced as part of the ongoing "narrative" of the class as it proceeds.

Developing Strategic Writers

In L2 teaching in general, a lot of attention has been given to the topics of language learning strategies and learner strategy training (e.g., Chamot & O'Malley, 1994; Oxford, 1990), which ideally elevates instruction from merely completing exercises and covering content to developing self-sufficient learners who can extend their knowledge and competence beyond the classroom. Grabe and Stoller (2011; Chapters 2–4) made a helpful distinction between *teaching reading strategies* and *developing strategic readers*, the latter being an intensive, intentional, and individualized process that takes place over time. Here we extend this construct to the goal of developing strategic *writers*. This section flows logically from the previous ones on instructional approaches and course design processes, as the ideas simultaneously flow from and influence both previous subtopics.

Types of Strategies Needed by L2 Writers

As the discussions in the above sections of this chapter have demonstrated, there are specific strategies that should be explicitly presented and practiced to the benefit of all student writers, regardless of language origin. These include *process strategies, rhetorical/genre awareness strategies, language development strategies,* and *interactive/collaborative strategies.* We discuss each category briefly below and then conclude with suggestions, again borrowed from Grabe and Stoller (2011), as to how L2 writing instructors can approach the process of developing strategic writers and integrate this goal into their course planning. The strategies are summarized for ease of reference in Figure 6.3.

Process Strategies

As discussed earlier in this chapter, process-oriented writing pedagogy has been around since the 1970s and is still common today, especially in U.S. composition or L2 writing classes. But *doing* process (because the teacher requires multiple drafts and so forth) and *understanding or managing* process are not identical endeavors. Many students, regardless of where they have been educated, have come to think of school-based writing as something they do for an examination, under time pressure, on a "cold" topic they may never

Figure 6.3 Overview of goals for developing strategic writers

General Strategy	Type
Specific Strategies to Develop Process Strategies	• Understanding what an assignment/task requires • Time management for a writing assignment (including when/where to write, and for how long, taking breaks and returning to a text) • Idea/content generation • Planning the initial draft (e.g., working thesis, outline, etc.) • Asking for and applying feedback from others • Revising an initial draft based upon feedback • Editing/polishing a near final draft
Rhetorical & Genre Awareness Strategies	• Articulating a purpose for writing • Understanding the need/exigency (the "so what?") in a writing task • Understanding the audience for a piece of writing • Analyzing evidence/rhetorical appeals that will be effective, considering the genre and audience • Researching the target genre and shaping the text according to genre expectations • Identifying language features appropriate for the task, genre, and audience
Language Development Strategies	• Becoming aware of error patterns and executing a plan to address those issues • Understanding and applying effective self-editing strategies to ongoing writing projects • Applying vocabulary learning strategies, especially to improve writing • Understanding how grammar can convey meaning (rhetorical grammar) and contribute to more effective writing style and applying that knowledge to composing and editing their own texts
Interactive & Collaborative Strategies	• Understanding and using technology to facilitate collaboration around writing • Giving and receiving feedback from peers • Understanding group dynamics and working effectively in pairs or groups to complete writing class activities and to produce co-authored texts

have thought about before. Composition students in the U.S., for example, have found Anne Lamott's essay, "Shitty First Drafts" from her book *Bird by Bird*, eye-opening and powerful in its message that good writing will emerge over time and no one, not even a successful professional writer, let alone a student, should expect perfection on a first attempt.

It can be helpful, at the beginning of a writing course, to talk explicitly about stages and strategies for the writing process: Approaches to under-standing and setting goals for a task, generating content and ideas (through reviewing personal experience, reading sources, conducting interviews, etc.), making an initial plan for how to shape those ideas into a coherent text (which involves not just mechanical outlining but investigating models of the target genre, as available), reviewing and revising an initial version of a text, and doing final polishing and editing of a text that is nearly finished.

Rhetorical and Genre Awareness Strategies

Young students do not typically have a conscious sense of audience or genre. They write papers because their teachers tell them to, and they (correctly) view the "audience" for their papers as being solely the instructor. They also, as previously noted, have been extensively exposed to writing in very constrained and artificial school genres, such as a literary analysis essay (in secondary English classes) or a five-paragraph opinion essay on an assigned topic (as test preparation for the SAT® or the TOEFL®).

It can be helpful, therefore, to help them become more aware of how frequently they *do* consider audience and genre when they write or otherwise communicate. For example, when they write a status update on Facebook or post a photo on Instagram, about whom are they thinking, and what do they expect the responses to be? Might they, for example, avoid making profanity-filled comments or posting photos of themselves drinking alcohol if they're aware that their parents, teachers, or grandparents might see them? How do the genre constraints built into social media applications such as Twitter (140-character limit) or Snapchat (posts and photos disappear after a short period of time) affect what they say and what they post? What about the public nature of any digital form of communication—text messages or emails that can be forwarded, photos or posts that can be screen-captured? How can or should those characteristics affect how they write and otherwise express themselves?

Beyond raising awareness about audience in writing, students need to understand that different rhetorical situations will require varying types of evidence or argumentation. In most academic writing, students will need to provide source-based and/or research-driven evidence for any claims they make, but in journalism or personal communication, storytelling and expressing strong emotions may be effective appeals for the rhetorical situation. Similarly, students should learn to analyze different target genres not only for general text structure (e.g., a research journal article begins with an abstract and a recipe begins with a list of ingredients) but for the language variations different genres may display, such as formal or informal vocabulary, simple or elaborate sentence structure, explicit transitions, and even certain types of punctuation (the informal dash vs. the formal semicolon, for instance).

Language Development Strategies

In the previous section, we discussed how instructors should build language development into their course planning and syllabus design. Here we focus specifically on the agency of the students themselves: How can they become more aware of and proactive about steps they need to take to gain better language control and to apply new linguistic knowledge to their writing?

Students need several different strategic interventions from their writing instructors. First, they need to know what their strengths and weaknesses are. Far too many students have been told they have "problems with grammar" or "need to improve their vocabulary," but that is not specific enough advice about the *what* ("grammar" encompasses a great deal of information, and not all "vocabulary" is equally important for student writers' purposes) or the *how* of language development.

As to the "what" of language study, students need concrete information about areas of weakness (i.e., error patterns and/or underdeveloped language with overly simple or repetitious syntax and lexical choices) that is based upon a current assessment from an expert (the teacher) and some self-evaluation. A detailed analysis of an early writing sample will help students to set and prioritize language learning goals at the beginning of the term. Figure 6.4 shows a suggested procedure for guided analysis of an early writing sample.

Students also need guidance as to the "how" of language development. For example, they should be presented with suggestions for self-editing their work (read the text aloud, check for known patterns of error, and so forth) and given repeated opportunities to practice self-editing with different texts throughout the term. They should also be provided with resources for further study on known language gaps (a handbook, a website, or in-class or one-on-one instruction). Importantly, students need guidance on which language features to study that will directly influence their assigned writing (e.g., verb tenses for narratives, passive voice for scientific writing), especially on target vocabulary, such as items from the Academic Word List (Coxhead, 2000) and key content-specific terms relevant to class reading and writing assignments.

Finally, students need guided practice in how to apply grammar knowledge to their own writing. For example, if the teacher wants them to focus on lexical variety, they could use an online text analyzer such as the Vocabulary Profiler in the *Compleat Lexical Tutor* (Cobb, n.d.) to find key terms that are repeated frequently, research and generate synonyms, and practice inserting alternative wording and phrasing into their paper drafts, asking peer readers or the teacher which lexical choices are better. Similarly, they could

Figure 6.4 Sample error analysis and goal-setting activity. Ferris (2016, p. 226)

1. Preselect particular errors on which to focus (e.g., verbs, plurals, articles, word choice, punctuation, etc.). Pick enough error types to get a good picture of student needs but not so many that the task will be overwhelming to you or to the students.
2. Go through the writing samples and mark (highlight, circle, or underline) all instances of errors in the categories you have chosen.
3. Return the papers to students in class and briefly go over a brief explanation of the error categories you marked, with examples of each type.
4. Ask the students to go through their texts, numbering each marked error and trying to categorize it. They can ask classmates or the teacher for help if they're confused about a particular error(s). Have them record their findings in an error chart you create for the activity.
5. Ask them to identify, below the chart, three patterns of errors they noticed most frequently when they were completing the exercise.
6. Collect the exercise, spot-check the students' work for accuracy, and record the information (make a spreadsheet or take copies of the exercise) for individual students and compile findings for the whole class. Now you have a fairly good sense of what the class as a whole might benefit from in terms of in-class instruction and of what each student might need help with individualized feedback.
7. Share the whole-class findings with the students so that they understand why you will focus more on certain issues than others for in-class work.

practice combining sentences using transitions and subordination (if their texts are overly simple in syntactic structure) or in separating and shortening sentences (if wordiness or out-of-control syntax are problems). In short, language issues are a major challenge for L2 writers, and teachers need to do more than mark errors and give students a few in-class grammar lessons. They need to help students develop and apply self-directed language learning strategies.

Collaborative Strategies

Much has been written over the years about both the benefits of collaborative work for L2 writers (and L2 learning) and about its challenges. Specifically, depending upon their cultural backgrounds and educational experiences, scholars have observed over the years that group work, especially when it involves giving or receiving critical feedback to/from peers, can be very uncomfortable for L2 writers (e.g., Carson & Nelson, 1994). However, student discomfort should not dissuade L2 writing teachers from using collaborative group work as an integral part of the class. Not only are there solid theoretical arguments in favor of it (specifically Vygotskyan sociocultural theory and interaction-based second language acquisition theory), but as the world of academic and professional communication has become increasingly collaborative due to technological advances, the ability to collaborate productively around a piece of writing or other form of communication has become a core skill for students and future professionals.

Teachers, therefore, need to help student writers develop not only comfort and the right attitude about collaborative work but also specific skills for handling such activities appropriately and effectively. For example, students need to understand the goals of peer response activities—that is, when students give each other constructive criticism about in-progress writing projects—that the purposes of such workshops are: (a) to read other peers' papers, getting ideas about their own; (b) to practice thinking critically about a piece of writing, which may help their self-evaluations of their own writing; and (c) to give the other writers specific reader feedback about what they are doing well so far and where the paper could benefit from additional thinking. The purpose of peer response workshops is *not*, as many student writers mistakenly believe, for the peer readers to "fix" the writer's paper so that it can receive a high grade. The primary purpose is to benefit the *reader*. With these goals in mind, students also need to understand that simply being vague and "nice" is not an optimal approach (because it neither promotes their own critical thinking, nor does it help the writer at all), nor is being harsh and overly negative (because it may discourage and anger the writer and because that doesn't help them learn how to be good collaborators).

A different type of collaborative activity is when students must co-create and co-edit a text that will be evaluated as a jointly authored (group) project. Students tend to resist such activities even more than they do peer feedback, but they are important because they help students understand group dynamics when there is shared responsibility for a work product and practice how they will behave in such settings. These are not easy lessons for students to learn and they are not necessarily enjoyable for teachers to plan, manage, or assess, but it is important to be intentional about building this set of strategies seriously within the design of a writing course (see Howard, 2001 and Kennedy & Howard, 2013 for excellent and accessible suggestions for collaborative writing pedagogy; see Ferris, 2015a, and Ferris & Hedgcock, 2014, for suggestions about implementing peer response successfully).

The Process of Developing Strategic Writers

Having outlined the range of overlapping strategies that L2 writers need to develop (or improve), how can such strategic writing skills be incorporated into the writing class syllabus? Here we take cues from Grabe and Stoller's (2011; see Chapter 2–4) suggestions for developing strategic readers. First, "the teacher should introduce a strategy and talk about when, how, and why to use it" (Grabe & Stoller, 2011, p. 146). For example, it is not enough to have students simply do prewriting exercises: The instructor should talk with students about why it is useful to take time to generate ideas and make a plan for writing, and how this process can transfer to most writing tasks they will do as students and beyond—even students taking timed writing examinations can benefit from a brief planning stage.

Second, teachers need to model the strategy (or combinations of strategies), providing some in-class practice and immediate application to students' own writing. Grabe and Stoller suggest that teachers could keep a running list of strategies that have been explicitly presented and practiced so that they and students can refer back to them regularly.

Third, the development of strategic writers should have an individualized component. The first two stages—presenting and modeling of strategies for the whole class—are important as they introduce a group of students to the range of options available to them. However, students come into writing courses with different strengths and weaknesses; some may already be very good at some of the strategies presented but need to improve in using others. Further, a long and detailed list of strategies to incorporate may be daunting to students, and it may be better for them, with input from the teacher, to identify a smaller list of goals to address during a specific assignment or throughout the writing course. They can write this list of goals early in the term, revisit it at key intervals (e.g., at midterm or at the end of an assignment unit), and write a self-evaluation at the end of the course about the progress they have made in developing better writing strategies (and what they still need to work on in the future). Teachers could even build thoughtful consideration of and progress toward fulfilling those goals into the grading scheme.

Chapter Summary

In this chapter, we have covered three major subtopics for teachers to consider when planning L2 writing classes (or courses that include L2 writers). We first looked broadly at historical and current pedagogical approaches to teaching composition and L2 writing, noting that many of these, while discussed separately in overview pieces, tend to co-exist and overlap in different programs and courses. We concluded this section with general themes that should guide teachers in planning their own L2 writing courses.

We then looked at a suggested set of stages for course design (see Figure 6.1), focusing specific attention on assignment design, language development, and calendaring. While not all of these stages may be possible in every teaching context (e.g., when the teacher has very little lead time before beginning a course and/or when the curriculum and textbook are predetermined by the program), the principles presented here are important for every teacher to at least think through and be aware of—before, during, and after teaching.

Finally, we took up the topic of developing *strategic writers* as a goal that underlies all other aspects of course design. In the end, neither the content (what topics students write about) nor even the specific writing tasks themselves are as important as what the students learn about writing and themselves as writers and how that awareness may help them in approaching future writing and communication tasks. In this section, we discussed both types of writing strategies on which teachers could focus and an overall process for how such strategies could be presented, practiced and applied, reinforced, individualized, and informally measured.

Curriculum design and course planning are inevitable parts of teaching. To do such preparation well takes time, research skills, and thoughtfulness. It also involves some flexibility and willingness to adjust one's preferences and prior experiences to a new situation. However, the alternative is simply to teach a class haphazardly and with poor results ("aim at nothing and you're sure to hit it"). In the next chapter, we will move from general suggestions for planning a whole course to specific ideas about how to teach the class once it has begun.

Discussion Questions and Tasks

1. The section on pedagogical approaches concludes with a six-point list that summarizes themes for course design that emerge from reviewing the different historical orientations to writing pedagogy. Examine this list carefully. Are there any you disagree with? That you are unsure about? Are there any you think are more important than the others and that should take top priority in designing a course? Are there any themes you think might be missing? What are they?
2. The middle section presents a suggested staged process for course design. Do you disagree with the inclusion of any of these steps? Which ones? Do you think the order of the steps is about right, or would you change it? In what ways?
3. The final section presents different strategies that should be built into the design of the writing course, followed by suggestions for how the instructor should help develop students as "strategic writers." Are there any strategies you think are missing from this framework? What are they? What did you think about the suggestions for individualizing the development of writing strategies for each student? Do those seem feasible and useful? Why or why not?

Further Reading

Ferris, D. R. & Hedgcock, J. S. (2014). *Teaching L2 composition: Purpose, process, & practice* (3rd Ed.). New York, NY: Routledge.

 In particular, chapters 3–5 discuss in more depth themes and topics touched upon in this chapter.

Hinkel, E. (2015). *Effective curriculum for teaching L2 writing*. New York, NY: Routledge.

This recent, full-length treatment of the topic of curriculum design for L2 writing instruction includes foundational chapters, a suggested set of processes, and a separate section on incorporating language instruction into L2 writing courses.

Tardy, C. M. (2009). Building genre knowledge (second language writing). West Lafayette, IN: Parlor Press.

This accessible and practical book lays the research foundation for genre-based instruction in L2 writing and provides many specific suggestions for teachers.

Yancey, K. B., Robertson, L., & Tacsak, K. (Eds.) (2014). *Writing across contexts: Transfer, composition, and cultures of writing.* Logan, UT: Utah State University Press.

This edited collection explores research and pedagogical approaches focused on "teaching for transfer" in writing and composition courses. Though it is not L2-focused, it presents principles and strategies that are important and useful for teachers of L2 writers.

7 Writing Instruction and Assessment

Activities, Feedback, and Options

Dana R. Ferris

In Chapters 5–6 we laid the groundwork for how to approach the teaching of second language writers: Understanding what is distinct or challenging about writing in a L2, the different contexts in which L2 writing is taught, and principles and strategies for designing courses for L2 writers. In the final chapter of this section on writing, we will discuss specific day-to-day concerns for teaching L2 writing. Specifically, we will examine (1) the types of in-class activities and lesson plans that are optimal for L2 writing classes; (2) the critical importance of designing response systems (teacher and peer feedback, self-evaluation) that help to structure the writing course to address course goals; and (3) how questions related to assessment of writing influence daily instruction and course design in general. These are three wide-ranging topics, and space will not permit us to discuss them in adequate depth, but readers/ instructors desiring more information are encouraged to consult the annotated "Further Reading" section that follows the chapter.

Lesson Design for L2 Writing Courses

If an instructor has done a good job of designing the course syllabus (including major assignment/thematic units within the plan that will guide subsections

---

Task 7.1

Think about classes you have taken as a student yourself (on any topic—not simply language or writing). How have those classes been conducted? What types of activities were included? Do you think those classes were carefully planned? Now consider any writing classes you may have taken (or taught or observed). Is lesson planning for a writing class different from, say, planning for a chemistry class or a history class (etc.)? If so, how?

of the calendar; see Chapter 6), individual daily lesson planning should flow naturally from that initial thinking. Nonetheless, structuring class time so that it is well spent takes considerable thought and effort—often more than new teachers anticipate. There is a cost to poorly designed class sessions: They can confuse and frustrate students, who may come to resent the teacher for being unprepared and/or for wasting their time, and they can represent missed opportunities for learning and practice to address larger course goals. With this in mind, we offer some principles for lesson planning in general and writing class lessons in particular.

Lesson Objectives

In the same way that a syllabus should involve the identification and articulation of course goals, an individual lesson plan (and a larger unit of multiple lesson plans) should include specific objectives or reasons for the various activities of the day. For example, the following simple lesson goals were identified for a 110-minute writing class session. Students had composed their first drafts of literacy narratives (reflecting upon their own histories as writers) and brought them to class for a peer workshop. The first three goals are related to that assignment. The fourth is a language mini-lesson, presented here because it is early in the course and students would need to apply the vocabulary analysis strategies presented here for subsequent reading/writing assignments, including a self-directed vocabulary journal.

1. Practice giving and receiving feedback to/from peers about writing on a literacy narrative first draft.
2. Identify and discuss strengths, weaknesses, and characteristics of literacy narrative models (by peers, by former students, and by professional writers).
3. Make specific revision plans for next draft of literacy narrative.
4. *Language focus:* Analyze how verb tenses are shifted in narratives and practice editing literacy narrative drafts for verb tense usage.

A couple of points should be made about these lesson goals. First, they are simple and straightforward. They could be shared with any audience, including the students themselves. Second, they include concrete verbs such as *identify, practice*, and *discuss* rather than verbs that cannot be observed or measured such as *learn* or *understand*. Third, these goals (and the entire lesson) build upon previous lessons (specifically, reading professional writers' narratives and composing the first draft) and anticipate future ones (later peer review sessions beyond the one for that day, revision processes useful not only for the literacy narrative but for future writing tasks, language analysis strategies for the writing course and beyond it). An individual lesson plan, therefore, should be seen as a chapter of the ongoing narrative of a course, rather than a stand-alone chapter in an edited collection.

Beginning, Middle, and End

As with a piece of writing, a lesson should have a beginning, a middle, and an end—and these stages of the class session should be planned for rather than haphazard. The beginning of a class session should preview the day's activities and help the students (and the teacher) to (re)focus on the goals they are pursuing in that course. Most students (and teachers) live busy lives with many other things competing for their attention. Teachers should not assume that their students are instantly ready to focus on the day's material. In a writing class, besides obvious "housekeeping" types of details such as attendance, collecting homework, or reminding about upcoming deadlines, teachers can also ask students to engage in the day's lesson content by completing a brief freewrite (e.g., to review a reading assignment they did for homework and/or to anticipate an in-class discussion or activity). This type of hands-on opening to a lesson immediately gets students engaged and thinking about the class material.

Similarly, the ending of a class helps students refocus on what has been discussed and accomplished that day. It is important for the teacher to manage time so that there is space for a lesson wrap-up, even if it is only for a couple of minutes. Again, students could be asked to freewrite and/or to write a question for the teacher to address the next time or a take-home point from the day's lesson that they will try to remember and apply. Such review and reflection moments are arguably more important even than the more typical "here's your homework" moment at the end of class.

The "middle" of a class consists of the main activity(ies) for the day, and this will vary according to the syllabus content—sometimes discussing a reading, sometimes practicing writing processes, sometimes doing a peer review workshop, sometimes participating in a language mini-lesson. The length and scope of the "middle" of a lesson will also, of course, differ according to the amount of time in a class period. In the example discussed above about lesson objectives, the class was nearly two hours long. Several extensive activities—preparation for peer review, the peer review itself, looking at models and making revision plans, and discussing verb tense shifts—were possible with this much time available. Obviously with less time, there would be fewer "middle" activities. In planning the body of the lesson plan, the teacher will also need to consider not just *what* students will do but also *how*—will it be individual, pair, small group, or whole-class work, the procedures for each activity, how much time each activity should take, and how to transition smoothly between activities.

Variety and Coherence

Students may experience writing classes as dry and/or stressful, so keeping them engaged and comfortable is a critical consideration. Perhaps more so than for other types of courses, variety in a writing class lesson plan can be important to student success. Variety can be achieved through both *content* (discussion of readings or other class materials such as videos, language issues, writing strategies) and through *mode* (teacher-fronted activities, group work, individual work). Though the types of activities will vary according to the syllabus (e.g., discussion of content early in an assignment cycle, peer review workshops toward the end of it), it is probably fair to generalize that no writing class lesson should have a disproportionate amount of time devoted to teacher-led whole-class activities. Writing (like reading, see Chapters 3–4) is not a spectator sport, and students are not likely to learn much from lengthy teacher lectures or from extended whole-class discussions (which tend to favor the most extroverted, confident students while the rest of the class tunes out).

While variety is important to the success of a lesson plan, that principle needs to be carefully balanced with the principle of *coherence*. Asking students to race through a choppy, rushed set of activities in which they career in and out of group work and cover many different instructional points can cause stress for students (they may not be able to keep up with the rapid changes in focus) and can lead to diminishing returns (they may not learn as much from a brief, hasty exercise as they would from something that was presented, discussed, and practiced in a more in-depth manner). To return the earlier example under "Lesson Objectives," students in this class did the following activities during the 110 minutes:

➤ They discussed (with the teacher) their previous experiences with peer review and what they saw as the benefits and drawbacks of peer feedback on evolving assignments.

➤ They examined a model literacy narrative from a former student and practiced identifying feedback points based upon a set of peer review questions. This activity was individual, followed by a brief whole-class discussion both of strengths and weaknesses in the paper and of how they would articulate suggestions (and praise) for the paper's author.

➤ In groups of three, they read, wrote comments about, and discussed each other's literacy narrative drafts.

➤ They were then given a sample of an excellent literacy narrative (from a former student) and were asked, in individual written work, to compare this model with their own paper and with their group members' drafts. Based upon this analysis, as well as previous class discussions of two professional writers' literacy narratives, they individually wrote revision goals for their own drafts.

➤ After a brief transition/break, the teacher delivered a mini-lesson on verb tense shifts in narratives. This included a PowerPoint® presentation with whole-class discussion prompts on the slides as well as brief practice activities that were completed individually, discussed with a partner or small group, and then debriefed as a class with the teacher.

This lesson was coherent and it had variety. The entire class session focused on students' ongoing work with their literacy narrative drafts, but it also had larger writing process lessons about feedback and revision and transferable information about the why and how of shifting verb tenses when writing narratives (useful not just for personal narratives, but for other academic genres such as summaries, history or literature papers, case studies, etc.). Despite the unified focus of those activities, there was still variation in mode (indi-vidual work, whole-class discussion, small group work) and content (the first model, peers' drafts, the excellent post-workshop model, grammar information about shifting between past and present tenses while writing narratives).

Timing

One of the hardest details for a new teacher (or a teacher of a new class/group of students) to anticipate is how long different activities in a lesson plan should take. While experience is truly the best teacher in this regard, there are some practical strategies teachers can use to plan lessons and consider timing. First, instructors should think in terms of ranges rather to-the-minute precision. For example, rather than saying something on a lesson plan will take "7 minutes," the teacher may wish to say "5–10 minutes." That way, if a class catches on quickly, the teacher can move on without belaboring the point, but if the class needs a bit more time to grasp an idea or finish an exercise, students can have the time they need.

Second, it is usually better to at least slightly overplan a lesson than to underplan it. Students may enjoy being dismissed 20 minutes early if the teacher runs out of material, but making a habit of that does not reflect well upon a teacher and is not a good use of precious class time. If the teacher has "leftover" activities, they can always be postponed to the next class session. Indeed, such flexibility is critical not only in planning but in on-the-spot execution of a lesson. It can be equally ineffective to have small group or whole class discussions drag on too long (losing students' attention and lower-ing the energy in the room) or to race students through activities or discus-sions when they need more time. In L2 writing classes, it should be noted, activities that involve in-class reading and writing (e.g., peer feedback work-shops or working on an outline or introduction for a longer paper) will often take more time than teachers anticipate, and rushing students through such tasks will frustrate them.

Lesson Planning: Putting It All Together

With the above principles (objectives, beginning/middle/end, variety and coherence, timing) in mind, it may be helpful to consider the types of activities that a writing (or reading/writing) lesson could include:

- Rhetorical strategies—understanding the genre(s) and audience(s) for a particular writing task (or analyzing the genre/audience awareness of a published author whom they have read).
- Research strategies: how to find, evaluate, and effectively utilize sources and content for writing assignments, including important subtopics such as citation and avoiding plagiarism.
- Reading/discussing course content—assigned readings and other materials that students will write about.
- Reading and vocabulary learning strategies and making effective reading-writing connections.
- Writing process—discuss and practice strategies for planning, receiving and applying feedback (from peers teacher, others), revision, and editing of ongoing writing projects.
- Language—discuss both common errors and ways to improve writing style (e.g., through syntactic variation, broader vocabulary usage).
- Workshops: opportunities for students to give and receive peer feedback, opportunities for students to work on their own writing in class, getting help from the instructor and peers.
- Reflection: focused opportunities for students to discuss and write about what they are learning about writing/language/content in the class.

See Chapters 5–6 for further definitions and justifications for these types of activities in L2 writing classes. Obviously, no individual lesson plan will include *all* of these possibilities, and the principle of variety (as to modes) can apply to any of them—they could be teacher-fronted explanation, small group discussion, and hands-on application, or, ideally, some combination of all of these modes.

To close this section, we offer a checklist that teachers of L2 writers (or L2 writing classes) might find useful in creating and evaluating lesson plans (Figure 7.1). Again, experienced teachers may not always need to write all of this down, but new teachers learning how to create lessons should go through this process multiple times until it becomes automatic.

Response Systems for L2 Writing Courses

Response to student writing, or "feedback," is one of the most important—and time-consuming—activities undertaken by any writing instructor. Not to be confused with, or reduced to, simply "grading" student writing, response is a formative activity designed to help students not only see how to improve the current assignment under review but also to apply lessons from the process to their future development as writers. It has been called by some teachers "the job of teaching writing" (Ferris, Liu, & Rabie, 2011); indeed, it could be argued that the creation and implementation of an effective "response system" (Ferris, 2015a) is the most critical part not only of course design (Chapter 6) but also of day-to-day instruction, the focus of this chapter.

Figure 7.1 A Lesson-Planning Checklist (adapted from Ferris & Hedgcock, 2014, p. 175)

✓   Summary list of lesson objectives
✓   Work previously completed (relevant to this specific lesson)
✓   Materials needed (books, handouts, technology, etc.)
✓   Class management (e.g., homework to collect, reminders)
✓   Lesson sequence (activities, timing, grouping)
✓   Assessment (how will the teacher know objectives have been accomplished?)
✓   Homework and future related work (to help the teacher keep track of the flow of lessons from one day to the next)
✓   Possible problems and contingency plans (if something doesn't go well or goes more slowly/quickly than planned)
✓   Post-lesson reflection and evaluation (what went well; what could be done better/differently)

Providing (from the teacher) or facilitating (from peers, tutors, or self-evaluation) effective response to student writers is a complex endeavor, and new writing teachers often have a daunting learning curve to climb. In this section, we will discuss the primary issues, questions, and priniciples around response, and readers desiring to learn more are encouraged to consult the suggestions for further reading given at the end of this chapter. This necessarily brief treatment here will be structured around the *sources* of feedback—teacher, peers, self, others—with issues and questions around each source included in those subsections.

Teacher Feedback

There are several important guiding principles for teacher feedback. First, the teacher need not be, and should not be, the only responder to student writing. Though expert guidance from an instructor *is* critical to student writers' development, there are benefits, as we discuss in later subsections, to peer response and self-evaluation that should not be neglected. Second, when giving feedback, teachers should not feel that they must address every single weakness or mark every single error in a student paper. Such an approach can over-burden teachers and overwhelm students with too much information. Third, teacher feedback can be written, oral, or some combination of the two. We turn to this third point next.

Written Teacher Feedback

There are several practical questions that teachers should consider when providing written commentary (or error corrections) on their students' papers:

- *When* (at what point in the writing process) should feedback be given?
- *On what issues* (ideas, organization, grammar, etc.) should feedback focus?
- *How much* commentary is necessary/appropriate for student learning?
- *Where* (within the text itself and/or in a summary note) should comments be placed?
- *How* can written feedback be constructive, encouraging, and clear?

As for the "when" question, answers may vary depending upon how the course syllabus is constructed, but typically in a process-oriented model, students may receive teacher feedback on at least one preliminary (i.e., not final) draft before the assignment is submitted for more formal evaluation. L1 and L2 composition instructors have stressed for decades that intermediate-draft feedback is more useful to students than is summative commentary about a paper that is already finished, though there may also be utility to final-draft feedback that looks forward to future writing tasks (Ferris, 1995; Sommers, 1982; Zamel, 1985).

There has been some controversy in the L2 response literature as to which issues teacher feedback should focus upon. One point of disagreement is whether instructors should give specific, language-focused correction on early drafts of student writing. It is argued that because students should be focused on more global revision issues at that stage (developing or refining ideas, improving organization), giving them word- or sentence-level feedback distracts them from the big picture (Sommers, 1982; Zamel, 1985). However, there is counterevidence in other research that L2 students are quite capable of addressing different types of feedback on the same draft of an assignment (Chandler, 2003; Fathman & Whalley, 1990; Ferris, 1997). A possible compromise approach is for teachers to prioritize global issues in their feedback on early drafts but also to point out, in general terms, any salient patterns of language error that they see in those drafts so that the student writer is aware of them while revising. For example, the teacher could write a summary comment along these lines: "I noticed some errors in verb tense and form, and I marked a few examples on page 1 for your information (but there are others). As you revise, you may want to pay attention to this issue."

A related issue is *how much* written feedback teachers should provide on a particular paper. Teachers often feel that they are being irresponsible if they do not comment on every problem they observe and/or mark every language error. However, there are diminishing returns to this approach, as excessive commenting can lead to teacher frustration and exhaustion (Ferris et al., 2011; Hairston, 1986) and can provide more information than students are able to process. It is best, therefore, to *prioritize*—to focus on the most major issues present in the current version of the paper—rather than to try to "fix" everything. After all, the goal of teacher feedback is not to co-produce with the student a "perfect" paper; rather, it is to help the student become a more competent, confident, and strategic writer (see Chapter 6). I have recommended elsewhere (Ferris, 2003, 2015a) that for any given draft paper, teachers read through the entire paper and identify 2–4 "feedback points," or specific issues for providing suggestions for revision (or for future papers, if it is a final draft). In my experience, if the suggestions are well chosen and clearly constructed, this is a substantive amount of feedback that will help students learn, but it is also focused enough that it will not overwhelm them.

A practical issue that follows from the above points is *where* written commentary should be placed. The choices are some combination of (a) written comments in the margins of the student's text; (b) a summary note provided at the beginning or (usually) end of the paper; and (c) a separate document that might include a completed grading rubric in addition to summary comments. Considering the principle of prioritizing the key issues, a well-constructed summary note (with the 2–4 feedback points mentioned earlier) may be the most important use of a teacher's feedback time. It may also be useful to add a few comments in the margins of the paper to give specific illustrations of points raised in the summary note, but the instructor should not add so much in-text commentary and correction that it becomes visually overwhelming (and possibly even discouraging) to the student writer. Appendix 7 provides an example of a short student paper with sample teacher commentary (a summary note plus marginal comments) to illustrate the possible balance suggested here.

The *how* of providing effective teacher commentary is arguably the most important question. If students do not understand what the teacher is suggesting, the feedback cannot help them. Research on teacher commentary to L2 writers has provided some insight about feedback characteristics that may be more or less helpful to student writers as they revise or otherwise try to apply the suggestions (Conrad & Goldstein, 1999; Ferris, 1997; Goldstein, 2005). The suggestions in Figure 7.2 below should be considered as general guidelines, rather than hard-and-fast rules.

Oral Teacher Commentary

Many teachers prefer in-person writing conferences with their students to providing extensive written commentary, finding such interactions more satisfying due to the two-way interaction and more efficient as to time spent. Teacher-student conferences, when logistically possible, can be an effective alternative approach for responding to writing, but there are several issues to keep in mind when planning and conducting these conferences with L2 students. First, some students are more comfortable with reading and writing in the L2 than with oral interactions. For these students, the teacher may wish to offer the option of written feedback, but if conferences are preferred, it can be useful to have the students take notes about what is discussed orally. One successful hybrid approach to in-person conferencing is having a discussion over a digital version of the student's paper, on either the teacher's computer or the student's. Suggestions and revisions discussed could be added to the paper using "comments" features (as in Microsoft Word® or

Figure 7.2 Suggestions for Writing Clear and Useful Commentary

1. Generally speaking, use statements rather than questions.
2. If questions are used, pair them with specific suggestions as to how the answer to the question could be integrated into a revision.
3. Avoid rhetorical or grammatical jargon ("thesis," "agreement," etc.) unless you are certain that you have taught those specific terms to the students.
4. Keep comments relatively brief (no more than 10–15 words per sentence), and for longer comments, consider breaking them out visually with bullet points or a numbered list.
5. Make comments as concrete and specific as possible. Abstract challenges to the student writer's thinking or argument should perhaps be saved for an in-person discussion.
6. For language issues, focus on patterns rather than simply marking many different types of errors.
7. When marking language errors, use words rather than symbols and provide at least a brief explanation (in the margins or in a summary comment) of the problem.
8. Do not forget to write notes of encouragement about what the student has done well (see Appendix 7).

Google Docs®) and saved for the student's future reference. In that way, the student benefits from both in-person discussion with the teacher (to ask questions and provide clarification) and from a written record of what was discussed. Virtual (not in-person) conferences can be similarly conducted using tools such as Google Hangouts® or through learning management system tools such as the Conferences tool on Canvas®.

Another issue for L2 students is that they may be uncomfortable meeting privately with the teacher, perhaps finding it intimidating or otherwise stressful. The teacher in that situation might wish to have small group conferences, in which 2–3 students meet with the teacher, allowing for peer interaction as well as teacher input. A third issue that arises in teacher–student conferences is how directive the teacher should be. Conferencing/tutoring literature focused on L1 students urges teachers/tutors to ask questions and let the student writer take the lead (see Newkirk, 1995; Patthey-Chavez & Ferris, 1997, for a discussion of this point). However, many students are culturally unfamiliar with such nondirective approaches and/or may not be ready to take the lead in asking questions during a conference. It can be helpful for teachers to ask students to fill out an "office visit" form before a conference and bring it with them (requiring students to give some advance thought to questions they may have or advice they may need), but the teacher may still need to be flexible in conducting the conferences according to student personalities and needs rather than a nondirective ideology.

Whether the teacher is providing written feedback, in-person or virtual oral feedback, or some combination, it is critical that the teacher keep the principles of prioritization, clarity, and encouragement in mind.

Peer Feedback

Though peer feedback has been a staple of L1 composition instruction since the 1970s (see Elbow, 1973; Ferris, 2003) and has strong theoretical support from L2 research (Liu & Hansen, 2002), as a teaching approach it has often been met with skepticism by teachers and students alike (e.g., Zhang, 1995). Students wonder if their peers are really capable of giving them appropriate and useful feedback, and teachers wonder if peer feedback sessions are a good use of class time. Despite these concerns, it *is* possible for L2 students to benefit from peer feedback as part of the writing class response system. Peer feedback gives student writers another audience who is not the teacher, promotes student interaction and classroom community, and encourages metacognition and critical thinking about writing.

That said, there are some important components needed to make peer feedback successful in the L2 writing class. These are summarized briefly in Figure 7.3.

Figure 7.3 Guidelines for Effective Peer Review Workshops

1. Have appropriate expectations for peer review (and convey them to the students).
2. Use peer review workshops regularly throughout the writing course.
3. Peer workshops do not only have to consider full and complete drafts. Peer review work could also include (for example), shorter tasks such as giving feedback on each other's thesis statements, outlines, or introductory paragraphs.
4. Provide training and modeling before beginning peer feedback sessions.
5. Think carefully about pairing/grouping of students for peer response.
6. Give students clear and concrete tasks to complete during peer review.
7. Allow adequate time for peer feedback workshops.
8. Provide students with reflection, analysis, and application opportunities after peer review.

Guided Self-Evaluation

Besides providing students with expert (instructor) feedback and facilitating opportunities for peer review, a final component for a writing class response system should be regular opportunities for "self" feedback—guided activities to help students critically evaluate their own work. Most writers find that they can improve their texts simply through the process of rereading and revision, even if no one else gives them feedback, so students should be encouraged/ required to do reflective and analytical passes through their own texts to learn and practice these self-feedback strategies (Andrade & Evans, 2013).

Self-evaluative work, like peer review, should be consistent and iterative throughout a writing course. For example, students could do guided reflection at the following junctures:

➤   at the beginning of the course, to reflect upon their own histories, strengths, and weaknesses as writers, and to set goals for the term;
➤   between drafts of a writing assignment and/or after a peer feedback session to review what they have learned and set revision goals;
➤   before a peer review session or receiving teacher feedback, to pose questions about issues they'd like help with;
➤   at the end of an assignment unit, to reflect upon what they have learned from the process of writing that particular paper;
➤   after receiving teacher feedback, to respond to, question, and think about how to apply suggestions received;
➤   at the end of the course, to review their progress as writers during the term.

One sample self-evaluation activity is shown in Figure 7.4; further examples can be found in Ferris (2015a).

Figure 7.4 Sample Self-Evaluation Activity (Source: Ferris, 2015a, p. 40)

Instructions: Now that you have written a first draft and read and responded to the drafts of several classmates, reread your own paper and the comments your classmates made.

Before making any revisions, save your file as a new draft ("Paper 1, Draft 2"). Then turn on "Track Changes" ("Tools" Menu in Microsoft Word®). Revise your essay and save it.

Then write a short memo (200–300 words, or about one double-spaced page) to me which addresses the following questions.

- How did your peer draft workshop go? What did you learn from (a) reading your peers' drafts; and (b) getting their comments on your own draft? What impact did this have on your revision?
- What changes did you make between Drafts 1–2, and what were the sources of those changes (peers' suggestions, ideas from peers' papers, your own rethinking)?
- As you approach your final draft of this paper, what are 1–3 specific questions or concerns you would like feedback about from me?

To summarize this section, feedback of various types is critically important for the progress of student writers. As the above discussion and examples demonstrate, different sources of feedback can and should interact and inform one another throughout a writing course. The activity shown in Figure 7.4, for example, moves from peer feedback to self-evaluation to posing specific questions to the teacher. Designing effective response systems is a critical part of syllabus design, and implementing them successfully is an important aspect of day-to-day instruction.

Assessment Issues for L2 Writing Courses

In this final section, we discuss issues that instructors should consider as they evaluate/assess/grade their students' progress in a L2 writing course. As with the response subtopic, assessment affects both course design (Chapter 6) and daily instructional choices. Obviously, in designing a course syllabus, the instructor will have to choose a grading scheme for the course (or adopt one if there are program policies as to grading mechanisms and criteria). For example, in the past, students' outcomes in L2 writing courses were often determined by an *exit examination*—an in-class writing task that (ostensibly) demonstrated the progress they had made in writing and what they had mastered. However, L2 writing experts currently recommend that timed in-class writing assessments be minimized, if not abandoned altogether, in grading decisions. Rather, teachers should consider multiple measures of student progress, completed at different points in time, under varying conditions, and on a range of tasks and topics (CCCC, 2014). For many programs and instructors, these suggestions are applied in the form of a final portfolio—a collection of different pieces of writing, usually introduced with a cover memo in which the student reflects on lessons learned and introduces the various pieces of writing submitted in the portfolio.

For day-to-day assessment, a L2 writing instructor has several decisions to make:

- Will a *rubric* (of criteria for success on the assignment) be utilized to determine and explain the grade/score on major papers? If so, what kind of rubric?
- How much will *language issues* (errors, style) influence overall assessments of student writing?
- How will the instructor assess other, less formal types of writing (e.g., preliminary drafts, in-class freewriting, responses to reading, reflective memos, etc.)?

In its *Statement on Second Language Writing and Writers*, CCCC (2014) recommends that instructors explicitly convey criteria for success to students. This not only helps students know what is expected but also helps instructors to give focused feedback that communicates clearly to students what they have or have not done well. A rubric is a good communication tool for all of these purposes. Rubrics can be *holistic* (one overall score or grade based on the text as a whole), *analytic* (various aspects of the text carry specific point values and may be weighted differently), or *trait-based* (varying from assignment to assignment depending upon the focus, task, and genre under consideration) (Ferris & Hedgcock, 2014).

If teachers are allowed to design their own rubrics, one choice they can make is how heavily to weight language errors. In L2 writing classes, some instructors spend a good deal of time working with students on remediating error patterns and developing a more effective style, and they may wish that effort to be reflected in the grading scheme. In other contexts, teachers may wish to focus more attention on ideas, organization, use of sources, and so forth in their grading schemes. One important principle argued by Matsuda (2012) is that students shouldn't be punished for "failing" at something the teacher hasn't covered in the class. In other words, if there is little to no in-class focus on language issues, it is not fair to students to weight errors heavily in a paper or class grading scheme.

Beyond formal assignments that may be assessed via individual rubrics and/or placed into a final portfolio, a well-designed L2 writing course will also include regular, more informal types of writing to build students' writing fluency and confidence. Teachers may decide to assess these based on good-faith completion of the task rather than feeling that they must rigorously mark errors, write comments, or apply rigid grading criteria to every word students write. Such lower-stress writing activities have value in and of themselves, and informal assessment practices reduce both labor for teachers and anxiety for their students.

Chapter Summary

In this final chapter of the section on teaching L2 writers, we covered three subtopics. First, we looked at principles and suggestions for designing effective daily lessons for L2 writing classes. Second, we examined the important topic of response to student writing, focusing on three sources of feedback (teacher, peers, self). Finally, we looked at several practical issues around the assessment, or grading, of student writing.

Teaching L2 writing is fascinating and challenging. It is also very hard work. It takes time to plan courses and lessons, and it especially takes time to respond thoughtfully and effectively to student writing. As we discussed in Chapter 5, L2 writing is even more challenging for the student writers themselves. They need their instructors to be engaged and committed to student success. Becoming a successful L2 writer, especially for academic purposes, takes years, not weeks or months. A well-prepared and dedicated L2 writing instructor can have a very significant role in student writers' long-term success in their academic and professional lives.

Discussion Questions and Tasks

1. Think about feedback or responses you have received about your own writing—from a teacher, classmates, a tutor, or a friend. What types of comments do you find helpful? What have you found less effective or frustrating?
2. This chapter argued that teachers should, in their feedback to student writers, prioritize the few most important issues rather than trying to comment about every issue or mark every error. To practice this principle, obtain a L2 student paper, and, if possible, the assignment prompt that generated it. Read through it and identify the 2–4 most important suggestions you would make if this were your student. Compare your list with those of your classmates and instructor.
3. When grading L2 student writing, how much should language error (or effective language use) be weighted, in comparison with other writing concerns, such as development of ideas, argument, or text organization? Why do you think so?

Further Reading

Andrade, M. S. & Evans, N. W. (2013). *Principles and practices for response in second language writing: Developing self-regulated learners.* New York, NY: Routledge.

This useful recent book highlights various practical aspects of responses to L2 writers, with special emphasis on developing student independence and autonomy.

Crusan, D. (2010). *Assessment in the second language writing classroom.* Ann Arbor, MI: University of Michigan Press.

This accessible book provides teachers and program administrators with an overview of issues and options for L2 writing assessment.

Ferris, D. R. (2011). *Treatment of error in second language student writing* (2nd Ed.) Ann Arbor, MI: University of Michigan Press.

This practical book highlights strategies for giving corrective feedback on written language error, for providing strategy training for student self-editing, and for delivering supplementary language instruction on vocabulary and grammar.

Ferris, D. R. & Hedgcock, J. S. (2014). *Teaching L2 writing: Purpose, process, and practice* (3rd Ed.). New York, NY: Routledge.

Chapters 5–9 in particular discuss themes covered in this chapter.

Appendix
Written Teacher Feedback on Sample Student Paper

Lucy,

You did a nice job of taking a clear stand on the essay question
by saying that "lying is not always wrong." Your two examples—the
surprise party and the shrimp dish—were both effective in illustrating
times when a lie may be harmless and even beneficial.
There are a couple of issues you need to think about as you write
your next draft:

1. You should also discuss times when lying **is** harmful. You hint
    at this a couple of times in your introduction and conclusion by
    saying that lying can be "manipulative" and "damaging," but the
    rest of your essay presents a very positive view of lying. I'd
    suggest adding a paragraph or two that defines the types of lies
    that are harmful and provides an example or two.

2. The story about your friend's birthday is confusing and needs a
    bit of work. See if you can make this clearer by explaining either
    (a) what you might have done differently or better; or (b) why you
    think the positive aspects of the surprise "erased" the hurt she
    felt when she thought you had forgotten her birthday.

3. You need to use Goodrich's article more in your essay. Be sure
    to introduce it clearly at the beginning—author's full name, article
    title, and a brief summary of the main idea(s)—and see if you can
    use facts, examples, or specific quotations to support your own
    arguments and examples throughout the paper.

You are off to a great start with clear organization and nice
examples. I will look forward to reading your next draft! Be sure to
e-mail me, talk to me in class, or come by my office if you need any
help as you revise!

Good luck!
—Teacher

Sample Student Paper

Lying is not always wrong, if it is used for good intentions. Lying can be very manipulative, yet that particular quality, Goodrich mentioned, "is also exciting". Instead of using it for evil, lying can be a vital source for good, whether it from sparing a child feelings or doing it just to get something out of it. There are numerous explanations why people would create white lies. One reason why people lie is to surprise or distract a love one. Another reason why people do it is to create a diversion, in order to escape the difficulties that may take place by telling the truth.

There is no greater rush than getting away with a good, harmless lie. For example, on one occasion, I have used lies for good intention. My close friend birthday was coming up. My friends and I were planning a surprise birthday. We did not want the birthday girl to know of this, so we manipulated her into thinking that we did not remember her birthday. Making up stories that we were busy on that day, to convince her so. Seeing the hurt in her eyes further greaten our smile. Like Goodrich said, "even though people lie for good reason, lying can be harmful". My friends and I knew that by lying to her, the surprise party would be a total success. Yes, our way of springing the party on her was wrong, but when the surprise was successful, seeing the joy on her face gave everyone involve a great rush, and that is exciting.

When Goodrich said that, "everyone lie" it could very well be the truth. People lie constantly to avoid difficult situation by telling the truth. For instant, I was at my friends' house for dinner. His mother was cooking her best dish that took hours to make. During the course of the meal she asked me how was it. The truth is that I didn't like it, maybe is because I hate shrimp, but to avoid being an unwanted guess, I bit my lips and told her that the meal was excellent. Besides my stomach hurting from the shrimp, no feelings got hurt.

To conclude, small, harmless lies can be exciting and fun. Not knowing if you will get caught in a lie, or knowing that you just got away with a lie is a great thrill. The truth is, some lies can be damaging when it is discovered, but if done properly, lies can be very benificial. No one really likes to lie, but not everyone is aware that they are lying. Lying is not always wrong.

Section 3

Introduction to Listening

Larry Vandergrift and Christine C. M. Goh

Listening is critical to academic success at every level of education. Students who study in their first language would have little problem hearing what is said by their teachers, professors and peers, but they would still need to relate what they hear to the topic and what they are thinking and attempting to learn. They would also need to learn to listen differently for different purposes. These demands that first language speakers face are experienced by all second/foreign language speakers of English in schools and colleges where English is the medium of instruction. Their learning, however, is made all the more challenging because they have problems hearing the words or utterances in speech during academic interactions. They may also find it difficult to recognize important information in a lecture or presentation because they are unfamiliar with the way such discourses are organized in English. It is therefore important that all students are taught how to listen effectively and become strategic listeners who can manage their comprehension and listening development well throughout their post-secondary/tertiary studies.

Many listening courses are available in the market for teaching ESL/EFL students how to listen to lectures and seminars and to take effective notes that can help them in their learning. There are also many online and published audio/video resources to help them practise their listening comprehension on their own. These are no doubt useful, but students need more than just materials for listening and note-taking practice. They need guidance and scaffolding to understand and develop the processes of listening so that they can develop their listening comprehension explicitly and systematically, just as they do for their reading, writing and speaking development. Effective teaching of listening requires that the often hidden cognitive, metacognitive, social and affective processes of listening comprehension be made explicit for learners. It also requires learning tasks that can help learners experience and reflect on these processes.

The section addresses what we know about listening in a second language and explains why it is important to focus on the process of learning how to listen rather than the outcomes of comprehension. It offers theoretical perspectives on cognitive processes during listening, addresses multi-faceted learner factors that can contribute to, or hamper, listening success, and identifies core listening skills which can guide teachers when they plan lessons and create listening tasks. It shows how teachers can build on theoretical knowledge about L2 listening and offers practical ideas for teaching listening processes and skills that students can acquire gradually and systematically. The chapters also offers practical guidelines for planning listening courses and curriculum for L2 listeners. Models are given for structuring listening lessons that integrate listening practice with metacognitive processes that can support learning. In addition, issues of assessing L2 listening will be discussed and ideas for assessing listening formatively to promote learning will be suggested. Each chapter also provides further reading references for teachers who want to read further about L2 listening or conduct classroom inquiry into this area.

8 How Listening Comprehension Works

Larry Vandergrift and Christine C. M. Goh

Much of teaching and learning in post-secondary contexts takes place through the spoken language. Students attend mass lectures, which require note-taking and comprehension skills; listen to and view materials that have been uploaded in electronic learning platforms; participate in face-to-face seminars and tutorials; make oral presentations and take questions from the audience; and research for information online which often includes videos and podcasts. Many academic institutions also practise flipped classroom teaching where learners view materials such as recordings of talks and lectures before coming to class for in-depth discussion of the topic. This makes listening an important skill for post-secondary students, not just for everyday social interactions with other speakers of English, but also for thinking and learning. Although listening is such an important skill, many tertiary-level second language (L2) learners still find it a challenge. They need to continue developing their listening skills even though they would have learnt English for a number of years by the time they enter tertiary institutions.

To add to their challenges of developing L2 listening, many EAP teachers also feel they are not sufficiently knowledgeable and skillful when it comes to teaching listening. In many classrooms, teachers would play audio and video recordings of spoken texts, such as short lectures and talks, to the class and ask students to answer comprehension questions by writing answers, filling in the blanks, completing diagrams and tables, taking notes, and selecting the right answer from a number of options. Teachers also encourage students to spend more time listening to the L2 after class using mass media resources and sources of texts available to the students. Teachers can only hope that their students' listening will improve with frequent listening activities such as those just described.

Unlike teaching other language skills, grammar and vocabulary, teaching listening requires teachers to engage with learning processes and texts that are hidden from view. While a reading teacher can point to the words and sentences on a page and model reading strategies as students focus their attention on the printed words, a listening teacher has to contend with texts and mental processes that are transient and not easily captured during a listening task. As comprehension processes occur inside learners' heads, it is difficult for teachers to find out how easy or difficult something is to their students when they are listening. Even when mistakes are identified after the learners have listened, teachers may not fully understand what has led to the comprehension problem. As a result, there is little evidence of this process that teachers can base their feedback on.

Teachers can become more effective listening teachers if they understand more about the mental and learning processes that learners need to engage in in order to achieve comprehension. They can then plan lessons that help to reveal some of these processes as well as making their students more aware of their own listening processes. Teachers also need to recognize internal and external factors that can influence language learners' listening performance so that they can plan learning activities that assist learners in overcoming some of these problems and find ways of improving their listening based on the students' existing strengths. In other words, teachers need to know what it is that they are trying to teach. With a good understanding of the construct of listening, teachers can plan listening lessons in a systematic and theoretically-principled manner.

A good listener is an active listener who constructs reasonable interpretations based on the input they receive (Brown, 1990). When they recognize that more information is needed, active L2 listeners will also adopt strategies that can assist them in getting the specific information either by asking others for it or listening for clues that can help them fill in the information gaps or construct a reasonably acceptable interpretation based on what they hear and know. It is, therefore, important for teachers to recognize that language learners have an active role to play in listening and in learning to listen. Just as important is the need for teachers to adopt an approach that teaches listening as process and one that tests it as comprehension outcomes, which is the nature of the activities described at the beginning of this chapter.

The purpose of this chapter is to explain how the process of L2 listening comprehension works and the challenges that L2 learners face. It will examine the theoretical bases for teaching listening by explaining listening as process and listening as a set of skills. It will discuss factors that can assist listening comprehension or create problems for language learners. Overall, this chapter will help teachers understand the rationale for designing a listening curriculum that can develop learners' listening processes and skills and support greater learner involvement in their own listening development in and beyond the language classroom.

What is Listening Comprehension?

Various cognitive processes come into play during the process of L2 listening comprehension. While these processes are common to all types of listening, different listening texts, demands and contexts may require the listener to engage with these processes differently; some processes may be more dominant on one occasion and less important on another. Rost (1990, 2013) describes listening comprehension as an inferential process of perceiving and interpreting cues from the text and context rather than simply matching sound to meaning directly. Listening is also described as a combination of basic low-level decoding of the speech stream and higher-level processing of meaning interpretation (Field, 2008), as well as the construction of meaning based on information from a number of knowledge sources applied through iterative cognitive processes (Vandergrift & Goh, 2012). These three descriptions of listening comprehension share the view that learners need to recognize sounds in a speech stream as well as use other kinds of information to generate a mental representation of a spoken text. This mental representation is an approximate model of the meaning of what is heard linguistically, but not a direct reproduction of the linguistic forms, i.e., grammatical structure and vocabulary. Comprehension is considered to have been achieved when there is a reasonable interpretation of the text, although the degree of "reasonableness" will clearly depend on the listening purpose. If the purpose is to identity precise facts in the text, providing approximations of these facts is unlikely to be acceptable.

There is, therefore, a continuum of acceptable comprehension levels in any communication environment. In post-secondary education contexts, learners would need to understand their purpose for listening and listen in the most effective way to achieve it. For example, when they are asked to note down some important terminology or a set of numbers from a lecture, students would need to listen and identify them exactly. On the other hand, there are also situations where they do not need to reproduce or record such details and deriving a gist of the main ideas in a lecture or a part of that lecture would suffice.

Task 8.1

List five occasions this week when you had to listen to something important or interesting. How are these listening events similar or different? Did you have to use a lot of effort to understand what you heard? Explain the reasons.

Listening as Process

When we listen, several of our cognitive processing systems—attention, perception and memory—work interactively to transform the linguistic information and create an interpretation by relating what is heard to information stored in our long-term memory. We need to attend to or focus on the sound signals and perceive these sounds as words that we recognize. At the same time, we also draw on various kinds of knowledge stored in long-term memory to act on the new information. A competent listener will attempt to process the information in the most efficient way, either by processing each unit of information at a time or by handling several simultaneously. There are three ways in which we can explain how our brain processes linguistic information: 1) top-down and bottom-up processing; 2) controlled and automatic processing; and 3) the reiterative process of perception, parsing and utilization. Each of these is discussed in more detail in the sections which follow.

When processing auditory information, listeners also mentally manage the on-going cognitive processes and the unfolding interpretation by checking their understanding. This is done through the listeners' metacognition, which is the mental capacity that regulates these cognitive processes by planning, monitoring and evaluating. Research suggests that L2 learners also engage in similar cognitive and metacognitive processes, albeit with some challenges because of their lack of facility with the language. Unlike L1 children who are able to process much of the everyday auditory input they hear by the time they are four or five, L2 language learners may still be developing their knowledge of the language (pronunciation, grammar and vocabulary), discourse routines (how different types of spoken texts are organized in the L2), and specific socio-cultural contexts in which the L2 is used. Nevertheless, with more opportunities to learn about and develop these listening processes, coupled with their increasing control over the L2, language learners will learn to listen more effectively. At the same time, they can also learn to adopt appropriate strategies to overcome problems and facilitate better comprehension and overall development of their listening.

Top-Down and Bottom-Up Processing

Fundamental to an understanding of comprehension processes is the broad distinction between bottom-up and top-down processing, the types of knowledge each process brings to the comprehension of a message, and the interaction between these processes. Doing the next task in a small group will help you understand the interrelationships between these cognitive processes in listening by a competent listener.

If this was the first time you came across this text, you would have attempted to hear every word and use the words to interpret the message. This process of segmenting the sound stream into words you recognize is referred to as lexical segmentation, and is part of the decoding process of sounds in spoken text (Field, 2008). In the past, theorists thought that listeners built up their understanding of a text by first perceiving the individual sounds, followed by larger units of individual words and phrases in an approach known as bottom-up processing. We know now that bottom-up processing is not an adequate explanation of how spoken texts are processed. This decoding process assumes that comprehension begins with information in the sound stream by drawing primarily on phonological, vocabulary, and grammar knowledge, with minimal contribution of information from prior knowledge of the world. This is untrue of L1 listeners and certainly untrue

Task 8.2

Speaker

(reads aloud this passage without showing the text to the other members in the group)

> Sally first tried setting loose a team of gophers. Her plan however backfired when a dog chased them away. She then entertained a group of teenagers and was delighted when they brought their motorcycles. Unfortunately, she failed to find a Peeping Tom listed in the Yellow Pages. She thought about calling a door-to-door salesman but decided to hang up a clothesline instead. It was the installation of blinking neon lights across the street that did the trick. She eventually framed the ad from the classified section.
>
> (adapted for listening from Richards,1990)

Listeners

1. As you listen to the text, try to answer this question: What is the text about?
2. After you have finished listening, discuss the following questions:

   a. Did you understand most or all the words in the text?
   b. What did you do to try to derive meaning from these seemingly disparate sentences?
   c. You would have recognized all or most of the words in the text and it is likely that you still have difficulty constructing a reasonable mental representation. Can you suggest why this might be so?

of L2 listeners. L1 and L2 listening are greatly assisted by another type of processing which draws on prior knowledge about the topic and the context for listening. This is referred to as top-down processing.

To illustrate this, let us review the listening task you have just performed. You were not able to make much sense of what appeared to be disparate sentences even though you understood the words and the literal meaning of each sentence. If you had been told before you listened that the title of the text was "Getting Rid of a Troublesome Neighbour", the meaning of the disparate sentences would have been clearer and the text would have had greater coherence. When applying this knowledge of the topic to the comprehension process, you are using top-down processing. Top-down processing primarily involves the application of context and prior knowledge to comprehension. This component of listening, seen as an interpretation process, assumes that comprehension begins with listener expectations about information in the text and subsequent application of appropriate knowledge sources to comprehend the sound stream. Used alone, this approach to comprehension is not adequate either, because listeners would not have all the prior knowledge required (or there would be no need for communication), or share enough of the speaker's perspective on the subject matter to interpret accurately without any linguistic input.

In reality, top-down and bottom-up processes rarely operate independently but occur in what is known as parallel processing. In some instances, one type of processing might take precedence over the other, depending on the amount of practice an individual has had on a particular task. Linguistic information gleaned from the decoding process, and prior knowledge applied during the interpretation process, are used by the listener in an interactive manner to create a mental representation of what is heard. The degree to which listeners may use one process more than another will depend on their purpose for listening. A listener who needs to verify specific details such as driving directions, for example, may engage in more bottom-up processing than a listener who is interested in obtaining an overview of a particular news story, for example. Research suggests that L2 listeners need to learn how to use both comprehension processes to their advantage, depending on the purpose for listening, learner characteristics (e.g., language proficiency, working memory capacity, age) and the context of the listening event. These processes are also largely affected through different skills employed for purposeful listening.

Controlled and Automatic Processing

When listening is fluent, as in L1 listening, cognitive processing occurs rapidly through an interaction of top-down and bottom-up processing as required to achieve comprehension. Less skilled listeners can struggle with decoding if their linguistic knowledge is limited and their processing skills inefficient (Cutler, 2012). Successful L2 listening depends, obviously, on the degree to which listeners can efficiently coordinate these processes. L1 listeners do this automatically (particularly bottom-up processing), with little conscious attention to individual sounds or words. L2 listeners, on the other hand, have limited language knowledge; therefore, they are not able to automatically process all the linguistic information that they receive. Depending on their L2 proficiency or their familiarity with the topic, listeners may need to focus consciously on some aspects of the text or pay attention only to basic elements of meaning, such as content words. Word recognition is particularly problematic as it takes L2 listeners more time and effort to identify the correct word from a number of lexical candidates that they might be considering (Broarsma & Cutler, 2011).

Controlled (as opposed to automatic) processing involves conscious attention to, and processing of, elements in the speech stream. This can become automatic with practice, in the same way we learn a skill like riding a bicycle. When we first begin, we need to pay deliberate attention to coordinate: 1) getting on the bike, 2) maintaining balance, 3) steering with the handle bars, and, 4) gaining momentum by moving the pedals with our feet. Eventually this becomes automatic and we no longer need to pay conscious attention to the coordination of these different elements. In the same way, the coordination of comprehension processes needs to become automatic so that we can efficiently process all of the elements in the sound stream. Controlled bottom-up processing of linguistic information is not efficient because the listener cannot keep up with the speed of the spoken text; consequently, comprehension breaks down unless listeners resort to compensatory strategies, contextual factors, and other relevant information available to them, to guess at what they did not understand.

The extent to which processing can occur with little interruption or extended manipulation of the linguistic input would depend on the cognitive system of memory. Memory consists of two main components: Long-term memory (LTM) and working memory (WM) and both play a crucial role in comprehension processing (Baddeley, 2000, 2003). LTM, as noted above in the discussion of top-down processing, is the bank of information (world knowledge) that listeners access to help them interpret what they are trying to understand. It also includes knowledge about language and its use, which learners draw on when decoding and interpreting spoken texts. WM, on the other hand, has limited capacity and its functions include temporarily storing and manipulating information for complex cognitive tasks, language comprehension being one of these. It comprizes a central executive (CE) which manages several other sub-systems, including the phonological loop, which stores verbal information such as the sounds from spoken texts. Due to its limited capacity, WM can only hold a limited number of phonological units before this information fades and new information overtakes it and has to be processed.

Generally, L2 learners who have a higher language proficiency will be able to decode the information in larger chunks and more quickly. This proficiency is built on their ability to efficiently recognize spoken words and chunks of speech, which in turn they will have developed through frequent exposure to the sounds of the L2 and opportunities to rehearse the decoding and interpreting of spoken input in a variety of situations. At the same time, their increased knowledge of the L2 grammar system and their enlarged store of vocabulary would also enable quicker lexical access when words are heard. The process of developing good L2 listening ability is a long and gradual one, and it can be greatly assisted if listening instruction is planned more systematically to improve students' ability to engage in the cognitive processes just described.

The interface between WM and LTM plays a critical role in successful listening comprehension. This is facilitated by the work of the episodic buffer, which is another sub-system in the WM model by Baddeley (2000). In listening, the episodic buffer provides a temporary connection between the WM sub-system of phonological loop and LTM, combining these various sources of information into "episodes" and storing them temporarily. The more listeners process linguistic information automatically, the more they can allocate the limited attentional resources of their WM to processing new information and to making connections with prior knowledge in LTM. In academic listening, for example, students often have to draw higher-level inferences when listening critically to information and points of view. The ability to process linguistic information automatically would therefore allow L2 learners the cognitive space to interpret the meaning of the input and evaluate it against their own understanding of the topic or context.

Perception, Parsing and Utilization

Another cognitive framework that can provide further insight into how listeners construct meaning is Anderson's (1995) classic model that differentiates comprehension into three interconnected and recursive phases: Perceptual processing (perception), parsing and utilization. Although this model may appear to suggest a sequence of phases, the three phases in fact have an iterative relationship with one another, illustrating the interaction between bottom-up and top-down processing.

In the perception phase, listeners use bottom-up processing to recognize sound categories of the language, pauses and acoustic emphases and hold these in WM. This is the initial stage in the lexical segmentation process. Developing lexical segmentation skills is a major challenge for L2 listeners. Unlike readers, listeners do not have the luxury of visual spaces to determine word boundaries which in spoken language are difficult to determine due to stress patterns, elisions and reduced forms. Even if they can recognize individual words when spoken in isolation or during reading, recognizing them within a connected speech stream is a key problem for many L2 listeners (Goh, 2000). Furthermore, lexical segmentation skills are language-specific and acquired early in life. L1 segmentation skills can be so solidly engrained in an individual's processing system that these are involuntarily applied when listening to an L2 (Cutler, 2012).

In the parsing phase, words are transformed into a mental representation of their combined meaning. This occurs when an utterance is segmented according to phonological (sound), syntactic (grammatical) or semantic (meaning-related) cues. These segments are in turn recombined to generate a meaningful representation of the intended meaning of the original sequence. Using any one or more of these cues, listeners create propositions (abstract representations of an idea) in order to hold a meaning-based representation of these words in WM as new information from the oral text is processed. Meaning is often the principal clue in segmentation. In the absence of semantic cues, L2 listeners are often unable to recognize words correctly because they are misled by the large number of possibilities (candidate words) that they activate (Hamrick & Pandza, 2014). As their vocabulary increases, L2 listeners will activate fewer relevant candidate words and be quicker to recognize words in the text.

Finally, in the utilization phase, listeners relate the resulting meaningful units to information sources in LTM in order to interpret the intended or implied meanings. This phase primarily involves top-down processing of the parsed speech. An important characteristic of this phase is that listeners use information from outside the linguistic input to interpret what they have retained. Using prior knowledge and knowledge of how language is used (pragmatic knowledge) (stored as schemata in LTM) and any relevant information in the listening context, listeners elaborate on the newly parsed information and monitor this interpretation for congruency with their previous knowledge and the evolving representation of the text in memory, as often as necessary, within the time available. Fluent listeners automatically reconcile what they perceive and parse with their accumulated store of prior knowledge, in order to determine meaning of the text.

These phases of comprehension neither work independently nor in a linear fashion, as Figure 8.1 shows. Arrows moving back and forth between the components suggest that cognitive processing at each level can influence and be influenced by the results of cognitive processing that precedes or follows. In fact, this occurs so rapidly in fully automatic, fluent listening that these

Figure 8.1 Cognitive processes and knowledge sources in listening comprehension (Source: Vandergrift & Goh, 2012, p. 27)

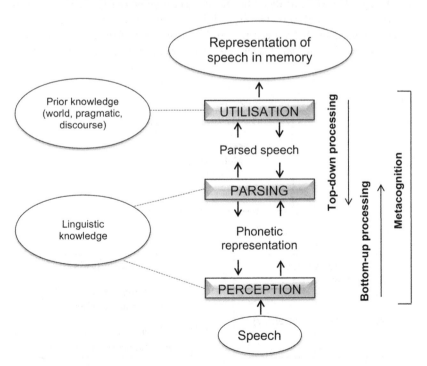

processes occur simultaneously as new speech is processed. As for L2 listeners, these processes can break down due to problems with perception and parsing and so many may not be able to accurately interpret what they hear. Some may even have so little parsed information to build on that they are unable to engage in the utilization phase at all. This is a very common problem among less proficient language learners. Language teachers will need to plan learning tasks that can develop more effective strategies for engaging in all three phases of language comprehension.

Metacognition

Metacognition is the human capacity to examine our own cognition or thinking. It enables us to think about what we are doing, why we are doing it and whether we are doing it correctly or appropriately. It also helps us ask and answer questions such as "how can I do this better now/next time", and "what makes this task easy/difficult". Metacognitive processes include planning, monitoring, evaluating and problem-solving. They can occur at any time during the comprehension process, from planning how and what to listen to, to monitoring or checking our comprehension during listening, and evaluating our interpretation after listening (see Figure 8.1). Metacognition also includes a component of prior knowledge about learning which is applied to managing and directing learning. Known as metacognitive knowledge, it comprizes the knowledge that we have about (a) ourselves (*person knowledge*), (b) the nature and the demands of the task (*task knowledge*) we undertake, and (c) the strategies or conscious steps that we can take to improve our performance or achieve a goal (*strategy knowledge*) (Flavell, 1979; Wenden, 1998). See Figure 8.2.

Figure 8.2 Components of metacognition

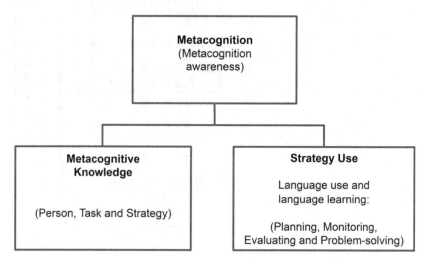

In L2 listening comprehension, metacognition helps language learners think about the way they process linguistic input and consider ways of better managing these cognitive processes to achieve communication and learning goals (Goh, 2008). A characteristic shared by many skillful L2 listeners is the ability to apply metacognitive knowledge and strategies to regulate the listening process and to draw on various relevant knowledge sources to arrive at comprehension more efficiently.

Working memory is the mental facility that enables metacognitive processes such as monitoring and evaluation to take place. This is accomplished through a sub-component called the Central Executive (CE), which manages the temporary storing and processing of information. Specifically, as listeners attend to the input, they have to decide whether they need to shift their attention from one source or unit of input to another in order to get as much meaning as possible out of what they hear. They also need to remember what they have heard and use incoming information to update or elaborate the interpretation that is being formed. Skillful listeners also know how to focus and direct their attention on the input or its relevant parts and stop their attention from wandering or getting fixated on one piece of information.

Learner Factors in Listening Success

The success of L2 listening comprehension and the development of listening ability are influenced by a number of internal and external factors. Knowledge of these cognitive, affective and social factors, and how they hinder or facilitate successful comprehension, is important for informed teaching of listening.

Cognitive Factors

L2 Vocabulary Knowledge

When L2 learners are asked what they consider to be the most important factor in L2 listening success, they often point to L2 vocabulary knowledge. Research appears to support this claim. Initial research by Mecartty (2000) examined the degree to which L2 vocabulary knowledge and syntactic knowledge contributed to listening and reading comprehension. Although the results for reading were higher, L2 vocabulary knowledge did emerge as a significant predictor for listening, explaining about 14 percent of L2 listening ability. In another investigation by Bonk (2000), learners listened to four texts of increasing lexical complexity and wrote recalls (learners write from memory, usually in L1, what they recall after listening). Overall, higher comprehension scores were associated with greater L2 vocabulary knowledge, although some listeners achieved high comprehension scores, in spite of limited vocabulary knowledge.

Stœhr (2009) presented impressive evidence for the relationship between L2 vocabulary knowledge and listening comprehension. He noted that over

51 percent of listening variance could be explained by L2 vocabulary; 49 percent could be attributed to vocabulary size (breadth of vocabulary); and depth of vocabulary contributed only 2 percent more (quality of knowledge related to different aspects of a word and other words associated with it). Similar to Bonk (2000), Stœhr also observed that many participants with low vocabulary scores were able to compensate for this weakness by using compensatory strategies. In the same vein, van Zeeland and Schmitt (2013) noted similar variation among L2 listeners as to their management of unknown or marginally known vocabulary. This capacity to compensate for the unknown may be related to their metacognition and ability to regulate L2 listening processes.

Vandergrift and Baker (2015) observed similar results for French immersion students at two different entry points. Using the French version of the *Peabody Picture Vocabulary Test* (Dunn & Dunn, 2007, 4th edition), *Échelle de vocabulaire en images Peabody* (Dunn, Dunn, & Theriault-Whalen, 1993), they determined that, among the different factors examined, L2 vocabulary was the strongest predictor of L2 listening success. For both groups of students, L2 vocabulary was able to explain about 26 percent of the variance in L2 listening success.

Syntactic Knowledge

Although syntactic knowledge plays an important role in L2 learning, it does not appear to play a strong role in L2 listening, as observed by Mecartty (2000). This might be explained, as suggested by Field (2008), by the cognitive demands of listening and the limitations listeners face when processing the text. This is also consistent with the literature on word segmentation which finds that meaning is often the principal clue in segmenting the sound stream (Cross, 2009). Function words are typically unstressed and, therefore, not salient. If listeners pay too much attention to syntactic cues (function words), they limit how much attention they can allocate to semantic cues that carry more meaning and are easier to retain in memory.

Discourse Knowledge

The role of discourse knowledge in listening has mostly been researched in the context of academic listening. Discourse signaling cues such as previews ("First, let's look at"), summarizers ("to sum up so far"), emphasis markers ("and, to repeat, this is why preparation is so important") and logical connectives ("first", "second", etc.) play an important role in facilitating lecture comprehension. L2 listeners who had the benefit of these cues were able to recall higher level information and supporting details better (Jung 2003). Young (1994) argues that the best way to help L2 learners improve lecture comprehension is to acquaint them with the general schematic structure of lectures by providing systematic instruction in the macro and micro features of lectures. As the discourse patterns of lectures across different disciplines may vary, some differentiations in instruction would benefit learners (Dudley-Evans 1994).

Pragmatic Knowledge

Pragmatic knowledge is knowledge about how meaning and language use are dependent on the speakers, the addressees and features of the context of interaction. An L2 listener can draw on this understanding to infer what is said or respond in ways that are appropriate. One of the main outcomes of research related to this factor is that activation of pragmatic knowledge during comprehension appears to depend on language proficiency: Lower-proficiency listeners have greater difficulty processing both contextual and linguistic information and, therefore, are less able to activate their pragmatic knowledge. The ability to process both pragmatic information and linguistic information simultaneously appears to be related to language proficiency, suggesting that the use of listening texts requiring L2 pragmatic knowledge for comprehension be reserved for intermediate-level classes and higher, or that learners be provided with this information as part of pre-listening activities (Taguchi, 2008). L2 students in mainstream English language classrooms benefitted from their learning when they were able to demonstrate pragmatic knowledge through behaviors such as asking for repetitions, rephrasing statements for clarification and back-channeling (Brice and Montgomery, 1996).

Metacognitive Knowledge

The importance of metacognition in reading comprehension has long been acknowledged (Grabe, 2009). Much of what we know about the relationship between metacognition and successful L2 listening comes from research into the strategies of skilled listeners (Goh, 2002; O'Malley, Chamot & Küpper, 1989; Vandergrift, 2003a). Skilled listeners appear to use about twice as many metacognitive strategies as their less-skilled counterparts; however, a closer examination of these differences suggests that successful L2 listening involves a skillful orchestration or clustering (Graham & Macaro, 2008) of strategies to regulate listening processes and achieve comprehension (Vandergrift, 2003b). In their validation of the Metacognitive Awareness Listening Questionnaire (MALQ), Vandergrift, Goh, Mareschal, and Tafaghodtari (2006) determined that metacognitive knowledge, was able to explain about 13 percent of the variance in L2 listening performance. When teachers help their L2 learners to develop their metacognitive knowledge about listening, the learners have been shown to improve both their listening performance and overall positive attitude to listening (Zeng, 2014).

Prior Knowledge

Prior knowledge refers to all the conceptual knowledge and life experiences that language learners have acquired and is available for comprehension purposes. It is organized in the form of schemata (networks of abstract mental structures) which listeners use as a framework to fill in missing information as they listen. The influential role of prior knowledge in L2 listening comprehension has been empirically established in a systematic review by Macaro, Vanderplank and Graham (2005). Activating this vital resource is particularly important when teaching adults because of their life experiences and knowledge on which they can draw to facilitate comprehension.

An important study by Long (1990) provides empirical evidence for the powerful role of prior knowledge in L2 listening. A large group (188) of American university learners of Spanish listened to two texts (the rock band U2 and the gold rush) deemed to be similar on a number of important characteristics except topic. As hypothesized, the participants possessed significantly less prior knowledge related to the gold rush (69 percent) compared to U2 (90 percent), and this influenced how much information they were able to recall after listening to the text. Similar results for prior knowledge were observed in a subsequent study by Chiang and Dunkel (1992) on knowledge of different religions.

The role of prior knowledge was further investigated by Tsui and Fullilove (1998) within the context of a widely-used, standardized high-stakes examination. Listeners were required to carefully monitor short listening texts in which some passages began with information that was not followed by information congruent with the opening (mismatched schema) and other passages where information was congruent throughout the text (matched schema). Two types of questions were also used: 1) global-type questions requiring overall comprehension and the ability to draw conclusions or inferences, and 2) local-type questions requiring comprehension of specific details. Skilled listeners were able to outperform less skilled listeners on both question types on the mismatched schema-type texts, probably because they were able to process the test effectively in a parallel manner. On the other hand, less skilled listeners managed better on "matching schema type" texts because they were able to use prior knowledge to compensate for what they were not able to understand, although this top-down approach did not always produce accurate answers in other questions.

L1 Listening Ability

L2 listeners already possess an acquired listening competence in their first language. Although the role of L1 in L2 comprehension has received significant research attention in L2 reading (see, for example, Schoonen, Hulstijn, & Bossers, 1998), the contribution of L1 listening to L2 listening ability has only recently been examined. Vandergrift (2006) found that L1 listening ability and L2 proficiency together could explain about 39 percent of the common variance in L2 listening ability. L2 proficiency explained about 25 percent and L1 listening ability about 14 percent. These results suggest that L1 listening ability may contribute in some way to L2 listening ability although the exact influence will need to be determined through more research.

L1 Vocabulary

The role of L1 vocabulary knowledge in L2 listening comprehension has only been recently investigated by Vandergrift and Baker (2015) who observed a moderate relationship (.23). Given the overall strong relationship between English and French vocabulary in their study, it is not surprising that these listeners, who are in the early stages of learning French, can transfer this L1 knowledge to facilitate their L2 listening efforts. When it came to explaining the variance that could be accounted for by L1 vocabulary, the percentage came to only a meager 1 percent, given the additional variables under examination in this same study.

Auditory Discrimination

Although auditory discrimination, the ability to receive, differentiate and process information through the ear, has been shown to correlate significantly with L1 development (e.g., Tsao, Lui & Kuhl, 2004), there is very little evidence available regarding the relationship between auditory discrimination ability and L2 listening ability. A recent study by Wilson, Kaneko, Lyddon, Okamoto and Ginsburg (2011) demonstrated significant correlations between auditory discrimination and several different L2 proficiency tests with Japanese learners of English. The researchers observed a moderate relationship (.36) between auditory discrimination and the two general language proficiency tests (as measured by an internal university test and a standardized test). The relationship between auditory discrimination and L2 listening comprehension (as measured by the listening sub-test in the standardized test) was also at the .36 level.

The Vandergrift and Baker study (2015) also confirmed the significant role of auditory discrimination in L2 listening ability. This variable was measured using two subtests of the Pimsleur Language Aptitude Battery (PLAB, Pimsleur, Reed & Stansfield, 2004 edition), normed and validated for students at this age. Results showed that there is indeed a positive and significant relationship between sound discrimination ability and L2 listening ability with medium-sized correlation for the Grade four (.39) group and a weaker relationship for the Grade seven (.22) group. In the end, some of the L2 listening variance could be explained by auditory discrimination: About 15 percent for the Grade 4 group and only .05 percent for the total Grade seven group (even though the variance for some of the individual Grade 7 cohorts approximated that of the Grade 4 group: 13 percent and 18 percent).

Working Memory

As explained previously, WM plays an important role in comprehension; however, little research has been done on the degree to which this variable might account for any differences in L2 listening achievement. WM is often measured using a Backward Digit Recall (BDR), where participants must maintain a forward sequence of digits while recalling them in reverse order (last one first), immediately after the spoken presentation of the sequence by a research assistant. Using the BDR, Kormos and Sáfár (2008) observed a moderate-sized (.37) relationship between WM and listening achievement. Working with higher-level learners of Dutch, Andringa, Olsthoorn, van Beuningen, Schoonen and Hulstijn (2012) observed an even weaker relationship of .21 while the study on French–English students by Vandergrift and Baker (2015) produced mixed results. The results of these studies suggest that, although there may be a relationship between listening ability and working memory, this relationship needs to be explored further through research.

Affective Factors

L2 listening involves more than paying attention to linguistic input and understanding the different cognitive demands made on the listener. In fact, the ability to maximize comprehension efforts can be influenced by a number of affective factors that, in turn, can impact the outcome of listening success.

Anxiety

L2 learners mostly associate listening with a high degree of anxiety, likely because listening is often considered the most difficult skill (Graham, 2006) and classroom practice often associates listening with testing (Mendelsohn, 1994). There are, not surprisingly, negative correlations between anxiety and final course grades (Elkhafaifi, 2005), but anxiety appears to decrease with a higher level of listening ability (Mills, Pajares, & Herron, 2006). The causes of listening anxiety most often cited are factors related to L2 input (speed, clarity, lack of visual support), followed by factors such as the use of inappropriate strategies (Vogely, 1999). When asked what could be done to alleviate listening comprehension anxiety, students suggested making input more comprehensible, increasing time for listening and combining listening with other skills. It should be noted, however, that not all anxiety is detrimental; a certain level can be facilitating, giving learners the "edge" to concentrate harder and be more successful (Horwitz, 2010).

Self-Efficacy

Self-efficacy, the basis for self-confidence and motivation, refers to learners' beliefs about their ability to participate successfully in learning activities.

Listeners with high self-efficacy feel confident about their ability to handle listening situations because they have learned to manage these challenges. They attribute their success mainly to their own efforts. On the other hand, listeners with low self-efficacy lack confidence in their listening ability and will hesitate to participate in listening activities for fear of revealing their inadequacies. They often feel incapable of improving their abilities because they attribute their listening ability to factors beyond their control. According to self-efficacy theory, when learners attribute success to factors within their control they will be more motivated to attempt future tasks (Bandura, 1993). This suggests that teaching L2 learners to manage their comprehension processes could help them perceive listening success as something within their control. As self-efficacy beliefs regarding listening improve, learners will be more motivated to persist in developing their listening skills. Graham and Macaro (2008) did indeed demonstrate that listening strategy instruction improved comprehension and had salutary effects on listener self-efficacy.

Motivation

The role of motivation in L2 learning has been investigated extensively; however, there is very little research on the relationship between L2 listening and language learning motivation. There is some evidence that language learners engaged in tasks that develop metacognitive knowledge about listening became more confident and motivated as a result (Goh & Taib, 2006; Vandergrift, 2003b; Zeng, 2014). Vandergrift (2005) further provided some supporting empirical evidence for the potential relationship between motivation, metacognitive control of listening processes, and comprehension outcomes. Listening comprehension correlated negatively with amotivation (−.34); however, correlations with extrinsic motivation (for personal gain such as a passing grade) and intrinsic motivation (for enjoyment only, or a desire to know speakers of the language) were only modest at .21 and .34, respectively.

In sum, the three affective factors discussed above greatly affect how language learners perceive a listening task, apply themselves to the task, and experience success in listening comprehension. These factors are also very much interrelated. Confident L2 listeners are likely more motivated and less anxious and possess higher levels of self-efficacy, and this has important implications for the teaching of L2 listening. More listening practice without the threat of evaluation, as well as opportunities to reflect and become aware of listening processes, can go a long way to make L2 listeners more proactive in their approach to listening tasks, reduce anxiety and, ultimately, achieve greater success in comprehension. This will have repercussions for both motivation and learner self-efficacy.

Listening Skills

A survey of the literature on L2/FL listening will show several lists of listening skills and sub-skills. One of the earliest inventories is by Munby (1978) which contained over a hundred subskills. Richards (1983) proposed a list of academic listening "micro-skills" that increase in complexity such as "identify purpose and scope of lecture" and "identify relationships among units within discourse" (pp. 229–239). Clearly, listening in a post-secondary academic context would require certain skills that are not common in general listening in social interactions (Flowerdew, 1994). One distinction is that tertiary-level students often have to listen to and understand long stretches of discourse. Field (2008) also identified a list of decoding and meaning-building skills which he called processes while Buck (2001) emphasizes abilities for understanding literal and implied meanings in spoken input. Based on the somewhat large inventories of "sub-skills" and "micro-skills" for listening in the literature, Vandergrift and Goh (2012) identified six core skills that are integral to the listening process and suggested that teachers can use these to plan listening lessons. See Figure 8.3.

Figure 8.3 Six core listening skills for planning listening lessons and tasks

1. Listen for details
    Identify specific information that is relevant to listening goal, for example, key words, numbers, names, dates, places, etc.

2. Listen selectively
    Pay attention to particular parts of the listening text and ignore others which are not relevant to listening goals or which contain too much information to attend to at the same time.

3. Listen for global understanding
    Understand the overall general idea, for example, the theme, the topic, the purpose, etc.

4. Listen for main ideas
    Understand the key points or propositions in a text, for example, points in support of an argument, directions for doing something, important events in a story.

5. Listen and infer
    Make up for information that is missing, unclear, or ambiguous in the listening text by using different resources, such as background knowledge, visual clues, speaker's tone.

6. Listen and predict
    Anticipate what is going to be said before or during listening by using clues from the context, from background knowledge, or knowledge about the speaker.

Chapter Summary

This chapter has presented a brief overview of what we currently know about the process of listening comprehension and some of the learner factors that can affect the outcome of this process. The discussion of cognitive processes in L2 listening comprehension unpacked many of the mental processes that occur in listeners, and, in particular, language learners. This knowledge will help teachers understand the complexities involved in listening, thereby offering a theoretical framework for teaching the processes of listening instead of merely focusing on the outcomes of listening comprehension. The discussion of cognitive and affective factors highlights some of the learner factors that appear to be related to L2 listening ability. However, since causality has not been established in these relationships, research needs to further explore the potential for causal relationships between learner variables and L2 listening comprehension. Nevertheless, knowing about how skillful and less skillful listeners differ in these qualitative features can help language teachers to be more sensitive to the diverse learning needs among their learners. The next two chapters will build on this knowledge to discuss how teachers can teach listening as process, design relevant listening activities and tasks for the classroom, and plan units of lessons, listening projects, and assessment tasks.

Discussion Questions and Tasks

1. Think back to the difficulties you experienced in listening to a new language. Based on your new awareness of the processes underlying listening comprehension described in this chapter, which of these difficulties are related to top-down processing or bottom-up processing? What factors might have influenced your listening ability? Share your reflections with one or two other members in your group. Identify those difficulties that all of you share and discuss how these insights can help you as a teacher of listening.

2. Work with a partner and read the following listening diary excerpts. List three or more things that the excerpts reveal about listening processes and learner factors that influence L2 listening success.

   a. Usually when I listen to the radio or watch TV I can hear clearly most of their words and paragraphs, but I can't connect the words quickly. So sometimes I couldn't catch what they said. On the other hand, when I talk about something to someone, mostly I can understand them. I think it is because that when I talk with somebody I make myself into the language surrounding but when I listen to the radio or watch TV, I don't.

   b. This week, I was listening to the radio. Many of the lectures are close to our life, so when I listen to it, I feel I can concentrate and also understand it better because of the existing idea about that.

I think the improving is really helpful and it always makes me be more confident.

c.   Every day I listen to the news, but only when I totally concentrate on the broadcast, I can catch what it says. There are also some intervals when I ponder upon the specific meaning of one word and lose the following words, which hinder me from coherent understanding. Mind-absent is the most dangerous and frequent barrier in my listening practice.

3.   Review the six core listening skills for planning listening lessons and tasks. Consider the listening instructional materials you have used or are familiar with. Which of these skills are frequently practiced and which are not? Make a list of listening situations in academic contexts where some of these skills are particularly important. Share your list with other members in your group or class and identify some of the most common situations and skills you have identified.

Further Reading

Buck, G. (2001). *Assessing listening* (Chapter 1). Cambridge, UK: Cambridge University Press.

The overview of theory and research on listening in the first chapter is both comprehensive and accessible.

Dörnyei, Z. (2005). *The psychology of the language learner: Individual differences in second language acquisition.* Mahwah, NJ: Erlbaum.

Although the focus of this book is on L2 learning in general, much of the discussion of the cognitive and affective variables related to the learner can be applied to L2 listening.

Vandergrift, L. & Goh, C. (2012). *Teaching and learning second language listening: Metacognition in action* (Chapters 2 and 4). New York, NY: Routledge.

These chapters provide further details on theoretical models for L2 listening.

9 Building a Listening Curriculum

Christine C. M. Goh

Listening in academic contexts shares many similarities with general L2 listening. The theories and research in the previous chapter help our understanding of listening processes during academic listening and their implications for instruction. This chapter gives an overview of approaches to teaching listening in second/foreign language situations. It recommends process-oriented pedagogies where the focus is not on the outcomes of listening but on helping learners to develop top-down and bottom-up skills for comprehension and to become strategic listeners who can manage the processes of listening comprehension and learning to listen. The chapter concludes with a summary of key guiding principles for building a listening curriculum and planning listening activities.

Teaching and Learning L2 Listening

Three decades ago, Brown (1987) wrote an article for teachers in which she reviewed the state of second language (L2) listening instruction from the 1960s. She noted that many teachers were not paying enough attention to teaching listening comprehension because many believed that it was caught and not taught. She observed that one of the reasons for this neglect was that, due to the hidden nature of listening processes, many teachers did not know how to teach listening. Indeed, knowledge within the field of ELT about second language listening processes and listening pedagogy was only emerging then. Although some empirical research on L2 listening had begun, very little of these insights were getting across to the professionals at the chalkface. In another conceptual article on the teaching of L2 listening, Dunkel (1991) noted a number of similarities between L1 and L2 listening and highlighted areas of research that could contribute further to a better understanding of L2 listening processes and how listening skill development for L2 learners could be enhanced. Interest in L2 listening instruction has since increased and there is now a fairly large body of works in both research and pedagogy (see Field, 2008; Flowerdew & Miller, 2005; Rost, 2013; Rubin, 1994; Vandergrift, 2004, 2007; and Vandergrift & Goh, 2012). Although the scope of L2 listening research has broadened, one point was consistently iterated by all: L2 listening needed to be taught in a more systematic and theoretically-informed manner.

Approaches to L2 Listening Instruction

Listening instruction has seen many changes in the past five decades, mainly as a result of theories and research about language learning and language use. Figure 9.1 offers a summary of three of the main approaches adopted by material writers and teachers. They are presented in chronological order as an indication of when these approaches became popular in the history of listening instruction. It does not mean, however, that elements of an earlier approach are completely absent today. Many of the practices we see in listening instruction today are in fact the result of accumulation of various practices in the past decades. Techniques introduced in the 1950s and 1960s, such as listen-and-answer, are still found in some language course books and classrooms to this day, even though the form of listening input may have changed from cassette recordings to videos or podcasts.

Approach 1: Text and Comprehension

Listening instruction in the 1960s was heavily influenced by reading and writing pedagogy and focused on learners comprehending listening passages that were written mainly as reading texts. Many of the listening passages, therefore, were grammatically and lexically dense and did not reflect the linguistic features of spoken texts where the grammar is less complex. Learners were also not exposed to different types of listening texts that they would have encountered in real-life second or foreign language contexts. Emphasis was given to accuracy in comprehension and teaching was influenced by a linear view of comprehension where understanding was built up from perception of the smallest units of sound to the final interpretation of the message. Learners learned to discriminate sounds at word- and sentence-levels to enable bottom-up processing. To demonstrate their understanding of what was heard, learners answered comprehension questions based on listening passages or completed written texts with details from the passages.

While there were plenty of listening activities, listening skills and processes were not taught and learners had to figure out the answers to the comprehension questions by themselves. Owing to this lack of scaffolding in comprehension processes, listening activities merely provided learners with regular spoken input to practise their listening without much in the way of informed teaching and learning opportunities. As Brown (1987) observed, teachers hoped that through regular listening practice, students would improve their listening comprehension abilities. There was also little awareness that such classroom practices were, in fact, testing rather than teaching listening and that, on the contrary, listening, like other language skills, needs to be taught explicitly and systematically.

Figure 9.1 Dominant approaches in listening instruction (based on Goh, 2008 and Vandergrift & Goh, 2012)

Instructional Orientation	Listening Input	Instructional Focus and Objectives
Text and comprehension: Learners demonstrate their accurate comprehension of what is in the texts through answering questions	• Words, phrases, sentences read aloud • Written passages read aloud	• Decode sounds: phonemes, word stress and sentence-level intonation • Listen to, imitate and memorize sound and grammar patterns • Identify relevant details from oral input • Demonstrate understanding of the meaning of the passage
Communication and comprehension: Learners demonstrate comprehension of what occurs during an interaction in order to achieve a communicative outcome	• Spontaneous learner–learner talk during interaction • Scripted or semi-scripted (transactional or interactional) recorded texts • Authentic listening/oral interaction materials	• Understand information appropriate to the purposes of the spoken texts • Practise main and sub-skills for listening • Respond to spoken input in socially appropriate ways
Learner awareness and the listening process: Learners experience and unpack the cognitive and social processes of listening, and use top-down and bottom-up skills and strategies to enhance comprehension and overall listening development	• Spontaneous learner–learner talk during interaction • Scripted or semi-scripted (transactional or interactional) recorded texts • Authentic listening/oral interaction materials	• Understand information appropriate to the purposes of the spoken texts • Practise main and sub-skills for listening • Respond to spoken input in socially appropriate ways • Increase metacognitive awareness about the listening process • Use strategies to enhance comprehension and cope with problems

Approach 2: Communication and Comprehension

A communication-oriented approach was the result of the phenomenal impact of the Communicative Language Teaching (CLT) methodology in the 1970s and 1980s, particularly in Europe. Unlike a text comprehension approach where the aim was to see how much of a listening passage could be understood, the focus of listening activities in CLT was on listening for a communicative purpose. Learners were typically given communicative scenarios where the information gleaned from listening inputs was used for a real or simulated goal, for example, listening to a telephone message and jotting down important points. Through communicative activities, learners practised skills such as listening for details and listening for gist. Listening practice also occurred as part of oral communication where learners develop their oral fluency. Learners worked in pairs and individually to respond to spoken texts in socially and contextually appropriate ways (e.g., infer attitude, respond to a question), complete missing information in texts or discourse (e.g., identify key words and phrases), and use information gleaned for other communicative purposes (e.g., prepare a talk).

A key feature of many CLT materials was that the four language skills of listening, speaking, reading and writing were often practised in an integrated manner through themes such as family, careers, culture, etc. It was common to find these integrated lessons culminating in the production of a written or spoken text. Listening, on the other hand, was often a means to achieving these productive language outcomes. The teaching of listening comprehension was often neglected as a result. Even in oral communication activities, listening often received less emphasis than speaking. Furthermore, when listening comprehension activities were conducted, teachers still focused mainly on learners' listening comprehension performance. This emphasis on accurate answers has been criticised to be yet another disguised form of testing listening comprehension (Sheerin, 1987).

An important pedagogical innovation during the CLT movement was the introduction of a pre-listening phase in listening lessons (see for example, Anderson & Lynch, 1988; Underwood, 1989; Ur, 1984). This was influenced by research insights into the constructive nature of first language text comprehension that drew on 'schemata' or sets of knowledge structures stored in long-term memory. Pre-listening activities helped to activate language learners' prior knowledge that they could use to interpret and complete meanings from listening texts. At about the same time, three linguistic concepts also began to inform listening instruction: 1) the difference between spoken and written language, 2) various dimensions of authenticity, and 3) contextualization of instructional tasks and language (Brown, 1987).

Approach 3: Learner Awareness and the Listening Process

Listening instruction was informed by further developments in applied linguistics about the role of the learner in second language acquisition in the early 1980s. Specifically, in the past three decades we have seen importance given to the development of learner autonomy where the use of learning and communication strategies was particularly valued. In L2 listening, a strategy-approach was proposed as a way of facilitating comprehension processes (Mendelsohn, 1998) and learners were taught to apply cognitive, metacognitive and social-affective strategies during listening (O'Malley & Chamot, 1990). Teachers were encouraged to use techniques such as modelling listening strategies for managing listening processes (Chamot, 1995; Mendelsohn, 1995, 1998) and verifying their inferences/guesses (Field, 1998). There was also a call to develop L2 listeners' metacognition, or ability to think about their own thinking and learning through introspective learning activities as well as process-oriented listening lessons (Goh, 1997; Vandergrift, 2004). Learners were encouraged to engage in various metacognitive activities such as reflecting on their listening experiences individually through listening diaries (Goh, 1997) as well as collaboratively through group discussions using metacognitive prompts (Cross, 2010; Goh & Taib, 2006). On the matter of explicit strategy instruction, research indicated that strategy instruction was more efficacious when carried out in the context of a listening activity instead of as standalone and decontextualized training (Cross, 2009; Graham & Macaro, 2008).

A common strategy identified among both proficient and less proficient L2 listeners was making inferences by applying prior knowledge to compensate for listening gaps. But such a top-down strategy needs to be counterbalanced by a focus on developing bottom-up decoding skills so that learners will have fewer perception problems interfering with accurate interpretation (Field, 2008). Merely learning to apply strategies without understanding the demands and nature of L2 listening was also inadequate, and so emphasis was given to metacognitive instruction. The aim of metacognitive instruction was to increase learners' metacognitive awareness of their listening and learning processes while developing their ability to self-manage their strategy use in contextualized listening activities as well as in personal reflective activities (Goh, 2008). Such learner-oriented approaches also orient towards the listening process because unlike approaches that focused on the product of listening, they emphasize teaching learners *how* to listen and helping learners to understand their own listening processes.

Process-Oriented Listening Instruction

Process-oriented instruction enables learners to experience selected listening processes at different parts of the lesson in order to develop greater metacognitive awareness about L2 listening. The aim is to develop strategic L2 listeners who not only do well in top-down and bottom-up process, but are also good at managing their overall learning of L2 listening. For example, learners can develop their knowledge of the language and discourse to decode speech signals, attend to discourse cues that signal text organization, use their prior and unfolding contextual knowledge to construct reasonable interpretations, and employ strategies for planning, monitoring and evaluating their listening task and performance. Process-oriented pedagogies enable learners to identify for themselves their listening weaknesses in language, discourse or other areas of language use thus allowing teachers to provide learning activities for addressing these specific weaknesses. As these processes are complex and not always immediately available for reflection, teachers need to provide learners with metacognitive tools to help them in their process of learning to listen.

A process-oriented pedagogy makes use of many common communicative listening activities while integrating them with metacognitive activities as a means of making the processes of comprehension and learning visible to learners. Listening lessons can also be carried out with a single listening text, as is commonly done in academic listening contexts such as listening to lectures and seminars. The learning of top-down and bottom-up processing skills is equally important in a process-oriented approach to listening instruction. Learners not only learn core listening skills and strategies through engagement with listening tasks and metacognitive activities, but also develop explicit knowledge of sounds and pronunciation, and improve their lexical segmentation, a key decoding process (Field, 2008).

There are four ways in which teachers can organize learning activities in process-oriented listening instruction, as Figure 9.2 shows:

Figure 9.2 Forms of process-oriented listening instruction

> a. *Metacognitive pedagogical sequence*—a five-stage lesson structure that guides learners through metacognitive processes of listening as they listen to a text several times.
> b. *Process-based reflections and discussions*—a three-stage lesson structure led by the teacher following a listen-and-answer activity.
> c. *Task-based metacognitive instruction*—communicative listening tasks that are framed by metacognitive activities in pre- and post-listening stages of a listening lesson.
> d. *Scaffolded extensive listening*—extensive listening projects which integrate listening practice beyond the classroom with metacognitive activities and tools.

The first three suggested pedagogies can form the mainstay of an in-class listening curriculum. They provide variety according to learner needs and listening texts and address diverse listening purposes in an academic listening programme. The fourth is a way of supporting learners' listening development beyond the classroom. Each of these forms of instruction will be explained in the sections that follow. Further details about specific listening tasks will be provided in the next chapter.

Metacognitive Pedagogical Sequence for Listening

Vandergrift (2004) argued that teachers should make thinking processes during listening more explicit to learners. To this end, he proposed the use of a lesson sequence that integrates metacognitive processes, such as prediction, verification, and evaluation, with listening at specific phases of a lesson. The purpose is to scaffold the learning of listening processes as learners work with listening texts. Four processes that are crucial to successful listening development are included in this sequence: 1) planning for the activity; 2) monitoring comprehension; 3) solving comprehension problems; and, 4) evaluating the approach and outcomes, and further planning. Research has shown that learners who were taught using this sequence improved their performance (Vandergrift & Tafaghodtari, 2010), developed greater awareness of what constituted effective strategies (Cross, 2010) and experienced increased motivation in learning to listen (Liu & Goh, 2006; Mareschal, 2007).

The metacognitive pedagogical sequence is most suited to tasks involving non-participatory listening, for example, listening to a recording of a talk or lecture in class without the need to interact with the speaker(s). Learners work in pairs and listen to the same text at least three times while the teacher guides them through different strategic processes with each listen. A complete metacognitive lesson sequence has five stages in which the learners listen to the text three times in all. During each listen, learners verify their understanding of the text as a way of gradually increasing their comprehension of the text content and control over their listening processes. Figure 9.3 shows how these stages are organized. This sequence provides a framework for planning

Figure 9.3 A metacognitive pedagogical sequence. (Adapted from Vandergrift & Goh 2012, p. 109. Used with permission.)

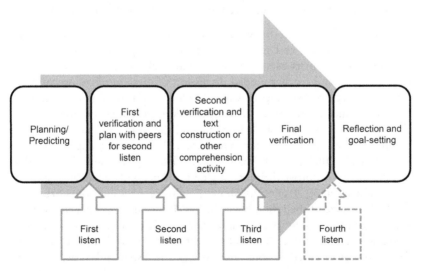

a complete listening lesson, which allows teachers to select the listening text and the strategies that are suited to the learners' needs and purpose for listening. Teachers can also offer just-in-time support on strategy use and guidance on lexical segmentation and other decoding skills after the main listening stages. Peer discussion and teacher modelling are also included.

In the planning stage, students define their listening goals, share with one another their prior knowledge about the topic and together predict and write down the information and words/phrases in the text. They also anticipate strategically any potential difficulties and prepare themselves with some strategies. During the first listen, students write down words that they have predicted. In pairs they compare what they have understood and describe the strategies they have used. Next they identify problems and tell each other what they should attend to when they listen again. (The teacher can also model thinking aloud strategies for listening selectively to problematic parts of the text). During the second listen, students listen selectively to the problematic parts they have identified and take down notes of new information. (The teacher can also lead a discussion to check students' comprehension and elicit from students the strategies that they have used. The teacher can also model some useful strategies). Before listening to the text a third time, students decide individually what strategies they would like to try out. They then listen to the text again to verify their understanding. Students may also decide to listen to the text one more time but with a transcript so as to notice how some problematic or unfamiliar words and utterances sound. In the final evaluation and planning stage, students are asked to reflect in writing what they have learnt from the listening processes and plan what they can do when they have to listen in similar situations in future. They can also be asked to write down what they have understood from the listening text.

Process-Based Listening with Reflections and Discussions

Another lesson sequence for working with non-participatory listening texts involves three stages and greater teacher scaffolding. This lesson structure uses a listening activity as a context for individual learner introspection after their listening and teacher-guided discussion of metacognitive processes for listening. It adapts listening activities that focus on text comprehension and adds to it a metacognitive dimension that develops learners' awareness about the nature and demands of L2 listening and the strategies that can enhance comprehension. It has been shown to work well with young language learners (Goh & Taib, 2006), as well as adult foreign language learners (Zeng, 2014), helping them to improve their listening performance and metacognitive awareness about listening. Figure 9.4 shows how these stages are organized.

The first stage of the lesson is a common classroom listening activity where the learner has to listen to a text and answer some comprehension questions. The lesson does not end there but this activity is, in fact, just the beginning for a process-oriented lesson. After doing the listen-and-answer activity,

Figure 9.4 A listening lesson sequence that integrates listen-and-answer activities with individual guided reflection and process-based discussions

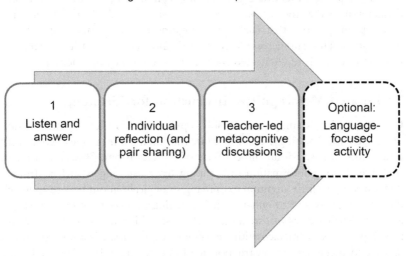

1	2	3	Optional:
Listen and answer	Individual reflection (and pair sharing)	Teacher-led metacognitive discussions	Language-focused activity

students are asked to reflect on their listening processes by writing down their reactions to some prompts. During this second stage, teachers use the reflection questions shown in Figure 9.5 to guide the learners in reporting their mental processes during the listening task while these are still fresh in their minds.

The students could share their written reflections with a partner first, or, if the class is small, they can also share it directly with the rest of the class. The third stage is a teacher-led whole-class discussion. In a big class, the teacher can nominate some students to read aloud their written reflections. As each student reports their observations, the others are encouraged to listen and ask questions or give comments. The teacher scaffolds this discussion by following up with questions that focus on strategies underlying four meta-cognitive processes: Planning, monitoring, evaluating, and problem-solving/inferencing. This stage enables learners to evaluate and apply their individual and collective metacognitive knowledge.

Figure 9.5 Reflection questions for listening

a. What did you listen to and what did you understand?
    (Purpose: Check comprehension)
b. What helped you to understand the text?
    (Purpose: Elicit task knowledge — factors that influenced listening)
c. What prevented you from getting the correct answers?
    (Purpose: Elicit task knowledge — factors that influenced listening)
d. What did you do to understand as much of the text as possible?
    (Purpose: Elicit strategy knowledge — ways of enhancing comprehension)

A fourth stage may also be added to increase learners' knowledge about how language works during listening. For example, if one of the problems that students report is that they are not able to hear some words clearly or correctly, a perception practice that facilitates recognition of segments of speech can be included. This can increase learners' task knowledge about how characteristics and demands of connected speech can influence comprehension.

Task-Based Metacognitive Instruction for Listening

Communicative listening tasks are still popular decades after the introduction of the CLT methodology. This is because they offer some degree of communication authenticity within the confines of the classroom. However, a lot of the time, getting information or meaning from listening is such a struggle that learners give little attention to thinking strategically about how to approach the listening task and to enhance their listening processes. In order to teach learners the processes of listening, teachers should combine communicative listening tasks with metacognitive development activities. We refer to this as task-based metacognitive instruction for listening (TBMIL). This pedagogy builds on familiar listening tasks where learners listen to texts and use the information for communicative outcomes. In addition to this, they also engage in metacognitive processes such as planning, monitoring, and evaluation at specific pre-listening and post-listening phases of the task-based lessons. By integrating metacognitive activities with listening tasks, learners become more strategic in their listening and also have the opportunities to work on weaknesses revealed in their listening tasks (Goh, 2010).

TBMIL makes use of a generic pre-listening, listening, and post-listening structure to develop a listening lesson that develops communication and metacognitive skills, as shown in Figure 9.6. In the generic lesson structure,

Figure 9.6 A lesson structure in task-based metacognitive instruction for listening

Pre-listening (strategic planning and language / knowledge oriented activities) → Listening task → Post-listening (utilising information from text for a communicative purpose) → Evaluation and reflection tasks

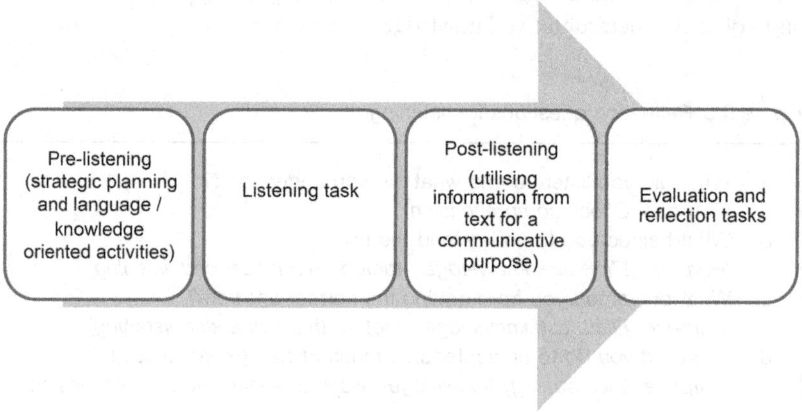

Figure 9.7 Guidelines for planning task-based metacognitive instruction (TBMI)
for listening

---

a. At least one pre-listening activity should precede a listening task.
    The pre-listening activity involves learners in predicting key words,
    activating prior knowledge, learning new words that they may hear,
    and identifying strategies to use for listening.
b. A post-listening activity should follow the listening task. Learners
    can apply, synthesize or evaluate information and interpretation from
    task.
c. A further extension activity can be included to develop further
    metacognitive knowledge and language/discourse knowledge from
    the task. Learners can analyze text for pronunciation, grammar and
    vocabulary; reflect on listening performance during the task; plan for
    future listening; and plan and carry out extensive listening.

---

pre–listening activities are used typically to activate learners' schema to assist
their comprehension during listening, while post-listening activities typically
involve learners in using the information from the listening text for some
other communitive purposes. TBMIL expands the scope of these two phases
so that learners can consider the listening process they are about to engage
in as well as evaluate how effective that process has been for them. You will
find descriptions of a variety of listening tasks and activities as well as a sample
instructional outline in the next chapter.

Figure 9.7 provides some guidelines for planning task-based metacognitive
instruction (TBMI) for listening and for reviewing existing materials so that
teachers can further enhance the lesson to teach the process of listening.

Scaffolded Extensive Listening Projects and Assignments

Learners should be encouraged to develop their listening beyond the language
classroom through extensive listening. There are two ways in which learners
are involved in extensive listening. The first is the typical individual practice
where learners access different kinds of listening resources available to them
on their computers, mobile devices or home facilities, such as the television
and radio. The second type of extensive listening comprises specially designed
assignments or projects which integrate listening practice with elements of
metacognitive instruction. In each assignment or project, learners work
individually or with their peers in process-based activities in which to listen
to the target language for communicative purposes and to achieve specific
outcomes. By providing learners with metacognitive tools, teachers offer them
the direction and focus that are often lacking in extensive listening learners
engage on their own.

Advanced learners can still benefit from engaging in authentic listening tasks beyond the classroom, but the weaker listeners will certainly benefit from these additional opportunities to develop their listening. Although listening practice is done during the learners' own time, teachers can still provide learners with guidance and support to help them use these opportunities well. One common practice among learners in this current age is to watch online videos and listen to podcasts. Teachers can help them in three ways. First, provide them with tools that can help them self-direct and evaluate their extensive listening efforts. Second, teachers can plan extensive listening projects that can help learners deepen their understanding of listening, use listening and learning strategies, and at the same time practise their perception and interpretation skills. Third, teachers can also curate a resource bank that learners can access. Teacher-scaffolded extensive listening can have a positive effect improving learners' metacognitive awareness, listening performance and overall confidence (Zeng & Goh, 2017, in-press). Teachers can also support learners in developing autonomy or ability to take control of their own learning beyond the classroom by capitalizing on technological affordances such as podcasts (Cross, 2016). Figure 9.8 presents three extensive listening projects/assignments which are suitable for listening in academic contexts.

Each extensive listening project should be distinguished from and add value to students' unguided individual learning. In other words, they should help learners develop awareness of the listening process which they would not otherwise do if left to practise their listening on their own. These projects should also offer them a chance to work cooperatively and creatively with their fellow learners. As a general rule of thumb, the project should be kept within two weeks followed by a quick review. Students and teachers can decide whether or not to extend it. When planning extensive listening activities, it is important to ensure that learners listen to as many different types of authentic listening texts as possible. Types of texts include narratives, recounts, information, reports, instructional/procedural texts, expository/argumentative texts and conversations. This will enable learners to become familiar with the way each type of text is structured. They should also have access to a wide variety of themes and topics so that they are exposed to a wider selection of vocabulary. Another option is to offer narrow listening tasks which focus on a small selection of themes so that they have opportunities to recycle the language. Learners should also be encouraged to follow a daily or weekly listening plan by setting their own goals and actions. It will be helpful to show them how to monitor their progress, and if necessary adjust their plans and revise their goals. This will enable them to be strategic in managing their own learning.

They should also be asked to listen to the selected texts a few times. This can be worked into the prompts and self-directed listening guides given to the students which require them to listen to something a few times and record their understanding and evaluations after each listen. The metacognitive pedagogical sequence can be modified so that the repeated listening normally

Figure 9.8 Examples of teacher-scaffolded extensive listening projects and assignments

Self-regulated listening programme *(non-participatory listening)*	Learners are provided with a selection of listening and viewing resources and a set of metacognitive tools to direct and monitor their own progress (checklists for assessing metacognitive awareness, templates for recording listening activities and tracking their progress in both metacognition and listening performance, self-directed listening guiding prompts and end-of-project evaluation prompts).
Authentic interview project *(interactive listening)*	Learners plan structured interviews with competent speakers using questions they formulate themselves. They plan the kinds of communication strategies they would need to support their learning and understanding, rehearse the questions through role play and prepare a report after the interviews. They also keep a journal of their experiences with prompts provided by the teacher.
The TED Talk listening assignment *(non-participatory listening)*	Learners are instructed to listen to TED Talks each week (the titles and URLs given by the teacher). When they listen to each of these authentic, lecture-style talks, they make notes about what they hear, evaluate their comprehension using English and translated transcripts, and write reflections on mis-hearings or misunderstandings and why they might have occurred. The teacher gives them a number of metacognitive prompts with instructions to guide them in their listening task and reflections on listening errors.

done in class can also be carried out individually as Elk (2014) did with her TED Talk listening assignments. Repeated listening helps reduce the learners' cognitive load as it enables them to become more familiar with the content, vocabulary and structure of the spoken text. This is part of the process of learning to listen which can help with greater automatization of cognitive processes eventually.

Becoming Strategic L2 Listeners

This chapter follows authors in other sections of this book in recognizing that the construct of a strategic L2 listener involves, not just a learner who can utilize effective strategies during communication, but one who can manage their learning and strategy development over a sustained period of time within and beyond the language classroom. An important aim of process-oriented pedagogies is to help learners become strategic in their listening comprehension and overall listening development. Research on L2 listeners has shown that more successful listeners are typically also more strategic in

Figure 9.9 Strategies for listening comprehension and development

1. Planning: Developing an awareness of what needs to be done and putting in place an action plan to overcome possible difficulties during listening and over the longer term learning process.
2. Focussing attention: Heeding the spoken input in different ways, avoiding distractions and focusing attention on action plans for improving listening in and outside the classroom.
3. Monitoring: Checking, confirming, or correcting one's comprehension during the task and individual progress in learning to listen.
4. Evaluation: Checking the outcomes of listening comprehension and listening plans against an internal or external measure of completeness, reasonableness and accuracy.
5. Inferencing: Using different kinds of prior knowledge and information within the text or conversational context to guess the meanings of unfamiliar language items or fill in missing information.
6. Elaboration: Using prior knowledge from outside the text or conversational context in order to extend and embellish one's interpretation of the text
7. Prediction: Anticipating the contents and the message of what one is going to hear and challenges that one may face when carrying out a learning plan for improving listening.
8. Contextualization: Placing what is heard in a specific context in order to prepare for listening or assist comprehension.
9. Reorganizing: Transferring what is understood into other forms to facilitate further understanding, storage, and retrieval.
10. Using linguistic and learning resources: Relying on one's knowledge of the first language or additional languages to make sense of what is heard, or consulting learning resources after listening to support listening and learning.
11. Cooperation: Working with others to get help on improving comprehension, language use and learning.
12. Managing emotions: Keeping track of one's negative emotions and finding ways to prevent them from affecting comprehension as well as attitudes and behaviours in learning.

that they orchestrate strategy use effectively to achieve better comprehension (Goh, 2002; Macaro et al., 2007; Vandergrift, 2003b) They also plan their overall listening development carefully by making good use of out-of-class opportunities (Zeng, 2012).

Some adult foreign language learners try to improve their listening by tuning in to radio broadcasts and viewing videos on the internet. They also find opportunities to talk to native or other competent speakers so that they could practise their speaking and listening. Of course, they do not become proficient in listening overnight. For many, learning to listen is a slow and painful process. Success does not come simply by hearing more or speaking more. Like children acquiring their first language through talk, many of these adult learners are also helped by the people they interact with. They are also 'bootstrapped' by their own learning strategies that enable them to make good use of the opportunities they have with the target language. Unfortunately, just as there are learners who successfully work on listening on their own, there are also numerous others who meet with less success.

Vandergrift and Goh (2012) identified 12 types of general strategies that are common in the L2 listening literature. These strategies perform various important functions of managing and controlling listening processes, solving comprehension and learning problems, and enhancing cognitive, social and affective processes in learning. The L2 strategies are described in Figure 9.9 and where possible they are explained in relation to both strategy use for enhancing comprehension during communications and learners' personal plans for developing L2 listening over time.

A comprehensive listening curriculum should develop learners' knowledge of these strategies and ability to use them flexibly for improving their listening comprehension and managing their overall listening development over time.

Curricular and Instructional Principles for L2 Listening

Based on the aforementioned reviews and discussions, we can derive a number of guiding principles for planning a listening curriculum and instructional activities. These principles can provide a reference for planning a complete unit of learning or a listening lesson and making decisions about the selection of suitable listening texts and strategies:

Teach Processes for Comprehension and Learning

1. Listening pedagogies should be learner-centred, focusing on helping learners understand, experience and control the various top-down and bottom-up processes in listening, as well as supporting them in learning endeavours for listening development over time.
2. Top-down learning processes should be complemented by perception activities that assist learners with recognizing sounds and sound patterns. Such decoding activities should be contextualized so that the learning

takes place within texts that learners have already encountered in earlier listening activities.

3. The teaching of thinking processes during listening should be made more explicit to learners so that they can understand that listening is an active and strategic process in which comprehension is constructed from a number of sources.

4. A comprehensive listening curriculum should develop learners' knowledge of strategies and their ability to use them flexibly for facilitating listening comprehension, as well as managing their overall listening development efforts.

Select Suitable Tasks and Texts

1. Learning activities should make the processes of comprehension and learning visible to learners. This enables learners to develop explicit knowledge of L2 listening processes and practise the use of core listening skills and strategies.

2. Process-oriented tasks should also aim to help learners identify for themselves their listening weaknesses in language, discourse or other areas of language use, and provide learning activities that will address these specific weaknesses.

3. Improvement in listening comprehension can be enhanced by learners' awareness and control of their mental processes. This can be supported by providing learners with metacognitive tools for reflection, problem-solving, evaluation, and self-direction.

4. Learners' metacognitive awareness about listening can be developed through individual reflections, teacher-led discussions, and collaborative student dialogue.

5. Learners should work with texts that match the academic genres of spoken texts encountered in academic listening.

Provide a Range of Listening Experience

1. Learners should engage in both wide-listening and narrow-listening, using different types of authentic listening texts in order to maximize opportunities to gain breadth and depth in their language development.

2. Include extensive listening activities as part of the listening curriculum, and learners should be encouraged to develop their listening by setting goals for extensive listening, supported by teacher guidance, and scaffolding.

3. Listening does not have to be individual work. Learners can work cooperatively and creatively with their fellow learners as part of their process of learning to listen in, and beyond, the classroom.

Chapter Summary

In a lot of listening lessons, students are passive or disengaged from the active process of learning to listen. This is often the result of too much emphasis on the product or outcome of listening which typically prioritizes accuracy and completeness of information. When the exercises are easy, learners can feel bored and when they are too challenging learners end up feeling anxious and frustrated. Listening instruction that focuses on the outcome of listening denies learners of opportunities to understand listening processes and discover how they might take better control of their listening development. It is therefore important that the teaching of listening helps learners focus on comprehension and learning processes. While outcomes are not completely ignored, the priority is on helping learners understand what L2 listening entails, the nature and demands of listening, their personal strengths and weaknesses and ways or strategies in compensating for these limitations. A way to do this is for teachers to be aware of the role of metacognition in teaching listening, a skill that consists of cognitive processes that are largely hidden but nonetheless active in the mind of the learners. Besides helping learners with new ways of learning to listen in an L2, metacognitive activities, when combined with authentic listening, also reduce language anxiety and improve confidence and performance as research has shown.

Discussion Questions

1. Select a listening course book and identify the approach it adopts for listening instruction. Choose one unit of work or chapter from the book and assess its strengths and limitations. If the material lacks a process-orientation, suggest how you might adapt the material to promote greater awareness about the listening process.
2. Discuss this statement: "Extensive listening activities for improving academic listening should be a combination of students' own initiative and teachers' planned activities."
3. Compare the four process-oriented pedagogies introduced in this chapter:

    a. Metacognitive pedagogical sequence
    b. Task-based metacognitive instruction
    c. Process-based reflection and discussion
    d. Scaffolded extensive listening

    Are there pedagogies that are more suited to learners of a specific age group? If there are, discuss why they may not be suitable for learners from another age group and discuss how you can adapt it for this group of learners.

4. Select two or three of the 12 guiding principles for listening instruction and explain how each one will inform the listening lessons or activities that you would plan.

5.   Interview some language teachers and language learners to find out what is normally done in their listening classes. Find out how they feel about these activities and compare the responses from the teachers and the students. What can you learn from these responses about teaching listening?

Further Reading

Cross, J. (2016). Podcasts and autonomous L2 listening: Pedagogical insights and research direction. *The European Journal of Applied Linguistics and TEFL*, 5 (2) 59–72.

This article provides clear and comprehensive discussion about autonomy and L2 listening and at the same time offers valuable suggestions for the use of podcasts as a learning vehicle.

Goh, C. C. M. (2017, forthcoming). Academic listening. In J. I. Liontas (Ed.), *The TESOL encyclopedia of English Language teaching: Teaching listening.* Wiley Blackwell.

This article describes the nature of academic listening, comparing it with general L2 listening and highlighting differences. Challenges that students face are discussed and considerations for instruction are proposed.

10 Listening Instruction and Assessment

Activities and Options

Christine C. M. Goh

In the last two chapters, we discussed theoretical perspectives on L2 listening and how the teaching of L2 listening has been approached in language and listening classes. This chapter will build specifically on ideas in the last chapter about process-based listening pedagogies and the overall curricular goal of developing strategic listeners. The chapter provides guidelines and examples of techniques that teachers, material writers, and curriculum designers can adopt and adapt for enhancing listening instruction. It covers: (a) instructional activities that promote listening skills for communication, metacognitive knowledge and skills, and decoding/lexical segmentation skills; (b) planning lessons and units of learning for listening; and (c) techniques for assessing *of* listening proficiency and assessing listening *for* learner development.

Designing Instructional Activities

In the previous chapter we explored how communicative listening tasks can form an important basis for process-oriented listening lessons. Listening tasks are defined here as learning activities which engage learners in listening to input in English or any other second/foreign language for a communicative purpose. The purpose would be to put to use the information or message obtained from the input. Listening tasks are, therefore, different from activities or exercises to improve learners' decoding skills for more effective bottom-up processing. We first discuss how teachers and material writers can design simple and effective communicative tasks for listening. This is followed by an explanation of metacognitive activities that can support learners' strategic processing of meanings of texts that they hear. Finally, perception activities are described to show teachers how to develop learners' decoding or lexical segmentation skills.

Communicative Listening Tasks

Effective listening practice involves the use of authentic language tasks that are appropriate to the age, language level, and life experience of the learners. These tasks should be similar to the types of listening experience that learners are likely to encounter in real-life contexts and communication. In academic contexts, these tasks would include listening to lectures and participating in seminars, listening to one another in group discussions, watching a video of a talk/speech/debate and taking notes for a summary or a report.

There are two kinds of listening in everyday language use: Non-participatory, and participatory or interactive listening. Non-participatory, one-way listening is most commonly found in language classrooms. Learners listen to a recording or the teacher so as to achieve a required communicative goal. It is often not necessary to give immediate responses and they have few opportunities, and in some situations no opportunity to stop the speaker(s) to ask questions or clarify what is said. Unlike real-time interactions, learners are also unable to ask for any repetition unless they control the device for a recorded input and so can stop it and play a part again.

Participatory or interactive listening, on the other hand, requires the ability to interact with speakers of the target language in academic and social situations, such as in group discussions and conversations. English learners in academic contexts will need to develop their ability to manage their listening comprehension in these situations where they not only have to understand reasonably well what is being said, but also to respond quickly and appropriately so as not to let the communication flag.

Listening tasks in the language classroom will have to address both types of listening. Interactive listening is practised together with speaking in oral communication activities. However, in such activities, the emphasis is typically

Figure 10.1 Listening comprehension tasks in one-way listening

1. Listen and restore: Listen for global understanding and details in order to amend a written text with mistakes.
2. Listen and sort: Listen for main ideas and details in order to sequence a set of texts or pictures.
3. Listen and compare: Listen for main ideas and details in order to make a list of similarities and differences.
4. Listen and match: Listen for global understanding in order to match different texts to their respective themes.
5. Listen and combine: Listening for main ideas and listen selectively in order to synthesis a combined summary based on information from different sources.
6. Listen and compose: Listen to predict and make inferences to compose the beginning or conclusion of a text.
7. Listen and evaluate: Listen for details and main ideas in order to make inferences about the merits of what is said.
8. Listen and reconstruct: Listen for global understanding, main ideas and details in order to reconstruct a written text based on the listening text.

on speaking and expression of meanings, so the development of listening skills may be overlooked. Teachers would, therefore, have to plan ways of developing skills and strategies for interactive listening alongside speaking practice.

Non-Participatory (One-Way) Listening Tasks

One-way listening tasks require learners to understand the meaning of what is said without the need to give immediate responses. Instead, learners are typically required to manipulate or use the information obtained from the listening texts in various ways that are similar to authentic academic contexts, for example, making lists, categorizing information, editing texts, drawing or completing diagrams and pictures, writing summaries, making notes, noting down questions, and making individual/group responses.

In Figure 10.1 you can find a number of listening tasks for practising comprehension. They form the main communicative component of a listening lesson around which other stages for task-based metacognitive instruction (TBMI) can be developed.

Below is an example of how one of the tasks above, *listen and evaluate*, can be conducted:

a. Students are each given a set of criteria to assess the information in some short listening texts based on predetermined criteria, such as clarity, interest level, accuracy and effectiveness.
b. They listen individually to three texts on a common theme or topic. (They can listen to each text more than once if they so wish).
c. After they have listened to each text, they record their opinion for each criterion.
d. When they have listened to all the texts, students work in groups of threes or in pairs and explain their choices.

Participatory (Interactive) Listening Tasks

In interactive listening tasks, the learner is often an active partner in an interaction and will be expected to offer information, express opinions or ask questions in response to what is heard. Such tasks will tap similar cognitive resources as those needed for non-participatory listening, but they will also develop different skills and processes. Interactive listening tasks involve talk of either a social interactional nature (e.g., conversations) or a transactional nature (e.g., service encounters), or a combination of both. In interactional talk, and some transactional talk, the turns between speakers and listeners may be short and more balanced. In some transactional talk, however, the person giving the information may do most of the talking, for example, when the speaker is giving detailed instructions, explanations or directions. However, the listener may still engage with the speaker.

In two-way listening tasks, students work in pairs or small groups and share information to achieve specific outcomes. A key consideration when planning these tasks is to create appropriate communication gaps relating to information and opinions. With some tasks, the turns between speakers are short and uneven, and not everyone gets the same opportunities to practise their listening. It would be helpful to learners if such tasks are repeated with different members in a group or pairs changing roles. The teacher takes on the role as a facilitator to structure and manage the tasks, which are shown in Figure 10.2.

Figure 10.2 Interactive listening tasks

1. Dictate and complete: Listen for details selectively and write down important information to complete a text.
2. Describe and draw: Listen for main ideas and details to draw pictures, maps, sketches, and other objects.
3. Simulate and discuss: Listen for main ideas and details; listen and make inferences and predict, so as to express views and recommendations.
4. Take notes and clarify: Listen for global understanding, main ideas and details; listen and make inferences. Produce a set of notes and questions for clarifying understanding.

Below is an example of how the task of *take notes and clarify* can be conducted:

a. Students listen to a presentation by fellow-students or a guest speaker.
b. They take short notes of the contents.
c. Whenever something is unclear, they write a question that they can ask after the talk.

Alternative: After they have reviewed the contents of their notes, students write down a few questions they would like to ask the speaker.

For more interactive-listening activities, you may also want to refer to the next section on speaking. Many of the activities described there will lend themselves to developing interactive listening skills and strategies. Teachers would need to focus on specific listening skills relevant to the task and emphasize to students that both listening and speaking skills are important for completing the tasks.

Metacognitive Activities

Metacognitive activities are learning activities that develop learners' metacognitive abilities to self-appraise and self-regulate their learning so that they

Figure 10.3 Metacognitive activities and tools for guiding learners' listening

1. Listening diaries with metacognitive prompts: Learners use guiding questions to reflect on a specific listening experience; learners record their responses to issues related to the three dimensions of meta-cognitive knowledge.
2. Self-report checklist: Learners evaluate their own knowledge and performance by referring to a list of pre-selected items of metacog-nitive knowledge about L2 listening.
3. Anxiety and motivation charts: Learners draw diagrams to show the changes in their anxiety and motivation levels for various listening tasks they do in and outside class.
4. Process-based discussion prompts: Learners use a set of prompts to guide them in their discussion about a listening task.
5. Self-directed listening prompts: Learners use a set of prompts to guide them in making pre-listening preparations, evaluating their performance and further planning for future listening tasks.
6. Guided self-evaluation of mistakes: Learners identify mistakes made during a listening task and suggest reasons for these mistakes. Used as a language-focused activity after listening, it can raise awareness of phonological features that affect decoding and interpretation.
7. Self-regulated listening portfolio: Learners build up a portfolio of their listening by using several tools including templates with prompts for recording listening activities and tracking their progress in both metacognition and listening performance.

become more strategic L2 listeners. Figure 10.3 presents some activities and learning tools to achieve this instructional goal.

These activities can be combined with listening tasks in process-oriented listening instruction in two ways: Integrated experiential listening tasks and guided reflections on listening (Goh, 2008; 2010). Integrated experiential listening tasks enable learners to experience cognitive and social-affective processes of listening comprehension while working on a listening-related task. The metacognitive pedagogical sequence and task-based metacognitive instruction in the previous chapter are examples of integrated experiential listening tasks. Guided reflection activities involve learners in evaluating their own listening performance and progress and in so doing focus their attention on specific aspects of their listening. These reflections can be carried out as part of a listening lesson or after class and as part of learners' extensive listening assignments.

Perception Activities

Perception activities strengthen learners' ability to recognize sounds and sound patterns in speech. Learners can develop lexical segmentation skills that help them recognize sounds in a speech stream as words or phrases that they know. In a process-oriented approach to teaching listening, perception activities are not conducted as isolated practice exercises, but are integrated with communicative and metacognitive activities as a pedagogical sequence, thereby improving their bottom-up processing abilities in context. These activities develop learners' metacognitive knowledge about phonological features so that they become more familiar with the way sounds of words appear in speech. Compared with decoding training in the form of standalone ear-training exercises, the use of contextualized perception activities builds on texts that learners have already encountered (Goh & Wallace, forthcoming; Vandergrift & Goh, 2012).

Including perception activities with listening tasks in a listening programme provides learners with discourse contexts within which to notice and rehearse how certain sounds, particularly problematic ones, are realized in speech. As part of a listening lesson, learners can also be asked to discover their own decoding errors (Wilson, 2003; Elk, 2014) and this also allows teachers to follow up with specific remediation through sound discrimination practice. The process of discovery and the remediation will further contribute to learners' knowledge of the sounds and pronunciation in the L2.

Perception activities work on many levels of sounds, from single syllables and words to longer sound patterns such as intonation, which can directly help with lexical segmentation or determining word boundaries. Learners can also find out about variations and irregularities in English pronunciations which hinder their recognition of words that they know. Here are some features of connected speech in English that learners may find challenging, particularly if they occur in words they are unfamiliar with:

- *Assimilation*: adjusting the sound of the end of a word to make it easier to move to the sound of the next word (e.g., these sheep → thee sheep);
- *Elision*: omitting individual sounds within a word when three or more consonants cluster together (e.g., grandmother → granmother);
- *Resyllabification or liaison/linking*: relocation of sounds so that the consonant at the end of a word is attached to the beginning of the next word (e.g., stand up ↑ stan dup);
- *Reduction*: reshaping less important words within a tone group to make them easier to pronounce (e.g., I am going to eat it → I'm gonna eat it).

Figure 10.4 presents some post-listening activities for building metacognitive awareness of bottom-up listening and contextualized remediation. The emphasis is on learners applying bottom-up processes to notice sounds, groups of sounds, words or segments of utterances in the listening text they have encountered earlier in a communication task.

Figure 10.4 Post-listening activities.

---

1. *Transcribe a listening text*:
   Learners listen to a segment of the text they heard earlier and transcribe it. When they have finished, they are given the original transcript for comparison. (Alternative: the teacher reads aloud the segment at normal speed and with natural features of connected speech.)

2. *Write down unfamiliar words*:
   Learners listen to the entire text again and write down the words or phrases that they did not recognise. They can try and write down how these words sound to them. After this, they compare what they have written with the original ones in the transcript.

3. *Listen and read*:
   Learners listen to the original listening text again but this time they follow along with the transcript. Whenever they come across words that they do not recognise from listening alone, they circle or underline the words.

Teachers can also develop bottom-up skills with dictation activities as they give learners practice in distinguishing between words in a speech stream and identify problematic phonemic features (Nation & Newton, 2009). In dictation activities, the texts can be repeated and the teacher or learners may choose to pause the text at any time after the first listen to get a better grasp of challenging sounds and words. At the end of each perception activity, learners can discuss with the teacher and among themselves why they had problem recognizing certain words and phrases. Repeating the text can help learners become increasingly familiar with the sounds of the connected speech in the text. The lesson can end with a final round of listening and learners can use their new phonological knowledge to perceive the challenging sounds and sound patterns.

Planning Lessons and Learning Units for Listening

Earlier chapters in this book have addressed key principles for lesson planning so these will not be repeated here. Instead, I will explain important principles for planning lessons that focus on one-way and interactive listening. Here we build on process-oriented pedagogies from earlier discussions and describe procedures for listening tasks, metacognitive activities, and perception activities to be integrated into a coherent unit. Three important considerations are discussed below: lesson objectives, lesson stages and listening texts. This is followed by a sample lesson/learning unit outline.

Lesson Objectives

Academic listening programmes typically have general aims, such as to listen and understand lectures, and to listen and participate in a seminar. Each lesson, nevertheless, should have specific learning objectives leading to the achievement of these listening comprehension goals. Objectives can be stated in terms of the communicative outcomes learners should achieve through a task, listening skills that learners can practise while listening, the strategies they need to support comprehension processes and the kinds of linguistic and metacognitive knowledge that learners can develop through the lesson. Figure 10.5 gives some examples.

Figure 10.5 Sample lesson objectives for listening

---

a. Make a set of handwritten notes of the talk.
b. Listen for global meaning to identify the theme of the talk.
c. Listen closely to details to identify five reasons the speaker gives for X.
d. Apply planning and evaluation strategies before and after a listening task.
e. Recognise features of assimilation and liaison/link-ups in natural connected speech.
f. Reflect on a listening event and explain how listening comprehension was helped or hampered.

Notice that the objectives (a) to (c) are skills applied to the contents of the listening input while (d) to (f) focus on the process of listening as well as knowledge of language/discourse that supports listening development. As listening is a multi-faceted process involving top-down and bottom-up processes, it is important that listening lessons provide learners with the right kind of scaffolding to facilitate comprehension. Listening lessons should also allow learners to understand these processes and learn strategies for listening development. Normally it would not be possible to have more than two or three objectives in a lesson, but when multiple lessons are planned to form a bigger learning unit, the content and process objectives can be spread over these lessons so that, by the end of the unit, learners would have had the opportunity to develop their skills, strategies, and knowledge in a comprehensive manner.

Lesson Phases

In many listening lessons, teachers just play a recording or read aloud a text while learners listen once or twice before answering questions or giving their responses. After this, the teachers check the correct answers with the class and move on to other tasks. This sequence of steps focuses largely on the outcomes of listening and offers little support to the language learners in *learning* how to listen; it is, in fact, a disguised form of testing because teachers are more concerned with how much the students can understand. We can address this problem by first identifying objectives for skills and processes. With these objectives in mind, we can develop different phases of a lesson or learning unit where the students can learn to use appropriate listening skills and engage in specific processes for facilitating comprehension. In other words, the teachers now unpack the multi-faceted listening process by leading learners through various stages and guiding them in using their internal and external resources to achieve comprehension. In so doing, we will be teaching listening, not testing it. More importantly, by giving learners support at every phase of a listening lesson, we will be motivating them to develop their listening ability gradually and systematically.

These stages were illustrated in three process-oriented pedagogies in the previous chapter. While traditional listening lessons focus on the content of the listening input, these pedagogies include a metacognitive dimension. In order to accommodate the communicative and metacognitive purposes of listening, a lesson should consist of at least three or four stages: Pre-listening activities, listening task, post-listening activities and extension activities. These will be elaborated further on in the chapter.

Listening Texts

Carefully selected listening texts can give learners strong motivation for listening. They can also be a very important source of language input to be further exploited for learning after the listening task. To prepare learners for academic contexts, there should be a variety of genres of listening texts that students encounter in their classes. It would also be helpful to have a mix of authentic unscripted texts and scripted ones that have a high degree of authenticity. Authentic recordings of natural speech taken from everyday academic sources are useful for familiarizing learners with what they can expect to hear in actual academic contexts. These texts also offer important pieces of language for analysis that can assist bottom-up decoding processes. Authentic speech, however, can be "messy" and care must be exercised in selecting only those that follow a clear organization generally expected of a particular genre. Speakers' pronunciation should also be reasonably clear. Some authentic texts, such as TED talks provide good input—they are short (under 10 minutes) and are well-structured—and can be used with suitable teacher support (see Elk, 2014). For beginning or lower intermediate learners, scripted or "semi-authentic" texts produced at a normal rate may be more helpful, so such texts should be used more frequently with a selection of less challenging authentic texts. Overall, all listening texts should allow students room to activate strategies and learn to cope with gaps in comprehension that they may encounter in real life.

Other aspects of authentic texts that we should also consider include:

a. The original intended communicative purpose.
b. The intended audience—age, background.
c. The characteristics of the speaker(s)—clarity, speed, number, accent.
d. Visual support, if any—presentation slides, accompanying images/figures/charts.
e. Appropriateness of the level of language used.
f. Length and duration—variations according to the genre.
g. Listenability—grammar of speech that can facilitate listening.

These considerations for selecting texts also apply to planning extensive listening assignments.

A Sample Outline for a Learning Unit on Listening

In the previous chapter we saw how learning activities are structured in three process-oriented pedagogies. Each structure is based on a listening comprehension task that is integrated with other kinds of learning activities. The structures can also be used in the planning of a learning unit of multiple lessons based on the same topic for listening. This may be necessary if the lessons are generally short (for example, under 45 minutes). For individual lessons of 100 minutes or more, the different activities can normally be completed within one lesson. Overall, it is important to ensure that the various activities created for each stage are integrated well. Figure 10.6 shows how listening tasks and other learning activities can be integrated into a coherent unit. The outline comprizes two stages: Planning considerations and the phasing of the lesson/learning unit.

Assessment Options for Listening

Assessment is an important part of the process of learning to listen. Through assessments, teachers can gather information about learner progress and determine the extent to which they can demonstrate proficiency in listening, thereby providing valuable feedback to both learners and teachers on areas that need improvement. From the perspective of programme administrators, learner performance will enable schools to gauge the success of their language programmes. This chapter explains options for assessing listening by drawing a distinction between assessing listening performance and assessing the learning of listening for learner development. It outlines formats that can be used for formal testing of listening, and discusses what teachers can do to ensure that the listening tests they construct have a high validity, that is to say that the tests measure listening comprehension accurately. We then consider alternative forms of assessment where learner self-evaluation and teacher support are emphasized for learning.

Figure 10.6 A sample outline for a lesson/learning unit on listening

Planning	
Listening outcome	Note-taking: a set of notes on a selected topic
Communication goal	Give a three-minute informal talk summarizing the arguments in a talk on a topic and expressing personal point of view.
Listening purpose	To listen critically to a short talk and understand the speaker's main and substantiating points.
Listening skills	Listen for global understanding, listen for main points, listen and infer.
Supporting task knowledge	Discourse structure of a spoken expository text Note-taking skills
Listening text	A podcast or a video of about 3–5 minutes on a topic of interest.
Listening proficiency level	Higher-intermediate or advanced
Learning unit duration	100–120 minutes
Lesson phases and listening activities	
Introduction	Teacher explains the listening outcome, communication goal, purpose for listening and listening skills required.
Pre-listening	**Content and strategy planning** Students review the structure of an expository talk and strategies needed to follow the talk to achieve comprehension. Students predict some points they will hear based on the topic and the title of the talk.

continued

Figure 10.6 continued

Listening task	**Comprehension and note-taking**
	First listen: Students listen to (or watch) a short talk for global understanding. In pairs they discuss their understanding of the speaker's purpose.
	Second listen: Students listen again and take notes. In pairs they compare their notes. Some students are asked to share with the class some points they have noted down. Teacher facilitates this sharing to focus both on content and strategies.
	Third listen: Students listen again to get further understanding of the text and improve their notes.
Post-listening	**Planning of a short informal talk** In pairs, students use their notes to prepare a short talk by a) summarizing the speakers' main points, and b) offering their responses and ideas. In a small class, students are asked to deliver the talk in class. If the number is large, they can record the talk and upload it in a common repository for the teacher and all to listen.
Evaluation	**Listening diary or checklist** Students write an entry in their listening diary to describe their experiences and lessons learned about the topic, their listening process and working with others. Alternatively, they can be given a checklist on similar items to guide their evaluation of their own learning.

Testing Listening Performance

A key difference between testing and teaching listening is that testing requires learners to complete a task within a specified time, and their ability is judged by the number of correct answers or the completeness of their comprehension. Teaching, on the other hand, offers learners various kinds of support to assist them in accomplishing a listening task and developing greater metacognitive awareness of the process. Listening tests are formal assessments of listening, i.e., learners are assessed on how well they are able to demonstrate their comprehension of spoken English or other target language over a term of study. This is also referred to as summative assessment. Figure 10.7 shows examples of testing formats for listening. The prompts and responses can be combined in any manner that suits the purpose and the time allocation for each test.

These are common formats for one-way or non-participatory listening. There are two main ways in which candidates participate in such tests. One is that they listen to the prompts and the questions first. This is followed by a short time of reading and selecting the corresponding responses in the answer scripts or writing or producing an appropriate response. Another way is for the candidates to listen to the prompts, followed by the questions while reading the items in the answer scripts. Where no responses are provided, they would need to produce items that demonstrate their comprehension. An example of this is while-listening assessment where learners make notes as they listen to a lecture.

Figure 10.7 Examples of listening test formats

Listening prompts (audio or video)	Responses
• Short passages • Talks • Lectures • Conversations/dialogues • News broadcasts • Telephone messages	• Select an answer from multiple choices • Determine true/false items • Fill in the blanks with single words or phrases • Complete a missing sentence in a dialogue • Write a summary • Match items from two sets of information • Transfer of information, e.g., complete a diagram • Write a response to a question • Repeat verbatim what is heard orally or in writing • Correct errors in a text • Rearrange/resequencing sets of information in text or graphic forms • Write notes

Issues in Assessing Listening

The modes of testing listening discussed above present different challenges to language learners that may not always be directly related to listening abilities. Hence, the validity of such forms are sometimes called into question. It is often difficult to be sure that the tests are indeed measuring listening comprehension and nothing else because candidates have to do several things in order to demonstrate their understanding. It may be argued that some of the additional demands, such as reading and writing while listening, may interfere with the candidates' cognitive processes during listening, thereby hindering their comprehension. Even in tests where responses are made only after the candidates have completed listening to the prompts, questions about short-term memory capacity linger. When constructing tests, teachers should bear in mind these challenges and endeavor to keep the test as true to its intentions as possible. Some ways in which these challenges can be mitigated is by making the various types of responses short so as to minimize reading, ensuring that the topics of listening texts are not totally unfamiliar to students, not penalizing students for mistakes in spelling, and shortening the interval between listening to the questions and answering them. These efforts can greatly enhance the validity of the tests.

Another challenge to writing listening tests pertains directly to the construct of listening. As we have seen earlier, listening involves many cognitive, social and affective skills and processes. For the purpose of assessment, Buck (2001) proposes a simple multi-dimensional listening construct that comprizes:

> The ability to 1) process extended samples of realistic spoken language, automatically and in real time; 2) understand the linguistic information that is unequivocally included in the text; and, 3) make whatever inferences that are unambiguously implicated by the content of the passage.
>
> (2001, p. 114)

Teachers should avoid the tendency to test listening skills narrowly, particularly by focusing too much on listening for detailed information, such as times, names, location and specific reasons. While the ability to focus on details is an important skill, listening tests should also assess other important skills that we naturally use in authentic listening situations such as listening for global understanding and making reasonable inferences.

Authenticity in Assessing Listening

Listening is an important component of spoken interaction, which is a real-life listening event that language learners are frequently involved in if they are learning English as a second language in English-speaking communities. Assessment of interactional listening abilities is a form of authentic assessment and it is typically conducted in an integrative manner with speaking during oral interviews in tests. The candidate engages in a conversation with the testers, who determine whether he/she is able to respond appropriately to their questions and prompts. In everyday interaction in social and academic settings, learners have to provide appropriate responses and use strategies effectively to manage their listening. The testers would therefore also be looking out for the use of interactional strategies during listening such as asking for clarification, seeking assistance and asking the interlocutor to repeat what is said. Language learners may also be assessed in pairs for their ability to interact with each other in English. However, as these are test environments, learners may also suffer from test anxiety which can affect their performance. In addition, the dynamics in examiner tester–candidate oral interaction are not the same as those found in real-life conversations with peers or even with teachers and university professors. Testing learners in such environments will give an indication of their abilities but never the complete picture of how they will actually listen and interact in a natural environment.

There are some things that teachers can do to improve the validity in the assessment of interactive listening abilities in class tests. First, they should choose a topic of conversation that their students are familiar with and it is likely to be something they would talk about in social or academic settings. They should also ensure that there is more balance of turns in the conversations with the teacher and the student both having almost similar amount of time to talk. In oral tests, it is common to see the student doing most of the talking as they want to demonstrate their fluency. To assess the students' listening abilities, the examiner can do more talking so that the student gets a chance to process the input and respond to it. It should never be a question and answer session, where the teacher asks a short question and the student produces a long answer. This is not authentic interaction and limits the opportunities for the learners to demonstrate their comprehension abilities.

Assessing Listening for Listening Development

To promote learner development in listening, it is important that teachers carry out regular formative assessments which can offer both themselves and learners valuable feedback about the latter's learning. The formats presented in figure 10.7 can also be used as tools for assessment for learning by including support from the teacher or peers. The learners can also use these tasks for self-assessment of their performance. For example, even an exercise of answering comprehension questions can be turned into a process-oriented assessment if learners are asked to focus on how they listen and reflect on the factors that facilitated or hindered comprehension. They can also evaluate how useful their strategies have been in helping them to arrive at the answers.

To assess listening development, teachers can use a number of formative assessment instruments that can provide feedback to learners and teachers. These include learner checklists, questionnaires, listening diaries, teacher checklists, interviews and portfolios (Vandergrift & Goh, 2012). Figure 10.8 below elaborates on some the instruments. These instruments are also an important part of a process-oriented approach to teaching listening which we discussed in the previous chapter—we can expect overlap between the areas of assessment for learning and teaching. Teachers can use learner responses to identify areas that are not well-developed to inform future planning of listening activities.

Figure 10.8 Formative assessment tools for listening development

Learner checklists	Statements that learners use to identify metacognitive behaviours in their process of listening, including planning, monitoring, evaluating and problem solving.
Teacher checklists	Statements that teachers use to identify learner behaviours in interactive listening situations, including use of clarification strategies, up-taking or back-channelling cues, and comprehension checks.
Listening questionnaire	Questionnaire items focus on important mental processes and strategies for listening which learners can use for self-assessment (see for example the Metacognitive Awareness Listening Questionnaire or the TELL).
Listening diaries	Diaries or journals enable learners to express thoughts, feelings, and reactions to particular in-class and outside-class listening activities. The format can be completely open or structured with prompts which the learners have to respond to.
Listening interviews	One-on-one interviews with learners regarding their progress in listening and listener thought processes. Authentic data can be collected in short episodes of listening to selected texts and students thinking aloud after listening.
Listening portfolios	Learners collect recordings and other listening materials (e.g., URLs of YouTube links) accompanied by reflections or some of the other formative tools mentioned above to demonstrate the learning and effort put into their listening development and goal-setting.

Chapter Summary

Listening is a multi-faceted language skill that involves cognitive, metacognitive, social and affective processes. Compared with the teaching of other language skills, listening needs to be taught more systematically, and in ways that involve learners in understanding their own comprehension and learning processes. This chapter offered practical ideas on how to plan and adapt listening tasks that build on the theoretical perspectives and pedagogical guidelines in the last two chapters. It has also shown how different listening tasks and metacognitive learning activities can be integrated into lessons/learning units. Assessment options were identified and some issues of validity of listening tests were highlighted. To encourage teachers to assess listening for the purpose of promoting further listening development, we also discussed ways in which formative assessment can be carried out.

Discussion Questions

1. Review the eight types of non-participatory (one-way) listening tasks.

   a. Select two or three of them and identify the main listening skills needed for the tasks. Specify the communicative outcome for each task. Plan a set of steps for carrying out these tasks. Follow the example given.

   b. Using the four-phase task-based metacognition instruction framework, suggest other activities that you can include in the pre-listening, post-listening and extended metacognitive phases.

2. Refer to the speaking activities described in Chapter 9/10. Select two or three of them and suggest how you would focus on developing interactive listening skills and strategies for learners engaged in these activities.

3. Develop a detailed outline of a learning unit for listening by using the format proposed in Figure 10.6. Suggest how much time you would allocate to the respective phases and learning activities.

4. Compare the similarities and differences between summative and formative assessment of listening. Suggest how some procedures for testing of listening comprehension can be adapted and modified to help learners become more reflective of their own listening abilities and development.

Further Reading

Field, J. (2008). *Listening in the language classroom*. New York, NY: Cambridge University Press.

   This comprehensive volume offers many activities for developing bottom-up processes involving lexical segmentation and decoding of sounds.

Nation, I. S. P., & Newton, J. (2008). *Teaching ESL/EFL listening and speaking.* New York, NY: Routledge.

There are many useful classroom ideas for L2 listening instruction that are backed up by sound theoretical discussions, all of which teachers will find helpful and relevant.

Rost, M., & Wilson, J. J. (2013). *Active listening.* Harlow, UK: Pearson Education.

This volume contains many pedagogical activities that teachers can use or adapt for L2 learners in academic environments.

Section 4

Introduction to Speaking

Jonathan M. Newton

There are good reasons for EAP programs to provide well-informed guidance and an appropriate range of opportunities for students to develop speaking skills. For students transitioning into academic study in English, spoken communication skills will be essential for participating in and learning through academic discourse. Equally, these skills provide access to the broader life of the academic community and to participating in the world of work for which they are preparing themselves.

But given the primacy of reading and writing in formal education it is all too easy to forget how important speech is for learning. Talk mediates the development of thought in young children and of literacy in the early school years. Throughout schooling it continues to play important roles associated with thinking, learning, communicating, democratic engagement, teaching and assessing (Alexander, 2012, pp. 3–4).

Perhaps even less appreciated is the role speaking plays in academic study and its importance for full intellectual and social participation in college or university life. Examples include discussion and Q&A segments in lectures, participation in tutorials and workshops, team-based lab work in the sciences, and project work in a wide range of disciplines (e.g., business studies, tourism and marketing, and architecture/design studies). Collaborative, interactive forms of learning in which talk is central are becoming even more important in 'flipped' classrooms in which students access online what used to be 'live' lecture material and do so independently and in their own time outside of the classroom. This then frees up classroom time for discursive modes of learning such as group discussions, Q&A sessions and problem and project based learning tasks. In academic assessment, speaking-based activities such as formal oral presentations and group work components for assignments are also widely used.

Beyond university, speaking skills are equally important in the workplaces in which graduates will seek employment, and more so as informal forms of discourse take on a greater role in the workplace. As Myles (2009) notes:

> The formal systems of command with written memos, formal letters and supervisors' orders have been replaced by multi-discipline or multi-function teams, which are much more dependent on informal, oral and interpersonally sensitive written forms, such as email messages.
>
> (p. 4)

Managing these informal forms of workplace talk can be particularly challenging linguistically and culturally for second language English users new to workplace communication in English. For them, even small talk can be challenging because of cross-cultural differences in the way it functions in work settings (Holmes, 2005).

The rise in internships as an integral component of many professional degree programmes means that these challenges are not so far removed from academic study either. Coping with communication in a new workplace will be challenging for all students, but more so for many ESL/EFL students who can face a steep linguistic and cultural learning curve. We see this in a small study by Myles (2009) who interviewed four ESL engineering students and their associates (e.g., tutors, trainers, employers) during their participation in an internship over six months in a large computer software company in Canada. The workplace was described as having an "intensely oral culture" (p. 60) which required the interns to participate in social talk, to use and understand colloquial expressions and to interpret the cultural connotations of indirect, idiomatic speech. Not surprisingly, all four interns described oral communication as the most challenging aspect of language use at work. Similarly, and also in Canada, Wood (2009) discusses the experience of host site managers for engineering student internships. These managers reported that students from non-English speaking backgrounds, while often highly skilled and proficient in their field of study, frequently struggled with the communication demands of an English speaking workplace.

How this Section is Organized

This final section of the book follows the pattern of the previous sections on reading, writing and listening by examining the teaching and learning of speaking in a second language from three perspectives. First, in Chapter 11 we look at what we know of L2 speaking from research and theory, and in so doing lay the groundwork for pedagogic considerations. In Chapter 12, a learning opportunities framework is presented and incorporated into a set of guidelines for managing speaking across an EAP curriculum. Finally, Chapter 13 introduces practical instructional activities and suggestions for assessing speaking.

11 Speaking in a Second Language

Jonathan M. Newton

This chapter begins our exploration of speaking in academic contexts by looking at the nature of speaking and the roles it plays in second language learning. We first consider what is unique about developing speaking skills in a second language in contrast to the other three language skills discussed in this volume. We then examine the roles of speaking, focusing on three aspects of speaking relevant to the language classroom: interactional speaking, corrective feedback, and controlled and communicative practice. These themes lay the groundwork for Chapters 12 and 13 in which each theme is revisited in relation to building an EAP speaking curriculum and designing instructional activities to use within it.

What's So Special About Speaking?

To understand speaking in a second language, it is worth keeping in mind three distinct features, each of which has repercussions for L2 instruction: the interactive nature of spoken language, the extent to which varieties and varietal features are fundamental to spoken English, and the physical nature of speaking.

Interactivity

More than the skills of reading, writing and listening, speaking requires the presence of someone else. As Alexander (2012) points out, "talk is, by its nature always dependent on others" (p. 10), a point expanded in Tannen's (2007) claim that "speaking entails simultaneously projecting the act of listening: In Bakhtin's sense, all language use is dialogue" (p. 27). To illustrate this point, consider how many times recently you have spoken without anyone else present, or spoken in a largely monologic mode? For most readers, the answer will be 'none' or 'not many'. While one can practice L2 reading, listening or writing to one's heart's content in almost any setting, speaking practice requires an interlocutor and a setting where one can hear and be heard. This feature of speaking naturally limits the amount of independent L2 speaking practice students can participate in beyond the classroom, especially in EFL contexts. Consequently, the English language classroom is, for many students, a primary site for speaking practice opportunities. For this reason, and as Alexander (2012) points out, "the teachers' own competence as a speaker and listener contributes significantly to the developing oral competencies of the student" (p. 11)

Variability and Transience

Second, in contrast to the highly standardized nature of writing, our everyday speaking is often fragmented and grammatically irregular. This is hardly surprizing given how transient speech is and thus how few opportunities speakers have to plan and repair compared to writers. Consequently, spoken language, whether by first or second language speakers, allows for some tolerance in the range of 'acceptable' varietal features, especially of pronunciation and prosody. In fact, these varietal features play the important role of marking out a speaker's first language and cultural identity, as well as characteristics such as class, gender, ethnicity, and nationality. Not surprizingly, therefore, speaking involves face-work—managing how we are perceived by others and interpreting how others wish to be perceived, and so is especially vulnerable to the influence of identity and affect. This includes factors such as communicative anxiety, willingness to communicate, motivational propensities, self-efficacy and imagined self, all of which have been extensively researched in relation to second language learning (e.g., Dörnyei, Henry, & MacIntyre, 2014).

The theme of variability brings us to the topic of non-native speaker (NNS) varieties of English. Recent years have seen rapid growth in the global use of English as a Lingua Franca for communication between NNSs. This has implications for the goals of instruction, especially goals concerning acceptability and accuracy (Matsuda, 2017). For instance, Jenkins (2002) proposed a set of EIL pronunciation priorities determined not by the full inventory of native-speaker (NS) phonemes and prosodic features but by those features that, she claims, most affect intelligibility in communication between NNSs from different L1 backgrounds. This proposal has proved controversial, although there is general consensus that the goal of pronunciation, teaching and learning for most English language learners, and especially those in EFL contexts, should be *intelligibility* rather than accent reduction (Derwing & Munro, 2015). But intelligibility, as a goal, also raises some challenging questions such as the three that follow, suggested by Roby Marlina (personal communication) and informed by McKay and Brown (2015):

- If teachers teach students to learn to be intelligible, to whom should they be intelligible? If I find a NNS intelligible/unintelligible, can we guarantee that this speaker will be intelligible/unintelligible to others?
- Should one learn or have the option to learn to be intranationally and/or internationally (locally, regionally, nationally, or internationally) intelligible?

- What are the pedagogic implications of treating intelligibility as an 'interactional' achievement involving speakers and listeners working together to achieve mutual intelligibility?

A Physical Skill

A third distinct feature of speaking that sets it apart from the other skills is that it is a distinctly physical skill requiring motor activity and involving musculature and speech organs (tongue, lips, teeth, hard and soft palate etc.). For this reason we need to consider carefully the pervasive influence of the first language on the habituated workings of the speech organs and, consequently, the possibility that L2 speaking might benefit from unique types of practice designed to address muscle memory. Another important implication is that, because our physical state is highly sensitive to stress and anxiety, teachers need to be sensitive to these factors when delivering speaking practice focused on pronunciation targets. Conversely, they need to recognize the facilitative effects of relaxation and a conducive environment on pronunciation practice.

Understanding How Speech Production Works

Levelt (1989) proposed a model of L1 speech production which has also been influential for shaping our understanding of L2 speaking (see Kormos, 2014). In this model, speech production consists of three broad processes: *conceptualization*, that is, establishing a communicative goal and intended meanings, and retrieving and sequencing propositional chunks relevant to the goal of communication; *formulation*, that is, selecting the linguistic forms for expressing this message, including relevant phonological forms, lexical items (words and formulaic sequences), and grammatical structures; and finally, *articulation*, the process of converting planned material into speech.

These processes typically run in parallel such that, when we are speaking in everyday contexts in our first language, they require little conscious effort. Note, though, how the seemingly effortless, automated nature of these processes can suddenly become effortful when speaking under stressful conditions such as in a job interview or when giving a formal speech. Such conditions expose the limited processing capacity of human cognition and the additional burden that conscious processing places on cognition and, consequently, on speech fluency.

For the second language learner, the effort required to activate these processes is significantly greater than that required of proficient English language users. To begin with, their L2 resources will be limited in size and richness. For example, the L2 learner's mental lexicon will be smaller, less well organized and lack collocational and semantic richness (Skehan, 2015). Consequently, formulating a message will be more effortful and attention-robbing. Furthermore, for the second language speaker, the complexity of the underlying processes involved in speaking and the fact that, unlike writing, these processes occur in real time and under communicative pressure, places considerable processing strain on a learner's attentional and L2 resources. As a consequence, the learners' speech may, for example, be marked by hesitation and false starts, by grammatical errors, or by a limited range of syntactic structures.

Fluency, Accuracy and Complexity (FAC)

The question of how second language learners draw on their attentional resources and manage the demands of speech production, as described above, is at the heart of Skehan's (2015) Limited Attention Capacity (LAC) model of task performance. The model identifies three distinct and independent dimensions of spoken L2 language performance: fluency, accuracy, and complexity (grammatical and lexical). Ellis (2003) defines these three terms in the following way:

> (1) fluency, the capacity of the learner to mobilize his/her system to communicate meaning in real time; (2) accuracy, the ability of the learner to handle whatever level of interlanguage complexity he/she has currently achieved; and (3) complexity, the utilization of interlanguage structures that are 'cutting edge', elaborate and structured.
>
> (p. 113)

Under the demands of spoken performance, these three dimensions compete for limited attentional resources and, where cognitive resources are strained, trade-offs between them are likely. Thus, in a time pressured task, resources may be devoted to aspects of fluent speaking—to getting the message out in time, thus robbing attention from attending to the accurate use of, say, grammatical or phonological forms. But if time is available for planning and practice, aspects of performance such as developing and organizing the message can be pre-constructed, thus freeing up attention to devote to other aspects of performance; perhaps to using more elegant syntactic structures and/or to clearer articulation or more dynamic prosody. Note how relevant Levelt's speech production model is here; when a learner has to allocate his or her attention simultaneously to constructing ideas (conceptualization), retrieving the necessary syntax and vocabulary to express these ideas (formulation), and expressing these ideas in clear and accurate speech, the potential for system overload and degraded performance is high.

Clearly, this model has important implications for pedagogy. It highlights the need for teachers to select, design, and implement speaking tasks in ways which are cognizant of the strain that speaking can put on attentional resources and especially of the potential for trade-offs between accuracy and complexity when the task is too demanding. Two of the most common and widely researched options for teachers are to give learners planning time (Ellis, 2005) or opportunities for task rehearsal or repetition (Kim & Payant, 2014). Both are discussed in the following two chapters.

What Role Does Speaking Play in Language Learning?

Task 11.1

Alexander (2012) has this to say about the importance of talk in education: "Talk that is cognitively demanding, reciprocal, accountable, and/or dialogic* has a direct and positive impact on measured standards in English, mathematics and science." (p. 5) (see the key below for explanations of terms.)

How might this apply to the role of talk in language learning? To answer this question, reflect on the role of talk in a recent lesson that you taught (or experienced as a language learner). Consider the following questions:

1. In what ways was talk used for classroom learning?
2. To what extent are the qualities listed in the quote above (e.g., "cognitively demanding", etc.) reflected in your experience?
3. What do your answers reveal about any unique roles that talk might play in language learning?

*Key:

Reciprocal—teachers and students listen to each other and consider various viewpoints.

Accountable—students ask for and provide evidence to support what they say.

Dialogic—talk which is collaborative and involves sustained interactions in which the teacher is a co-participant and in which student contributions are varied (i.e., not just responding to teacher questions) and substantive. (For further description see http://class.wceruw.org/dialogicinstruction.html)

It's hardly surprising that students need a wide range of opportunities for meaning-focused speaking to develop speaking skills. But it is also worth noting how important speaking is for supporting learning in the other skill areas. We see this when students talk about what they have read or listened to, or discuss each other's writing in peer feedback sessions. In addition, the need to discuss a topic fosters deeper intellectual engagement with ideas and with other views on the topic.

Equally as important, speaking (and writing) pushes language development forward. This is a less intuitively obvious role for speaking and one that is poorly served by the widely used metaphor of 'output'. Think of what the term 'output' refers to in the more literal sense of, say, industrial processes. Aluminum, for example, is the output from the processing in smelters of the input bauxite, an aluminum-rich mineral. Closer to home, your morning café latte is the output of coffee beans being ground and brewed by your local barister. In both cases, outputs are produced from the processing of various inputs. The quality of the output provides the factory manager and the barister with information on how well the process is working. But, in neither case does the 'output' also function as input or play any role in the construction of the machinery. And yet, in language learning, what we refer to as 'output' plays both these roles. How does it do this?

Merrill Swain's ground breaking work on the Output Hypothesis offers an answer (Swain, 1985). She showed how having to produce a message pushes learners to pay attention to lexico-grammatical structures, such as deciding on where to place an adverbial clause or what tense to use and how to mark that tense morphologically. In Levelt's (1989) speech production model (discussed above), this involves the dual processes of conceptualization and formulation, the latter forming thoughts into linguistic plans. In doing so, Swain argues, the learner not only uses existing linguistic resources but *expands* these resources through using them. In part, this expansion happens as the learner composes utterances on the basis of working hypotheses about the language grammar, and then has these hypotheses confirmed or discon-firmed by their interlocutor's response. Disconfirmation in the form of a quizzical look or a correction provides a feedback loop for the learner's developing interlanguage as in the following (made-up) example:

Teacher: Where did you go after class yesterday?
Student: I go to the bank
Teacher: Oh, you *went* to the bank
Student: Oh, right. I *went* to the bank

Speaking plays a number of useful roles in language acquisition. The following list is loosely based on Ellis (2003, p.111).

> *Speaking encourages the noticing of new structures and vocabulary in input.* We see this in the example above. We pay closer attention to something someone is saying if we have to say something similar or if it models what we have attempted to say. In the classroom, if students know they

will do a certain speaking task then they will be motivated to pay attention to input that will help them with the task. This is the idea behind Willis's (1996) proposal that students study a recording of advanced speakers doing a task similar to one that they will or have performed. In doing so, the teacher guides them to notice language features which they either compare with their own recent attempt at the same task or adopt for their upcoming performance of the task.

Speaking assists the learning of set phrases/formulaic sequences. Through learning set phrases, speaking helps learners to communicate before they fully understand the way the language works. This has a number of benefits: It is motivating, attracts input, and familiarizes learners with important language structures. Through noticing regular patterns across these set phrases the learner constructs a grammar of the language.

Speaking provides L2 pronunciation and prosody practice. Speaking practice is obviously necessary for developing motor control over articulation of unfamiliar sound patterns and for developing a natural 'feel' for the way the language is used. In classroom settings, songs, shadowing, jazz chants and dialogue practice are simple examples of speaking activities that play this role.

Speaking provides opportunities to develop conversation skills and strategic awareness of how to manage conversation in the L2. Evelyn Hatch made the important observation in the early years of second language acquisition research that:

> Language learning evolves out of learning how to carry on conversations . . . one learns how to do conversation, one learns how to interact verbally, and out of this interaction syntactic structures are developed.
>
> (Hatch, 1978, p. 404)

What Role Does Interaction Play?

Interactive speaking is worth treating as a separate category to highlight the collaborative nature of much of our spoken communication and the important role joint construction of meaning plays in learning from speaking. The process of negotiation for meaning (NfM) is pivotal here. NfM involves interlocutors working interactively to resolve communication problems triggered by comprehension or comprehensibility difficulties. This process can optimize the quality of input for acquisition by drawing learners' attention to learnable language features in the input and in their output. Newton (2013), for example, found that when adult ESL learners negotiated the meaning of unfamiliar words encountered in the process of performing classroom communication tasks, there was a much greater likelihood that they could subsequently recall the meaning of these words than for unfamiliar words they met in the tasks but did not negotiate for meaning. An oft-cited quote by Long (1996) points to the pedagogic relevance of NfM:

> ... tasks that stimulate negotiation for meaning may turn out to be one among several useful language-learning situations, in or out of classrooms, for they may be one of the easiest ways to facilitate a learner's focus on form without losing sight of a lesson's (or conversation's) predominant focus on meaning.

(p. 454)

Elaborating on this claim, Long (1996) identified seven roles for NfM:

1.   NfM makes input understandable without simplifying it, so that learnable language features are retained.
2.   NfM breaks the input into smaller digestible pieces.
3.   NfM raises awareness of formal features of the input.
4.   NfM gives learners opportunities for direct learning of new forms.
5.   NfM provides a 'scaffold' within which learners can produce increasingly complex utterances.
6.   NfM pushes learners to express themselves more clearly and precisely, i.e., 'pushed output'.
7.   NfM makes learners more sensitive to their need to be comprehensible (p. 445–454).

Task 11.2

Below are two NfM sequences that occurred as small groups of adult ESL students in an EAP program carried out classroom communication tasks (Newton, personal data). Which of the seven roles for NfM listed above can you see in these two extracts?

Extract 1. An information gap task

S6   above foundry, located pottery, above foundry
S4   yeah
S5   what?   pot-?
S6   pottery pottery
S4   ahh yeah pottery   pot-?   P. O.?
S6   P. O. T. T. E. R. Y.
S4   Y
S5   what does it mean?
S6   potter, not sure, but pot it means pot it means kitchen equipment
S5   a pot, yes

Extract 2. A problem-solving task.

S2 hypnotist
S3 hypnotist, y'know?
S2 yes
S1 I don't know
S3 y'know?
S2 when you make person like sleep and you sleep and I ma-, when I said something you do that
S3 ahhh hypnostic
S2 do you know? and you sleep and I go and -
S1 - ahh I know
S2 I say you, you take off your—
S3 - yeah, yeah

Teachers can use this list of NfM roles to monitor the quality of interaction in communication tasks; that is, to check that students are making effective use of interaction for learning and that the tasks teachers use are promoting these interactional learning processes. In Chapter 13 we look more closely at how to choose and implement speaking tasks to achieve these outcomes.

The general consensus from research on NfM is that communication tasks containing an information gap and requiring a single convergent outcome (i.e., there is only one solution and all participants must agree on it) require higher levels of mutual comprehension and comprehensibility and so generate more NfM than tasks without these design features (Long, 1996; Pica, Kanagy & Falodun, 1993). Chapter 13 describes different types of information gap tasks in more detail. The case for information gap tasks is not so strong when we look at a broader range of the learning affordances available in other types of communication. For instance, Nakahama, Tyler and van Lier (2001) compared the NfM that occurred in information gap activities verses unstructured conversations between native speaker and non-native speaker (NS-NNS) interlocutors. They found more NfM in information gap tasks. But a closer look at the syntactic and pragmatic features of the interactions revealed a rich range of learning affordances in the unstructured conversations, including co-construction of meaning and self- and other-corrections.

Similar conclusions were reached by Foster and Ohta (2005). They investigated interactions between young adult learners performing information gap tasks in pairs. They found that the learners rarely engaged in NfM. However, as with the learners in Nakahama et al.'s (2001) study, these learners adopted other forms of peer–peer assistance such as co-constructing utterances which, Foster and Ohta argue, show language development in progress. So while NfM is clearly a useful learning process that teachers should seek to foster in classroom speaking tasks, they should be aware of a wider range of ways in which the process of learners communicating together creates affordances for language and skill development.

As we have seen, scholarship on NfM views the role of interaction in learning in psycholinguistic terms; through interaction learners make input more comprehensible and get feedback on their spoken output. But, as important as these processes are, interaction also plays important social and psychological roles through building a sense of community in the classroom and through its positive impact on motivation and attitudes. This point is illustrated in a study by Aubrey (2017) which investigated the effect of face-to-face intercultural contact on Japanese university EFL students' L2 motivation and language learning. He found that students who were given opportunities for interactive speaking tasks with non-Japanese interlocutors made statistically significant gains in self-confidence, task engagement and interactivity, and attitudes towards learning English and the international community compared to non-significant gains by students who completed the same tasks with other Japanese students.

What Role Does Corrective Feedback Play?

Teachers and researchers in applied linguistics alike take a keen interest in corrective feedback (CF), especially in communicative classrooms in which incidental focus on form (of which corrective feedback is a prime example) is argued to play a valuable role in language development (Long, 2015). CF can be explicit, as in explicit corrections and metalinguistic feedback (i.e., information about the targeted error) or implicit, as in clarification requests, recasts and elicitations. Examples of each type of feedback are provided below.

Explicit correction

Student: Last year I go to Blue River College.
Interlocutor: You should say, 'I went (with emphasis) to Blue River College'.

Metalinguistic feedback

Student: Last year I go to Blue River College.
Interlocutor: Remember that the past tense form of the verb 'go' is 'went'.

Clarification request

Student: Last year I go to Blue River College.
Interlocutor: Sorry, I don't understand. Are you still a student there?

Recast

Student: Last year I go to Blue River College.
Interlocutor: Oh, you went to Blue River College.

Elicitation (prompt)

Student: Last year I go to Blue River College.
Interlocutor: Can you try again? 'Last year I . . .'

Evidence from research highlights the valuable role CF plays in language development (Lyster, Saito, & Sato, 2013). More explicit types of feedback have been shown to be more effective than implicit feedback. However, Ellis and Shintani (2013) caution that over-correction, including not being selective in which errors are corrected, is counter-productive, and that learning is more durable when the learner and not the teacher corrects the error. Note though that the explicit/implicit distinction is not clear cut; a recast, for example, can be made more explicit by emphasizing the erroneous part of the student's utterance. Also, these different feedback moves can be combined in various ways. As Lyster, et al. (2013) conclude:

> [T]he most effective teachers are likely to be those who are willing and able to orchestrate, in accordance with their students' language abilities and content familiarity, a wide range of CF types that fit the instructional context.
>
> (p. 30)

Interestingly, research reveals some distance between teacher and learner preferences for feedback. Learners are reported to prefer more feedback than teachers feel comfortable providing. Teachers on the other hand tend to be concerned with the negative impact of feedback on learner confidence and the communicative flow of a lesson (Lyster, Saito & Sato, 2013). For this reason, teachers have been shown to prefer less direct forms of feedback and especially recasts (Lyster & Ranta, 1997).

One way for EAP teachers to refine their feedback practice is to engage students in conversation about how they experience feedback and what their preferences are. Students are unlikely to be fully aware of the range of types of feedback and how to most effectively use it and manage it, and so this kind of discussion can raise students' awareness and help them learn how to maximize their learning from feedback.

Task 11.3

Reflect on how you give feedback as a teacher and on the kind of feedback you have received as a language learner and how you have responded to it. Reflect also on your expectations, successes and frustrations in relation to both experiences. How do these two perspectives—those of the teacher and of the learner align?

What Role Does Practice Play?

In its broadest sense, any time a learner uses the language could be seen as 'practice'. But this section is about practice in the more narrow sense of "repeated performance of the same (or closely similar) routines" (Carlson, 1997, p. 56), or in language learning terms, "specific activities in the second language, engaged in systematically, deliberately, with the goal of developing knowledge of and skills in the second language" (DeKeyser, 2007, p. 1).

Controlled Practice

Controlled speaking practice (e.g., drills and substitution tables) tended to go out of favor in the wake of the movement towards communicative language teaching (CLT) in the 1970s. The potential value of this kind of speaking practice has been hamstrung by two negative associations. First, it drew on behaviorist theories of learning and on the discredited belief that language is best acquired through sequentially staged practice of rule-based structures (Wong & VanPatten, 2003). Second, controlled practice too often involved mechanistic choral drills and tightly scripted, stilted dialogues.

> **Quote:** As DeKeyser (2007) argues, "mechanical drills can only serve a very limited purpose, because they do not make the learner engage in what is the essence of language processing, i.e., establishing form-meaning connections" (p. 11).

Despite these negative associations, Skill Learning Theory (SLT) posits a valuable role for focused practice of the sub-skills which make up skilled performance (DeKeyser, 2014). According to SLT, skill development goes through three stages: declarative, procedural and automatic, each distinguished by how knowledge is represented and used. In the declarative stage, knowledge is conscious and is typically *about* some aspect of the target skill. In the procedural stage, declarative knowledge is deliberately drawn on to perform the procedure but with this knowledge now chunked into set sequences of words which can be accessed with increasing efficiency and thus speed. As DeKeyser (1998) explains it, " . . .proceduralization is achieved by engaging in the target behavior—or procedure—while temporarily leaning on declarative clutches . . ." (p. 49). The final stage, automatization, is achieved through extensive practice and results in performance which is more fluent, contains fewer errors and makes less demands on conscious attention.

But, perhaps because of the communicative orthodoxy in language teaching, there is little recent empirical classroom-based research on the role of controlled practice in language learning. One exception is the technique of shadowing in which the learner repeats, either completely or selectively, what an interlocutor says or what they hear on a recording. de Guerrero and Commander (2013) investigated shadow-reading by pairs of Spanish-L1 learners of English shadowing each other reading aloud. The researchers showed how the shadowing tasks encouraged the learners to focus on 'chunking' speech units thus "providing affordances for persistent, meaningful imitation and internalization of second language (L2) exemplars as well as story comprehension and retention." (p. 433). Shadowing has also been implicated in improving listening skills and in particular with improved phonemic perception (Hamada, 2016).

Task 11.4

a. Watch Tim Murphy explain shadowing and see students doing different types of shadowing in this YouTube clip: *www.youtube.com/watch?v=Bri4tpCbjR4*
b. Then try shadowing someone speaking a language that you do not speak fluently or speak at all. Experiment with both complete and selective shadowing. Reverse roles and experience being shadowed.
c. Reflect on the experience and on its value for developing L2 listening and speaking skills.

In another study into controlled, non-communicative forms of practice, Ding (2007) investigated the role of memorization and imitation in the learning of English by three university English major students who had won prizes in nationwide English speaking competitions and debate tournaments in China. All three students used these techniques extensively and spoke positively of the value of this approach to learning. Ding concluded that "the study shows that text memorization and imitation have a legitimate place in second language education" (p. 279).

Communicative Practice

Although repeated practice is typically associated with traditional lock-step teaching approaches, its value in communicative settings is also widely recognized. For example, in the three separate studies described in Skehan, Xiaoyue, Qian and Wang (2012), task repetition had "huge" effect sizes for the accuracy and fluency of language production by tertiary EFL students in Mainland China and Hong Kong SAR. Similarly, in the context of Vietnamese high school EFL classes, Nguyen (2013) showed how opportunities to rehearse a task prior to performing it in front of the class prompted the students to engage in form-focused episodes as they co-constructed talk. Their subsequent public performances of the task were not only more confident and fluent, but much more accurate, reflecting the hard work they had invested in resolving language issues in rehearsal. Here is an example from one pair of students:

Excerpt 1: Rehearsal	Excerpt 2: Performance
S1: I'm erm mình nói kinh doanh have business à? (I want to say "do business". Should it be "have business"?)	S1: Hi Linh. How are you doing?
	S2: I'm fine. And what's your job?
S2: I do business thôi! *(I do business!)*	S1: **I *do business*** and I ***earn*** a lot of money and I want to take uhm part in volunteer work
S2: I do business and erm I gain kiếm được . . . kiếm được là chi? (earn . . . how to say "earn money"?) raise (.) uhm kiếm được là chi hè	S2: Ok. That's a good idea and erm what are you going to do with this money?
S2: *(how to say "earn ") (.) earn (.) earn!*	
S1: *and I earn a lot of money*	

We can see two other interesting processes in this example. The most obvious, perhaps, is the way the students use their first language (Vietnamese) to resource the upcoming performance. The second, closely related, point is that in the rehearsal the students engaged in frequent language-related episodes (LREs) in which they *talk about talk*. In the terms of Levelt's (1989) speech production model, we can see how rehearsal provides space for the conceptualizer and formulator to do their work so that articulation becomes the main focus of the subsequent performance.

In sum, the studies discussed in this section show both controlled and communicative forms of practice being effectively integrated into instruction.

Chapter Summary

In the body of second language acquisition research on which this chapter has drawn speaking is sometimes unintentionally reduced to verbalizing lexical and grammatical competence; speaking is seen as a vehicle for learning language without reference to its rich communicative and semiotic functions. We might describe this as a speaking-to-learn-language perspective.

But in a volume focused on the four skills, we need to give due consideration to the reverse version of this phrase—learning-to-speak in L2. After all, a competent second language speaker isn't just a live dictionary. They have learned how to participate successfully in a range of spoken genre and social and transactional exchanges and to navigate the often tacit rules of discourse and interaction in the new communities of practice which they have joined or come in contact with through their second language.

And so, from a learning-to-speak perspective, an important job for EAP programs is to identify and provide instruction on the particular L2 speaking skills relevant to functioning effectively in academic study. Just what these speaking skills are is a question tackled in Chapter 13 where five speaking skill priorities are proposed and exemplified: spoken accuracy, conversational ease, discursive reasoning skills, fluency, and formal speaking. But this focus on speaking skills notwithstanding, it is worth concluding with an important theme of the current chapter, that speaking isn't just something learners do *with* their learning, it is also *how* they do their learning.

In the following two chapters, the topics introduced in this chapter are expanded on with a particular focus on the implications for curricula and instructional activities.

Discussion Questions and Tasks

1. What have you learned about L2 speaking from reading this chapter that you didn't know before? What difference might this make to the way you approach the teaching of speaking?
2. Have a conversation with an English language student and then do an information gap activity with them.

    a. How much and what type of NfM took place in each type of interaction?
    b. What type of language issues/errors triggered NfM?
    c. How were they resolved?
    d. What evidence did you see of NfM fulfilling any of the seven roles for NfM listed above?
    e. What learning do you think might have resulted from this NfM?
    f. In what other ways apart from NfM did participating in interaction appear to assist the student to produce more accurate, complex or fluent language?

3. Look for examples of different kinds of controlled and communicative speaking practice in ELT textbooks. What role for 'practice' in language learning is implied in the examples you find? Do your findings align with what you believe about the role of practice in language learning? Why?/ Why not?

Further Reading

Hughes, R. (2011) *Teaching and Researching Speaking* (2nd ed.). Harlow, UK: Longman.

This book provides a comprehensive, scholarly account of the nature of spoken language and a principled approach to teaching speaking skills.

12 Building an Effective Speaking Curriculum
Guiding Principles

Jonathan M. Newton

Teachers are not usually expected to plan a speaking curriculum from scratch, although they should be able to draw on a set of sound principles for evaluating the sufficiency of the curriculum within which they work and, on this basis, make informed decisions about what aspects of speaking to emphasize and de-emphasize in their teaching. To this end, this chapter introduces seven guidelines for managing speaking in an EAP curriculum, as listed in Figure 12.1.

Figure 12.1 Seven guidelines for building a speaking curriculum

Guideline 1:	Use cooperative learning principles to organize group work
Guideline 2:	Use principles of task-based language teaching (TBLT) to plan speaking lessons
Guideline 3:	Integrate rather than isolate
Guideline 4:	Look for intercultural learning opportunities
Guideline 5:	Establish roles for learners' own languages in the classroom
Guideline 6:	Utilize technology
Guideline 7:	Focus on learning opportunities

These guidelines reflect well-established pedagogic principles grounded in extensive scholarship in languages education. They are relevant not only to planning a speaking curriculum, but to the broader work of building EAP curricula. Naturally, therefore, they will, in most cases, resonate with themes introduced earlier in the volume in the sections on reading, writing and listening.

Guideline 1: Use Cooperative Learning Principles to Organize Group Work

Cooperative learning has been described as one of the great success stories in education. However, it is important to realize that not all group work (including pair work) involves cooperative learning and, as many teachers and students will know from experience, group work done badly can be frustrating, demotivating, and lead to little tangible learning. Group work done well, on the other hand, has numerous benefits. These include providing a non-threatening environment in which all students can contribute, giving students experience with a variety of roles including leadership, encouraging independent thinking, reducing reliance on the teacher, and allowing the teacher to differentiate learning tasks. (See Killen (2016, p. 187) for a fuller description of these and other features of group work.)

For effective cooperative learning in group work, Kagan (1994) identified four key elements that need to be present (represented by the acronym 'PIES'):

1. Positive interdependence—I need your contribution and you need mine—your success is important for my success.
2. Individual accountability—The group supports individual effort and is accountable for individual participation and learning, and each individual must demonstrate their understanding.
3. Equal interaction—Each group member has a role to play or job to do in the group so that no one member is able to do all the work.
4. Simultaneous interaction—Groups work simultaneously rather than sequentially so that at any one time multiple students are actively interacting[1].

Teachers in transition from a more traditional teacher-centered approach to teaching will benefit from opportunities to develop the expertize needed to manage effective collaborative learning, and may need planned professional learning opportunities to achieve this. Without this expertize, group work is likely to remain the poor cousin of learning in more traditional ways in the classroom. But it is not only the teacher who must develop skills in this area. Students also need careful guidance if their cooperative learning is to be effective. To this end, in group tasks, group members should be given the opportunity to evaluate how well they are working together.

Guideline 2: Use Principles of Task-Based Language Teaching (TBLT) to Plan Speaking Lessons

TBLT offers teachers a well-developed approach for organizing both the curriculum and individual lessons and units of work. In fact, the EAP classroom has been described as "a natural fit for task based language teaching (TBLT) because it allows the students to use language and skills in situations they will face in their academic lives" (Douglas & Kim, 2015, p. 2). A task, in simple terms, is "an activity which requires learners to use language, with an emphasis on meaning in order to attain an objective" (Ellis, 2003, p. 4). The value of tasks is that they replicate in the classroom the purposeful use of language which is so central to the function of language in our lives. They thus provide opportunities to develop not just knowledge about language but, more importantly, the meaning-making cognitive resources and skills (including social skills) for doing things with language.

> **Quote:** Van den Branden, Bygate and Norris (2009) makes the following claims about the power of tasks in language learning:
>
> "Tasks, potentially at least, offer a uniquely powerful resource both for the teaching and testing of language. In particular, they provide a locus for bringing together the various dimensions of language, social context, and the mental processes of individual learners that are a key to learning."
>
> (p. 11)
>
> And to push the argument further, they argue that:
>
> "[t]here are theoretical grounds, and empirical evidence, for believing that tasks might be able to offer all the affordances needed for successful instructed language development, whoever the learners might be, and whatever the context."
>
> (p. 11)

TBLT offers teachers two valuable ways to guide curriculum planning and implementation. First, at the macro level of planning, the process of identifying the target tasks that students need to be able to perform in English informs needs analysis and provides the basis for selecting pedagogic tasks that prepare students for target tasks (Long, 2015). For example, students studying social sciences and humanities subjects are often required to discuss ideas from a set reading list and/or from recent lectures in tutorials. It follows then that speaking tasks in the EAP classroom should mimic this requirement by involving students in pair, group and whole class discussions of input from reading and listening.

Second, at the micro-level, teachers can draw on well-developed TBLT models of speaking lessons to design sequences of task-based activities within and across lessons. One of the better known models is that presented by Willis and Willis (2007). In simple terms the model consists of three main phases as outlined below.

Pre-task phase

Activities to:

- Orient students to task objectives and learning goals.
- Introduce and encourage engagement with the topic.
- Introduce key vocabulary for the task.

Task phase

- Task performance.
- Groups prepare to report to the class.
- Groups present reports orally, on posters, or in uploaded content to a webpage.

Post-task phase

- Form-focused activities based on gaps and accomplishments in the task phase.
- Review of learning goals.

This is a considerable simplification of the range of options available in TBLT, but it does highlight the position of meaningful, purposeful language use at the center of the instructional experience, with opportunities for language-focused and form-focused learning available throughout the sequence of activities to support the students as they pursue a task objective. An important point to make about this sequence of activities is that while the speaking task itself is at the center of the sequence, it is only one component. Rather than the assumption that learning will take care of itself through this activity, TBLT requires principled attention by the teacher to the instructional opportunities that should be built around a task to support and enrich learning in the task.

Guideline 3: Integrate Rather Than Isolate

From a language learning point of view, integrated skills work offers huge efficiency benefits because new language is naturally recycled when it is used in reading, writing, speaking and listening. It follows that, across a program, the goal should be to integrate all four skills wherever possible. This shouldn't be difficult—the skills naturally flow together, as when reading and listening provide input for speaking and writing or when using cycles of activities within a task-based sequence as outlined in the previous section. Organizing a curriculum around themes or topics provides a ready basis for integrated skills work. An advantage of this approach is that it reflects the fundamentally thematic nature of academic study. We provide an example of the outline of an integrated skills unit as part of a discussion of integrated skills development in Chapter 14.

Guideline 4: Look for Intercultural Learning Opportunities

Whether they know it or not, the language teacher is a teacher of culture. And nowhere is this more true than in the teaching of speaking. Culture and language are intertwined; language constructs and sustains culture just as culture shapes the language choices available to us. Culture also mediates the impact of the language choices we make on others and, through others, back on ourselves as members of culturally shaped communities of practice. As Kramsch (1993) has argued, every time we speak we perform a cultural act.

Unfortunately, EFL often strips language of its cultural valiance and of the potential for the experience of learning English to open the student up to new worlds and new ways of being in the world. This does students a profound disservice. It denies them the opportunity to deepen their understanding of the choices available to them as users of English. In turn it denies them the opportunity to develop the competencies necessary to function effectively in a world in which encounters with the cultural 'other' are increasingly part of our lives.

For university graduates, opportunities for careers in which business is transacted internationally in English between interlocutors from many different cultural and language backgrounds are increasingly common and desirable. Universities have an obligation to ensure their graduates are prepared for such futures. Universities across the globe increasingly recognize this need, with global mindedness and intercultural competence recognized as fundamental graduate attributes. Here is an example in a graduate attribute statement:

> The University supports its graduates to be active and engaged global citizens who demonstrate international perspectives and can engage constructively with their local and international communities.
>
> (www.victoria.ac.nz/learning-teaching/learning-partnerships/graduate-profile)

There is now widespread acceptance in languages education that linguistic and communicative competences are incomplete learning outcomes which need to be complemented by the pursuit of plurilingual, pluricultural, and intercultural competences, and global-mindedness. (Newton, Milligan, Yates & Meyer, 2010). Following are five starting points to help teachers to enrich the intercultural learning opportunities in their EAP classrooms:

Figure 12.2 Guidelines for fostering intercultural communicative language teaching (Newton, 2016)

---

1. Start with self (i.e., encourage students to take a reflective stance on their attitudes and experiences).
2. Situate language in real communicative events/genre/tasks.
3. Encourage experiential learning; encourage students to put learning into practice in and beyond the classroom.
4. Provide opportunities for students to compare experiences and reflect on what the experiences felt like, what judgments arise, and for both feelings and thinking, why they feel/think in this way.
5. Guide students to construct understandings: Replace transmission of cultural facts with discovery learning.

Guideline 5: Establish Roles for Students' Own Languages in the Classroom

There are good reasons to take an informed and well thought through approach to the languages students bring with them into the classroom and how this resource will be managed. The students' own language(s) (OL) (and for many students it is *languages* in the plural) have a pervasive effect on all aspects of language learning, and so harnessing this in productive ways makes sense. As James (2005 cited in Laufer & Girsai 2008, p. 712) argues, ignoring this influence or repressing OLs is "burying your head in the sand and hoping that effortless acquisition will take place in time". To give but one example, as Nation (2013) argues, there is strong evidence to show that translation (as for example in the use of flash cards) is one of the most efficient L2 vocabulary learning strategies.

Furthermore, many of our students will need to operate bilingually in their future lives as a matter of course. Translanguaging, a term which has emerged in recent scholarship is relevant to this point. It has been defined as "the ability of multilingual speakers to shuttle between languages, treating the diverse languages that form their repertoire as an integrated system" (Canagarajah, 2011, p. 401). Essentially, this approach treats translanguaging behaviors as normal rather than as a deviation from a monolingual norm. The benefits of strategically utilizing students' OL resources in the EAP classroom include the following:

1. OL is a valuable resource that aids the central learning process of noticing (the gap) via deliberate contrastive analysis (Laufer and Girsai, 2008).
2. OL use eases the processing burden of academically demanding tasks and allows for greater conceptual accomplishment and linguistic complexity as well as greater critical engagement with the curriculum.

3. OL use affords students emotional sustenance and recognition of their metalinguistic competence.

For teachers, engaging in learning conversations with their students about OL use can be a valuable awareness-raising experience, and especially for monolingual teachers whose own language learning experience may be lost in the mists of time. In preparation for such learning conversations, teachers can begin by listing the range of interactions in which OL use occurs in class and the purposes for which it is used. These might include those listed in Figure 12.3 below. This list then provides a starting point for the learning conversation on OL use.

Figure 12.3 Domains and functions of own-language use in the language classroom

Setting	Function
Teacher talk	• Clarifying understanding of difficult concepts or instructions • Translanguaging (moving between languages as normal practice) • Metalinguistic feedback
Teacher-class interaction	• Fostering solidarity • Learning to learn – talking about learning • Conversations on metacognitive awareness • Using translation as a deliberate pedagogic strategy • Conversations about intercultural awareness and intercultural communication experiences
Interaction between students	• Conceptual planning • Language Related Episodes (LREs) – talking about language
Independent learning	• Private speech • Vocabulary learning using flash cards and word/phrase translations (paired-associate learning)

A final point is that teachers may wish to consider a policy of more OL use at the beginning of a course with a gradual shift to English. This approach treats the students' OLs as a scaffold which is gradually removed over time. Alternatively, from a translanguaging perspective, the metaphor of a bridge is preferred since it emphasizes the instructional goal of developing even stronger skills of moving between languages rather than OL use being a temporary linguistic crutch.

Guideline 6: Utilize Technology

The potential of new technologies to shape the way speaking instruction is structured has inevitable consequences for curriculum design. Computer mediated communication (CMC), for example, offers students opportunities to develop their productive language skills using interactive platforms such as Skype, text chat and Twitter unhindered by time or space, that is, by classrooms or timetables. Similarly, learning platforms such as Tandem Exchange are available to link classrooms in different parts of the world, thus allowing teachers readymade opportunities for intercultural communication and structured cross-cultural enquiry tasks.

Virtual worlds such as those available through Open Sim or Second Life provide students with immersive environments in which to communicate in English (Milton, 2012), with the portable nature of these capabilities via mobile technology pushing pedagogy innovations that extend well beyond the physical classroom (Godwin-Jones, 2012). For teachers and students who wish to focus on aspects of accurate speech production, technology allows students to record themselves, compare their recording to a model and to use visual display of wave forms and pitch contours, and animations of the movement of articulatory organs to analyze their speech in detail. A well-established practice is for teachers to require students to record and upload spoken performances to wiki or similar sites for sharing and assessment.

Overall, these technologies provide scope for more individualized instruction and autonomous learning. A curriculum must make space for these modes of learning. The corollary is that the teacher roles of facilitator and curator of resources and opportunities take on greater importance. With these roles comes the challenge for teachers of keeping up with the rapid rate of innovation in educational technology and the continuing expansion of online learning and teaching resources.

Guideline 7: Focus on Learning Opportunities

Guideline 7 presents a framework of seven categories of learning opportunity that a curriculum should provide, as proposed by Crabbe (2007) (See Figure 12.4). Within the seven categories, we revisit the themes of output, practice, interaction and feedback that were discussed in the previous chapter, but this time with a focus on their relevance to building a speaking curriculum. This framework is broad in its scope and so takes up the remainder of the chapter, with each learning opportunity discussed under a separate sub-heading.

Opportunity 1: Input

It might seem odd to discuss opportunities for language input in a chapter on speaking. There are two reasons to do so. First, it highlights the point that speaking rarely occurs without listening; not only is one person's speaking

Figure 12.4 Types of learning opportunities important for ELT programs
(Adapted from Crabbe, 2007, pp. 118–119)

Opportunity category	Learning activity covered by the concept
Input	Listening to/reading a text that can be understood with some ease and with a primary focus on meaning/message.
Output	Writing/speaking with an emphasis on meaning/messages.
Interaction	Speaking and writing with one or more interlocutors in real or simulated communicative situations.
Feedback	Receiving information relating to one's own performance as a second language user, including indirect feedback (for example, that one has not been understood) or direct feedback (for example, that one has made a specific error).
Rehearsal	Deliberately repeating specific aspects of performance, including experimentation with pronunciation, memorization of words or word patterns, and repeated role-play or rehearsal of a piece of communication.
Language understanding	Consciously attending to information about language usage or use in order to be able to understand an aspect of vocabulary, grammar or sociolinguistic conventions.
Learning understanding (Metacognition)	Consciously attending to the process of one's own language learning in order to establish better metacognitive control over that learning, including understanding the nature of language learning, an analysis of the specific difficulties encountered in performance and an awareness of strategies to overcome these difficulties.

another person's listening, but the vast majority of the speaking we do is interactive, with listening and speaking juxtaposed and interdependent. Second, the learning opportunities available to students through classroom speaking activities are greatly enhanced by the reading and listening they often have to do in preparation for, or follow up to speaking. We see this in activities such as 'Be an expert' and 'Jigsaw listening' which are described in the next chapter. In jigsaw listening, for example, the expectation that each student will tell another student about what they have listened to motivates them to listen carefully because they have a real communicative purpose for doing so.

Furthermore, the opportunity to do this listening in groups provides a colla-borative space for students to talk about and clarify what they have listened to before they each have to tell other students who have not heard this material what it is about.

We can take this one step further by supplementing even basic oral com-munication tasks with listening and reading opportunities that can greatly enhance the learning from these tasks. Here is one way to do this, as proposed by Willis & Willis (2007). They suggest that, once the teacher has selected or designed a speaking task, they record competent speakers of English per-forming the same task, and, if time allows, transcribe relevant sections of the performances. This material is then used either before or after the students perform the same task. If the task involves a relatively open topic such as 'Discuss your experience of moving to a new city/country' the teacher can use this material in the pre-task phase since it doesn't give away an answer. The teacher might first use the recording for listening activities such as those described in Chapters 9 and 10 of this volume. Students might then be given transcribed parts of the recording to study in more detail so as to notice chunks of spoken language that may have been difficult to comprehend, or for language study focused on the devices the speaker(s) used to structure their message. Tasks which lead to a single solution such as exchanging infor-mation in pairs to find the differences between two versions of a picture should be used in the post-task phase so the answer is not given away before the students do the task.

Opportunities 2 and 3: Output and Interaction

Since output and interaction are the main topics of all three chapters in this speaking section of the volume they are not revisited here. Clearly, a primary responsibility for curriculum designers and teachers is to ensure that speaking practice opportunities in an EAP curriculum are sufficient in kind and quantity to help prepare students for the demands of speaking in high stakes English proficiency exams and in the academic environment.

Opportunity 4: Feedback

Thinking about opportunities for feedback from a curriculum perspective allows teachers to be more principled and strategic in how they manage what is often a rather spontaneous, reactive teaching activity. To this end, feedback practices are an ideal topic for action research and reflective practice. Here are some prompt questions to guide teacher reflection:

1. Who gives feedback and to whom? (i.e.. Teacher to individual students in whole-class or one-to-one settings, peer-to-peer.)
2. Who initiates this feedback?
3. What kind of feedback is given? (i.e., explicit/implicit, brief/extended.)

4. When is it given? (i.e., immediate or delayed.)
5. How is feedback acted on? (i.e., immediate uptake, ignored, written down, etc.)
6. What characteristics of feedback appear to help or hinder uptake? (i.e., setting, type of activity, provision of time for repair, etc.)
7. What dimensions of speaking (e.g., pronunciation, vocabulary, paralinguistic features, voice quality etc.) and what particular language forms (e.g., tense marking or article use) require the most feedback? Why these, and what instructional options might be needed to supplement feedback?

Task 12.1

Use the questions above to analyze the following examples of feedback

Example 1: PPP lesson (Presentation, Practice, Production)
The lesson focused on the construction *'used to + verb'* to talk about things that happened at an earlier stage in your life and are now finished. This example occurred in the production phase of the lesson.

S: I use_ to go to Sacred Heart College.
T: I us**ed** (with emphasis) to go to Sacred Heart College.
S: I use*d* to go to Sacred Heart College.

Example 2: During a communication activity (Braidi, 2002, p. 40)

S_1:   They have a smile
S2:   They're smiling?
S_1:   Yes, they're smiling and they go to the river.
S_2:   OK.

Example 3: During a communication activity (Braidi, 2002, p: 40)

T: What happened?
S: Oh, after they catch the fish? One fish eat other fish.
T: The fish eats another fish?
S: One—a fish eat other fish.

Example 4: During a communication activity
        (Mackey & Philp, 1998, p. 342)

NNS: Yeah and they're eat lunch
NS: They're eating lunch
NNS: . . . and finished its rain getting rain.

Opportunity 5: Rehearsal (Fluency Practice)

ELT curricula typically identify the language content and skills to be taught and learnt in a program. What may be less well specified are the rehearsal opportunities for students to become fluent users of what they have learned. Consequently, students may experience the frustration of struggling to put their language learning to communicative use despite investing many hours in language study. In fact only a relatively small amount of L2 knowledge is needed to engage in simple communication. But, where the goal is fluency, students need substantial opportunities for communicative rehearsal. As Brumfit (2001) argues, "[r]ight from the beginning of the course, about a third of the total time could be spent on this sort of fluency activity, and the proportion will inevitably increase as time goes on" (p. 12). However, fluency is often a neglected strand of a course, often because teachers are under pressure to present new material in each lesson. Thus, a critical issue for English language teachers and curriculum designers is to ensure fluency opportunities are given due attention in a program.

Gatbonton and Segalowitz (2005) point out that communicative language teaching (CLT) has largely failed to provide a satisfactory role for systematic practice. Consequently, they argue, teachers too often fall back on mechanistic pattern practice. But rehearsal can be arranged in many ways in communicative curricula, notably through task repetition. Tasks such as the 4–3–2, poster carousel and ACCESS (see Chapter 13) build repeated performance into their design, as does the 'think-pair-share' strategy for engaging students in discussion. Rehearsal is also built into the model of task-based language teaching (TBLT) proposed by Willis and Wills (2007) in which the task cycle involves students performing a task, then preparing to report to the class about the outcome of that performance, and then reporting to the class.

These approaches to rehearsal stand in contrast to a widely used approach to controlled and communicative practice, that of PPP—the 'Presentation, Practice and Production' approach. Here, students are first presented (P1) with target rules and structures which they then practice (P2) in carefully controlled ways before producing (P3) the structures in communicative activities. Advocates of the PPP view communicative use of language as a goal or outcome of practice. An alternative view, and one that is associated with TBLT (see Guideline 3 below), treats communicative use as a starting point not an end point. Willis and Willis (2007), for instance, propose that communicative performance should lead *to* rather than *from* a focus on form. They argue that the appropriate place for controlled speaking practice is in the post-task phase; in effect, PPP in reverse. The value of PPP is hotly debated in ELT reflecting ongoing disagreement about the value and place of controlled forms of practice in language learning.

Often, when I ask teachers to list the activities in their program that explicitly focus on developing fluency with using known language and that meet the conditions for fluency development (see Chapter 13), they discover that little time in class is allocated to fluency development. We so often lament the inability of students to gain fluent control over the language they have spent so much time studying and yet it really should be no surprise given how seldom real fluency practice takes place. This point mirrors core principles of teaching reading outlined in Chapter 2—students must read extensively for meaning in order to learn to read.

Task 12.2

Look at the classroom work done by a group of EAP students in a typical week. What opportunities for fluency development are available in class and out of class? How are these opportunities organized?

- as follow-on activities from accuracy activities
- as separate classes focused on fluency goals

Overall, is fluency valued in this program? If not, why not?

Opportunity 6: Language Understanding

Speaking can provide valuable opportunities for students to focus their attention on aspects of the language system—word meanings, pronunciation, grammatical forms and structures and so on. We have seen how this can happen when, for example, students use speaking to try out a language form they hypothesize is correct, or when they negotiate the meaning of each other's language use during task-based interaction.

In addition, speaking can nurture awareness of how the language works through students engaging in what are known as Language Related Episodes (LREs). These are occasions during meaningful interaction where students "talk about language they are producing, question their language use, or other- or self-correct their language production" (Swain & Lapkin, 1995, p. 104). LREs are distinct from NfM in that the emphasis is not on making the message more comprehensible but on identifying linguistic problems and finding solutions. Here is an example from a pair of students rehearsing a communication task in a Vietnamese high school classroom before they perform it in front of the class (Nguyen, 2013). Notice how valuable the students' first language, Vietnamese, is in this LRE, and how in using it, Student 1 fills a gap in her use of English.

S1: Ê, they are poor hay they poor thôi hè?
      (Hey, they are poor or just they poor?)

S2:   Er they are poor. Poor nớ tính từ mà, phải có động từ!
      (Poor is an adjective, it needs a verb!)
S1:   They are poor. They are poor.

LREs are likely to occur in activities in which students are asked to rehearse in pairs or groups in preparation for a more polished performance or report to the class or to other groups. LREs are also a typical part of the process of group reconstruction of a text which the class has listened to in what is known as a Dictogloss activity. In a Dictogloss, the teacher reads a short passage or plays a recording of it and students just listen. It is played a second time (again, at normal speed) and students write key words as they listen. Then they work in pairs or small groups to prepare a version of the passage based on their key words. It is here that students are likely to engage in LREs such as the following example from Storch (2008). In this example, two students performing a Dictogloss in an EAP program at an Australian university are discussing the use of the adverb 'particularly'.

M: the immigrants particular
C: south
M: is particularly
C: why is 'ly'?
M: or in particular . . . because is, is adjective and in this context this
     not adjective here
C: mm (some agreement)
M: yeah . . . particularly . . . in south . . . maybe in . . . in
C: the immigrants particularly

(Storch, 2008, p. 100)

Finally, groups compare their versions and the teacher leads a discussion of pertinent language issues.

An even more direct way to engage students in talking about language is to use communication tasks in which the subject of the task is, in fact, grammar. Ellis (2003) refers to these as **grammar consciousness-raising tasks**. Nassaji and Fotos (2011) give the example of a task focused on discovering rules *for* and *since*. In the task, pairs or groups of students are given task cards containing sentences in which these words are used and asked to figure out when *for* is used and when *since* is used. The groups then develop rules to explain when *for* and *since* are used. Here are the example sentences the students see:

Ms. Smith has been working for her company for most of her life.
Mr. Jones has been working for his company since 1970.
Ms. Williams has been working for her company for 9 months.
Mr. Thomas has been working for his company since February.

(p. 98)

From a curriculum perspective, the point is to ensure that, where possible, when speaking activities are planned, they are accompanied by opportunities such as these to strengthen the learning of forms encountered in the activities.

Opportunity 7: Learning Understanding

Learning understanding is broadly equivalent to metacognitive awareness, a strong thread throughout this volume [see for example Goh, Chapter 12, this volume]. Evidence from research shows that when students know how to manage their own learning and to develop a reflective awareness of the learning processes they are experiencing, their self-efficacy and learning outcomes improve. For the teaching of speaking, this has a number of implications.

Students should be made aware of the principles around which a curriculum is organized, and, in relation to speaking, the principles that underlie the range of speaking activities in the program. That is to say, students should be 'let in on the secret' rather than this knowledge of pedagogic principles being hidden inside the teacher's head. Of course this does not mean that the teacher lectures the students on the principles of curriculum design. In fact, the process may be best begun with the students reflecting on and discussing their beliefs, expectations, experiences and questions about how to develop their L2 speaking skills. This can prove to be a powerful process of empowerment. One way to start the process is through students completing a questionnaire about their understanding of learning, and this questionnaire then becoming the basis for group and class discussion. The questionnaire could also address inhibiting personal factors such as lack of self-confidence, reluctance to be seen to make mistakes and fear of being corrected in front of the class. This is important information for the teacher to be aware of when they plan the curriculum and decide how to implement speaking activities. For some students and some cultural contexts these issues can be quite acute and in such cases an important goal of the course is to help students address such inhibitions.

As a program progresses, written summaries of these initial statements of students' beliefs and of negotiated understandings can be used as points of reference for students to track their emerging understandings and growing confidence. We should expect that, at the conclusion of an EAP program, students will have gained not only proficiency but also become experts in how to learn and how to manage their own learning beyond a formal course of instruction. This might remind the reader of the rather tired old trope of giving someone a fish to provide food for a day or teaching them to fish to provide food for a lifetime.

Here is an example adapted in part from Crabbe (2007) of how learning-to-learn is used to raise awareness of how to negotiate for meaning during communication tasks: The teacher carries out a short communication task with a student or small group of students in front of the class so as to model the process of negotiating meaning, such as asking for clarification or checking comprehension. Practising negotiation then becomes an explicit goal of a follow-up communication task.

If students are reluctant to interrupt and seek clarification, the activity **'Control the teacher'** (Nation & Newton, 2009) can be used to help them overcome this inhibition. In this activity, the teacher reads a passage or talks about a topic and/or at a speed of delivery which is a little challenging for the students who have to complete an information grid as they listen. The goal of the activity is for students to practice interrupting using a variety of pragmatic routines (e.g., "Excuse me, I didn't quite catch that", "Sorry, would you mind explaining what you mean by X") in order to comprehend the message fully so they can complete the grid. For students who may be tempted to feign comprehension for the sake of face, this activity offers the chance to experience being a more active interlocutor.

Students also need space at the end of speaking activity cycles to discuss any difficulties they experienced and what strategies they can adopt to address these difficulties in private rehearsal and subsequent classroom tasks. The common practice of concluding a class with a **'One-minute paper'** can be adopted here for the purpose of fostering learning awareness. This requires the students to write short reflective answers (in either English or their language of choice) to two or three questions about the lesson they have participated in, such as the following questions:

1.   What did I do to manage my learning in this activity?
2.   What aspects of my speaking in the activity were a challenge?
3.   What independent learning strategies can I adopt to help me to overcome these challenges?

Learning Opportunities—Concluding Points

We have explored ways of applying a framework of seven categories of learning opportunity to the job of building a speaking curriculum in an EAP context. This framework provides the teacher with a way of checking for balance: Is each opportunity present? Where, to what extent, and in what combination or sequence? Of course all seven opportunities need not be present all the time. Nevertheless, because they build on each other in mutually supportive ways such as when rehearsal primes the students' attention to feedback or language understanding, leading to higher quality language output, it makes sense for teachers to facilitate students' access to all the learning opportunities across a unit of work or activity cycle.

We can illustrate this point with the example of planning the formal speaking component in a program in which students are expected to prepare and present a formal talk to the class (described in Chapter 13). In planning for this, the teacher should incorporate *input* opportunities in which students analyze recordings of TED talks, *rehearsal* opportunities which include *feedback* from *interaction* with the teacher and/or peers, opportunities to focus on *language issues*, particularly clear articulation, use of prosodic devices such as emphasis, intonation and pausing, and *learning-to-learn* opportunities focused on developing self-awareness and self-management strategies to cope with the stressful nature of public speaking.

Finally, teachers should give careful thought to where these opportunities take place, whether in formal classroom lessons or in the students' independent study beyond the classroom. This issue becomes more important as technology erodes the boundary between the classroom and the world beyond, and between learning/communicating in physical vs. virtual classrooms. Similarly, the move towards 'flipped' classrooms has implications for how an EAP curriculum should prepare students to participate in academic life. In flipped classrooms, traditional lecture material is accessed by students independently and out of formal class time so that when students gather together in class, time is spent responding to this material in more personalized and dialogic ways.

Task 12.3

What sort of learning opportunities should an EAP program provide in order to prepare students to engage effectively in learning in 'flipped' classrooms?

Chapter Summary

This chapter introduced a set of seven guidelines for building a speaking curriculum within an EAP program. The seven guidelines, including the framework of seven categories of learning opportunity embedded in the seventh guideline, are designed to provoke reflection and further exploration beyond this volume of six key themes: cooperative learning, task-based language teaching, intercultural language teaching, first language use, technology, and a view of teaching as fostering learning opportunities. Each of these topics has ramifications for how an EAP curriculum is planned and implemented, and each is supported by a huge body of scholarship which this chapter can only hint at.

The next chapter introduces a range of instructional activities for realizing the principles outlined in the current chapter.

Discussion Questions and Tasks

1. L2 speaking doesn't just occur in lessons or activities designated for speaking practice. What other 'invisible' speaking opportunities might be present incidentally in a program? How valuable might they be for strengthening learning?

2. With reference to your recent experience of either language teaching or learning, think of examples of each of the seven types of learning opportunity listed under guideline 1 that involve speaking in some way. Which types of opportunities are well represented and which are less well represented?

3. Brainstorm a list of the different kinds of speaking that occurred in classes you taught recently or, if you haven't taught, in your experience as a language learner. Consider, for example, the kinds of activities, who talked to who, and about what. Group these items into categories that make sense to you (e.g., teacher-fronted, meaning-focused, controlled practice etc.). What categories emerge and in what proportion? Compare them with another person.

4. Your students are reluctant to engage in group work because they are concerned they will pick up errors from one another. How will you respond?

Further Reading

Goh, C., & Burns, A. (2012). *Teaching speaking: A holistic approach*. Cambridge, UK: Cambridge University Press.

In this book, the authors present a principled framework for planning and teaching speaking which is particularly useful for guiding the development of a speaking curriculum.

Richards, J. C. (2017). *Curriculum development in language teaching* (2nd ed.). Cambridge, UK: Cambridge University Press.

While not specifically about speaking, this book provides a rich source of ideas for building curricula, many of which are relevant to, or focused on, academically-oriented programs.

Notes

1   See Killen (2016, pp. 209–235) for a useful expansion of these points.

13 Speaking Instruction and Assessment
Activities and Options

Jonathan M. Newton

This chapter introduces a range of activities for teaching and assessing communicative speaking skills in the EAP classroom. The activities are organized into five categories, each addressing an aspect of being able to success-fully convey messages and meaning in spoken English. The categories are as follows:

1. Clarity of spoken communication (i.e., focus on intelligibility).
2. Communicative and conversational ease (i.e., focus on sociopragmatic skills).
3. Dialogic reasoning skills and negotiating points of view (i.e., focus on pragmalinguistic skills/lexical and grammatical complexity).
4. Fluency.
5. Formal speaking skills.

We can treat these categories as *goals* of speaking instruction. While broad in their coverage, each is an important component of academic speaking and will typically need to be covered by teachers involved in preparing EAP students for high stakes English proficiency exams such as IELTS and TOEFL. As such, they reflect the main emphasis of this volume on equipping students at an intermediate level of proficiency or above (i.e., B1-B2 in the CEFR[1]) to perform in academic settings and for academic purposes with confidence and skill. For EAP students with lower proficiency than this, simpler, controlled speaking activities such as scripted dialogue practice, substitution table practice, and pronunciation practice activities may be suitable, and may also be used to support the more advanced activities described in this chapter. But these lower level activities are not the focus of this chapter.

Let me add a note on integrated skills teaching. There will be times when teachers will need to use activities to develop a specific speaking skill or to give students additional speaking practice. But in many EAP lessons and units of work speaking activities don't stand alone but are integrated into cycles of activities involving most or all four skills. We see this when students are asked to discuss a topic prior to reading or listening to a text about this topic, or work in pairs to talk about the main ideas from a short talk they have listened to. While the activities we discuss in this chapter can work for both these approaches, we encourage teachers to consider how each of the stand-alone activities described below can be systematically embedded into integrated cycles of activities involving different language skills.

Goal 1: Developing Clarity in Spoken Communication

The term clarity is loosely synonymous with the terms intelligibility and accuracy. But in research on L2 speaking, accuracy is typically defined in linguistic terms and measured in the number of grammatical or lexical errors per 100 words. As such, it is a quality of spoken language, but not necessarily of *communication.* Clarity, on the other hand, implies successfully conveying your message to another person. Crucially, achieving clarity is often an interactional achievement since it involves interlocutors negotiating understandings in order to achieve communicative outcomes. In this sense, clarity involves not just accurate language use but also sensitivity to how and how well one's message is being received, and the ability to resolve communication breakdowns caused by miscomprehension or language errors. Negotiation for meaning (NfM) is a key process here. As described in Chapter 11 of this volume, NfM can play seven different roles in facilitating learning from interaction. It is worth keeping these roles in mind when reading about the tasks described in this section. In particular, information gap tasks have been shown in many studies to generate substantial amounts of NfM in interaction between students or between a teacher and students.

In preferring the term clarity to accuracy we do not mean to dismiss the importance of accuracy. Students should be encouraged to attend to the accuracy of their spoken language in *all* the activities described in this chapter. As discussed in Chapter 11 and in the section on fluency below, the teacher can implement speaking activities in ways such as providing planning time, repeating the task, providing more task structure, and doing form-focused study in the post-task phase, that give students multiple opportunities to attend to the accuracy of their language even when the main task goal is a more broadly communicative one.

So what types of communication tasks can be used to encourage students to attend to the *clarity* of their English communication? Perhaps the most widely used are information gap tasks which come in many forms, including the ones described below: Listen and Draw, Same or Different, Problem-Solving, Know the World and the Jigsaw arrangement. In these tasks, essential information is shared among students whose job it is to convey this information to each other clearly and accurately in order to achieve the task goal.

Information gap tasks can be one-way or two-way. In one-way tasks, one student has information they must share with a partner or group who must write or draw what they hear from this student. In two-way tasks, each student in a pair or group has unique information which they must share orally with others to complete the task. The essential feature of information gap activities is that only by working together can the students complete the task. Students cannot find the answer simply by looking at their own material. In both one-way and two-way information gap activities, the emphasis is on describing and conveying information clearly and accurately enough for interlocutors to be able to replicate this information in some form. To achieve this, students will typically seek clarification of what they heard, or confirm that what they said was understood, i.e., negotiate for meaning.

For these activities to work effectively, the teacher needs to plan carefully to ensure students keep the written information they are responsible for describing hidden from other group members. This involves ensuring that the layout of desks and chairs allows students to face each other, 'toe to toe and eye to eye', and that different pairs or groups are not so close to each other that information 'leaks' to others. Likewise, separation of written information is more easily managed when students work off clip-boards or on either side of a physical barrier.

Listen and Draw

Listen and draw is a good example of a **one-way** task which works well for students at all levels of proficiency. For young adult students preparing for academic study, content matter can be selected to suit more academic topics. For example, the speaker in each pair is given a diagram outlining the organizational structure of an organization, or an industrial process (such as how steel is made) which they describe to their partner who uses the description to draft a version of what they hear or to fill-in a schematic outline of the information. These types of activity provide opportunities for vocabulary learning. For example, the labels can be new words, and the students discover what objects to label by listening to the description. Another example which is effective in a heterogeneous ESL classroom in which students come from different parts of the world, is for each student to describe their country to a partner who has a blank map of the country to fill in, highlighting places, cultural features, and economic activities typical of various parts of the country. Again, this activity is more effective if the listener has an outline map of the country with some numbered points on it.

Same or Different?

This is a simple example of a **two-way** information gap task. In this task, each student has a different version of the same picture or diagram. The goal of the activity is for students to describe their respective versions of the picture/ diagram to each other in order to spot the differences. A more challenging picture-based task involves pairs or groups of students being given different pictures from a picture story with the goal of reconstructing the story and sequencing the pictures accordingly. This requires each partner to carefully describe what is happening in their picture. To push the students to accurately use the language of a recount or narrative, a second phase of this activity can be added in which the story has to be written down or retold without recourse to the pictures.

Problem-Solving with an Information Gap

More challenging two-way information gap activities involve students exchanging complex or detailed information on a topic and then having to do something such as solve a problem with this information. For example, students can be given the job of scheduling an appointment on the basis of two people's timetables. First, pairs of students are given two incomplete versions of two peoples' timetables/schedules for the coming week. They share the schedule information they've been given to fill the gaps in these timetable. Each student is also given the role of one of the people along with a list of two or three additional constraints on when they cannot meet, for example, "Rolando can't meet after 4pm on any day because he has to pick up his children from school". Without first disclosing what these constraints are, the students have to negotiate to find a mutually agreeable time to meet.

Know the World

Topics can also be based on more global themes. For example, in the 'Know the world' task students in pairs or small groups can be given incomplete versions of a country description grid containing partial descriptions of five countries. They must share information in order to complete the grid and then attempt to deduce from this information what countries are described in the grid. The same approach can be taken to other topics such as famous world leaders, or to discipline-specific topics in economics, geography and so on. Such materials are not difficult to design and once made can be reused many times.

The Jigsaw Arrangement

Because of the high degree of cooperative learning it entails, the jigsaw arrangement is particularly useful for implementing information gap tasks. First, students are placed in groups and each group is given one part of a text or picture sequence or recording. The group works together to under-stand the input and perhaps to rehearse describing it. Then, students form new groups comprized of one member from each of the first set of groups.

In these new groups each member shares their information so that in doing so, the new group can complete the whole passage; all of the pieces of the 'jigsaw' are put together as it were. The jigsaw arrangement is ideally suited for developing the academic skill of synthesizing ideas from different sources on a topic.

The jigsaw arrangement in its most simple form involves dividing a single text into two parts with the two halves of a class each working on one part before they reconfigure in pairs to share details from their respective halves of the text. This is known as 'jigsaw reading'. For more advanced students, groups can be given different texts on the same topic so that the second phase involves not just sharing information but identifying different perspectives and constructions of an issue. In this way, the jigsaw arrangement is useful for developing critical literacy and intertextual competencies which are so important in academic study. '**Be an expert**' is a variation of this arrangement in which each group works together to prepare a presentation on a unique aspect of a common theme which one or two group members from each group present to the whole class. The class need to listen to each group presentation because of the unique information each group contributes.

As Crabbe (2007) points out, a communication task is only ever a starting point for learning. Students should be given the opportunity to identify how they can get more learning value from tasks through class conversations about how to add learning value to an upcoming speaking activity. If students engage in an information gap task, for example, with the sole aim of completing the task successfully, they may miss many opportunities to use the task for its actual purpose, namely to provide a vehicle for learning. This might include noting any new words or phrases that come up in the task, asking for feedback, engaging in LREs to better understand a language point that arose during the task, and so on.

Goal 2: Developing Communicative and Conversational Ease

English language instruction for academic purposes often emphasizes 'transactional' talk, that is, getting things done and information shared, with less attention given to the interpersonal dimensions of spoken communication. This is despite the importance of the latter in the academic, social and current/future working lives of our students. As discussed in the introduction to Section 4 of this volume, ESL interns in the final year of their degree studies often struggle with interpersonal communication in the workplace despite having the requisite technical knowledge to perform in their jobs. So how can academic English programmes provide students with opportunities to develop these skills?

$Q \rightarrow SA + EI + Q2$

A simple heuristic for helping students to maintain a conversation and manage small talk is $Q \rightarrow SA + EI + Q2$. That is, when asked a question (Q), give a short answer (SA), add extra information (EI) and ask a follow-up question (Q2). For example, in response to the question, "What career do you hope to pursue when you graduate?" a response might be, "I hope to be recruited by an international bank. I am really attracted to opportunities to work in different parts of the world. Is this something that interests you as well?"

The Donut Arrangement

This is a useful way to physically arrange the class to allow for practicing simple social interactions such as the $Q \rightarrow SA + EI + Q2$ technique. The donut arrangement simply involves dividing the class into two halves with one half sitting or standing around the walls of the classroom facing inwards and the other half forming the inside circle of the donut and facing outwards. Each inner circle student is thus paired with an outer circle student. With this arrangement in place, it is easy to give the class short, timed communicative activities which they can repeat with new partners as many times as required simply by moving the inner circle one 'click' clockwise each time. It is a little like speed dating. The topics can be as simple as practising 'small talk' which, as Holmes (2005) shows, is often a challenge for people who are unsure of the conventions and acceptable topics for small talk in English in new cultural environments.

Role-Play

An approach developed by Riddiford and Newton (2010) is to provide students with an authentic academic or workplace scenario which requires them to develop a role-play of a face to face (or email) interaction. They do this with the goal of developing confidence with managing cross-cultural dimensions of challenging speech acts such as disagreeing, apologizing, making requests and giving instructions. Students first analyze the key dimensions of the scenario—the status and relationship of interlocutors and the degree of imposition involved. In pairs or groups, students then develop a role play which they write out and perform. These are then compared to a transcript and recording of the original interaction on which the scenario was based, and salient aspects of pragmatics highlighted in the process. If such authentic data is not available, teachers can either create their own or simply allow the process of groups comparing and discussing how they approached the situation to develop their sensitivity to managing pragmatic dimensions of communication in English.

Here is a short adapted excerpt from one of the lessons in the book to show how this approach works. Although this example is drawn from a white collar workplace, there are plenty of scenarios in academic contexts that would suit this approach such as requesting an assignment extension, expressing dissatisfaction with some aspect of a course, and seeking clarification concerning unclear course content.

Figure 13.1 A role-play scenario (adapted from Riddiford & Newton, 2009)

Speech act: Making requests

The context
Tom and Greg have worked closely together for some time so know each other well. Greg is Tom's boss. Tom enters Greg's office to request a day's leave.

1. Thinking about context
Working with a partner, use the context information above and complete the table:

Tom and Greg:	High	Medium	Low
Status difference			
Level of familiarity			
Level of difficulty (how hard is it to make the request?)			

2. Role-play
The first part of the conversation between Tom and Greg is provided below. Work with a partner to role-play the conversation. When you have role-played, write down your conversation.

3. Comparison and analysis
(a) Listen to and discuss your impressions of each other's role plays. Identify the strategies used to manage both the *transactional* and *relational* aspects of the communication.
(b) Now listen to a recording and read a transcript of the original interaction. Carry out the same analysis as in (a) above.

Here is the authentic conversation recorded in a New Zealand workplace that students listen to and analyze once they have developed their own short role plays.

Figure 13.2 The authentic conversation for the 'making requests' unit

---

Tom enters Greg's office to request a day's leave.

Tom: Can I just have a quick word?
Greg: Yeah sure, have a seat.
Tom: [sitting down] Great weather, eh?
Greg: mm . . .
Tom: Yeah, been a good week. Did you get away skiing at the weekend?
Greg: Yeah, we did. Now, how can I help you?
Tom: I was just wondering if I could take Friday off and make it a long weekend?
Greg: mm . . . I don't see any problem with that . . . you will have finished that report by then, won't you?

This example reveals a number of principles about social dimensions of communication for students to explore:

- Talk is functionally complex; an utterance performs more than one function at the same time, and one form often has many layers of meaning (e.g., informative, relational, and attitudinal).
- Expressing degrees of politeness involves selecting contextually appropriate discourse strategies.
- Likewise, interpreting polite and impolite behavior involves taking account of appropriateness in context.
- Language provides a range of strategies and devices for boosting and softening the strength of an utterance.
- Language provides direct and indirect ways of expressing meaning.

Survey-Based Projects

Survey-based projects, which involve students collecting interview data, provide an opportunity for students to develop a range of social skills, especially with respect to making requests and asking questions. In a survey task, students work in groups to develop a set of survey questions on a topic they have been given or one they choose to investigate. Once the questions have been settled on, they can be handed to the teacher for feedback and language checking. Group members are then required to either circulate around the class and ask the survey questions or, an alternative that is particularly viable in ESL contexts, to find informants to interview in the wider community— neighbors, friends, and so on. The group then aggregates the information they obtained and uses it to prepare a presentation to the class or a poster (see a later section for organizing poster sessions and formal presentations).

An EAP programme in New Zealand developed a survey task around the topic of earthquake preparedness which had the additional benefit of raising the awareness of students who had not experienced earthquakes about how to prepare for one. Students chose to conduct their survey by asking strangers on the street, students on campus, neighbors, and service attendants in shops. The task outcome was in the form of a written report using the standard genre features of report writing and including a set of recommendations for government agencies.

For or Against?

This is an example of a survey task from Rossiter, Derwing, Manimtim and Thompson (2010). The instructor and/or students choose a topic of current interest in the local media (e.g., Should the government ban the use of cell phones by drivers?). With the instructor's guidance, students formulate a series of questions related to the issue (including open-ended questions), along with openers (Excuse me, . . .) and closers (Thanks for your time). Students practice asking and answering the questions among themselves in class. For homework, they gather responses to the survey questions from six English speakers in the community. Results are tallied, reported, and analyzed in the following class.

Survey-based projects have four notable strengths:

1. Almost any topic can provide the basis for a survey.
2. They are an excellent example of integrated skills teaching since students need to combine speaking, listening, reading and writing as well as presentation skills, including how to effectively represent data visually.
3. Throughout the process of planning, conducting and reporting on a survey, there are multiple opportunities to focus on language issues and to develop fluency through repeatedly working on the same material.
4. The responsibility to plan the project, the need to analyze and present data, and the collaborative team work required all help develop important academic skills.

Goal 3: Developing Dialogic Reasoning Skills and Negotiating Points of View

The ability to reason dialogically, that is, to express a point of view and respond to opinions given by others, is frequently called upon in academic study, especially in tutorial discussions, interactive lecture segments and project-based assessment tasks. This is especially so in 'flipped classrooms' in which students engage with lecture material and readings outside of class so that classroom learning is no longer dominated by lecturer monologues but by discussion, Q&A and debate. Flipped classrooms are likely to become a more common way of organizing academic learning and so EAP students will, more than ever, need the skills to participate in these new forms of learning.

Dialogic Teaching/Inquiry

We might intuitively think of group work as the place to develop these skills, but they can also be effectively modelled and developed in teacher-led whole class interaction in what is known in dialogic teaching/inquiry. In dialogic teaching "the teacher and students act as co-inquirers, collaboratively engaging in a generation and evaluation of new interpretations of texts" (Reznitskaya, 2012, p. 446). Dialogic teaching has been extensively researched and promoted in elementary and secondary school education, notably in the work of British educationalist, Robin Alexander (2012). It deserves more attention in EAP contexts for the role it can play in modelling and developing higher order thinking through in-class dialogue. In fact, the interactive component of lectures often constitutes forms of dialogic inquiry and, as such, provides one of the main opportunities for students to speak publically in academic contexts. It makes sense, therefore, to provide students with opportunities to develop these skills in EAP programmes. In a synthesis of research in this area, Reznitskaya (2012) identifies the following six characteristics of dialogic teaching:

1. Power relations are flexible with students given responsibility to maintain discussion.
2. Questioning is open and divergent.
3. Feedback is meaningful and specific.
4. Meta-level reflection through which students 'pay attention to the process and quality of their reasoning' (p. 448) is frequent.
5. 'Why' and 'how' questions encourage students to present lengthy elaborate explanations.
6. Knowledge is co-constructed through collaborative listening and sharing.

(pp. 447–448)

Although dialogic teaching is closely associated with responding to texts, and so to literature discussions, it can, of course, be extended to include discussion of academic topics, current events and themes that emerge from study. A simple strategy for ensuring more equal participation in whole class discussions is to write the names of all students on a pack of cards and to flick these over to call on another student to contribute. But truly dialogic inquiry involves cross-class participation rather than all contributions being initiated by or directed at the teacher.

Problem-Solving Tasks

Problem-solving tasks are an important teaching tool for developing students' dialogic reasoning and discussion skills. Problem-solving tasks can be open or closed. Open tasks have a range of possible solutions while in closed tasks only one solution or a very narrow range of solutions is possible. Since open tasks allow much more scope for students to explore different points of view, they are preferred for developing argument skills and so will be our focus here. Open tasks can be either convergent (students have to agree on a solution) or divergent (students sustain divergent positions as in a debate). Here is a simple example of an open, convergent problem-solving task.

The study group dilemma. You have joined a study group of students in your economics class at university. One of the students is quite talkative during the study group sessions but rarely talks about study. He is popular and is someone you want to become friends with but his behavior is really undermining your learning in the study group sessions. What do you do?

Adapted from www.lessonplansdigger.com/wp-content/
uploads/2016/07/Moreproblemsolvingactivities.pdf

For lower proficiency students, a list of possible solutions can also be provided. This gives weaker students more of the core vocabulary they will need to keep the discussion going. Problem-solving tasks are ideal for more challenging academic topics such as environmental issues (e.g., How can we reduce our dependence on plastic? How can we help others be less wasteful and more environmentally aware?) and social issues (e.g., What can be done to improve the quality of life in your community?).

Think-Pair-Share

To implement problem-solving tasks, students should first be asked to think individually about the problem and to make notes on possible solutions. This is an important step for increasingly the likelihood that all students will have an opinion to share. Teachers too often throw students into group work without this step, making it much more likely that weaker or less confident students will flounder under the pressure to simultaneously think creatively and share ideas. Next, the students work in small groups to reach an agreement. The third step involves whole-class work in which groups compare their rankings and the teacher facilitates discussion of the solutions. This whole class discussion should follow the principles of dialogic teaching discussed above. In simple terms, individual thinking precedes pair interaction which in turn leads to sharing in bigger groups and then with the whole class.

Ranking Tasks

These are a popular form of open, convergent, problem solving tasks. In ranking tasks, students must agree together on priorities from among a list of given options. Balloon tasks are a rather distasteful version of ranking tasks in which groups have to decide, for example, who, from a group of people in a rapidly descending balloon, should be the first to jump out in order to reduce the weight of the balloon and so slow its descent. Less morally dubious topics are preferable, such as the topic of survival in the task that follows.

Figure *13.3* A simple ranking task (adapted from Nation & Newton, 2009)

Survival

You are alone and lost in the jungle; put the following things in order of importance for your survival;

a sleeping bag;
a radio (for listening only);
an axe;
a gun and ten bullets;
matches;
a tent;
a torch;
a map of the area;
a cooking pot;
three cans of food;
three meters of rope;
a story book.

Although this is a rather simple, non-academic ranking task, the language students must bring to the task to justify points of view and reach consensus is not necessarily so. Newton and Kennedy (1996) showed how students performing ranking tasks such as this produced a significantly greater number of complex sentences than when they performed information gap tasks.

Activities like ranking, which focus on reaching consensus can encourage students to negotiate language items. This is simply because if students need to reach agreement, then they must understand each other. Again, the 'think-pair-share' steps provide an effective way to implement the task. Once a teacher is familiar with the principles for designing and implementing ranking tasks it is not difficult to design tasks to suit the needs and interests of students, or to target discipline specific topics. Here is an example.

Figure 13.4 An example of an academically-focused ranking task

---

Designing a history/social studies syllabus

Scenario: You have been asked to assist with the redesign of a high school history syllabus for grade 10 students. Your first job is to identify five key 20th to 21st century events of global significance to include in the syllabus.

Instructions:

Step 1:   Students individually write their personal list of topics without consulting with other students

Step 2:   In pairs, students share their lists and work to reach agreement on a single pair list of five topics.

Step 3:   Pairs join to make groups of four. The groups go through the same process of sharing lists and agreeing on a single group list of five topics.

Step 4:   Groups share their lists with the class and justify choices. This can be done using the poster carousel arrangement (see below) or a jigsaw reconfiguration of groups. Another option, which uses technology, is for groups to record a short multimedia presentation on their syllabus and post this in a wiki or common folder accessible to all groups.

A range of other topics can be inserted into this scenario include environmental issues, political figures, scientific discoveries and current global issues. Ranking tasks on topics like these involves students in deep engagement with the topic and requires them to produce complex language as they justify decisions and negotiate consensus.

Values Clarification Tasks

In a values clarification task (Manning, 2017), groups of students are given a list of controversial statements such as "Every child needs at least one brother and sister." They first individually rate each statement as to whether they agree or disagree with the statement and then work in pairs or groups to make changes to the statements so that everybody in the group can agree with them. As a final step, the whole class is involved in a discussion of the different group perspectives. In this final step, the teacher's skills in encouraging dialogic inquiry, as discussed above, are crucial. Note also how the 'Think-Pair-Share' approach to implementing the task is again utilized.

Figure 13.5 A values clarification task (Manning, 2017)

Statement	SD	D	A	SA
(1) I find learning other languages to be interesting and easy. *Reason:*		— — — —		
(2) You cannot learn a new language properly without living for a long time in the country in which it is spoken, *Reason:*		— — — —		
(3) If there were no English tests, I would not have studied English very hard. *Reason:*		— — — —		
(4) A classroom is not a good place to learn English. *Reason:*		— — — —		
(5) You can learn a language very well without speaking it to other people. *Reason:*		— — — —		

Goal 4: Developing Formal Speaking Skills

Formal speaking in the form of short talks or seminars presented by students to their peers is an important and common part of many EAP courses. It requires control of content, audience awareness and the rather unsettling experience of being the focus of attention. In these ways it requires students to use language under difficult and demanding circumstances and so pushes their speaking skill development. As it is not a typical part of everyday language use, it is a skill that needs to be taught.

The first step for teaching formal speaking is to give students the opportunity to listen to good examples of formal talks or lectures and to analyze how they are structured and presented. TED talks®[2] are an excellent resource for this purpose. If possible, students should be given the opportunity outside of class to watch one or two TED talks selected by the teacher so that, when these talks are analyzed in class, students are already familiar with the content and language. Ideally, these talks would model important text structures such as problem–solution, compare–contrast and cause-and-effect.

Next, students may need help identifying a topic, generating ideas and gathering information on the topic. Instruction on brainstorming techniques and mind mapping will be valuable for this purpose. Once students have begun to generate ideas they will need to plan and structure their talks. The teacher can encourage students to draw on conventional text structures that they have seen modelled and can provide text structure planning templates for this purpose.

Initially at least, formal talks may be scripted. But it is not usually desirable for the talk to consist of simply reading a written paper aloud. Students thus need to practice presenting an unscripted talk using notes and/or content on PowerPoint® or Prezi® slides. To encourage rehearsal, students can first present talks in pairs and get feedback from the listener. They can then present the talk to a small group of three or four students. Finally, the talk is presented to the whole class or another class with little reliance on written notes.

When listening to formal talks both teachers and students assess where the strengths and weaknesses of the speaker lie. A checklist such as the one shown in Figure 13.6 below can assist with this process.

Students should be encouraged to reflect on their own formal speaking, noting what they do well, and where they need to make improvement. A detailed

Figure 13.6 A formal speaking checklist for self-reflection or peer-feedback (Adapted from Nation & Newton, 2009)

Qualities of a formal talk

Goals and audience
- Is the speaker showing awareness of the audience through the use of appropriate language, pace of presentation, and shared experience?
- Is the speaker's goal clear?

Ideas
- Has the speaker enough relevant things to talk about?
- Is the speaker trying to present too much information?

Organization
- Is the talk well organized?
- Is the organization of the talk clear to the listeners?

Notes
- Is the speaker talking to the audience?

Presentation
- Is the delivery fluent?
- Does the speaker keep the attention of the listeners?
- Are there enough changes of focus of attention?

description of how to integrate self- and peer-assessment into an EAP seminar program is presented in the section below on monitoring and assessing speaking.

Goal 5: Developing Fluency

Students demonstrate fluency when they take part in message-focused speaking and do it with speed and ease without holding up the flow of talk, i.e., they are able to process language in real time. Fluency activities should meet three main conditions:

1. The students are communicating a message and experience the "real time" pressures and demands of normal meaning-focused communication.
2. The content and language required to perform the task is known to the students. This means that the students work with largely familiar topics and types of discourse for which they make use of known vocabulary and structures. It is very difficult to maintain fluent speaking if conscious attention and effort are required to think of new ideas, recall poorly known vocabulary, construct coherent sentences and attend to articulation. If we think of any activity as requiring attention to four areas—Language, Ideas, Skills and Text types (L I S T), then fluency activities will be most effective when the 'L', 'I' and 'T' are largely under the student's control so that their primary focus is on the skill ('S') of speaking fluently.
3. A fluency development activity pushes students to perform at a higher level, often by using time pressure. For example, students should be speaking and comprehending faster, hesitating less, and using larger planned chunks than they do in their normal use of language. In essence, a fluency activity involves students making the best possible use of *what they already know*.

Planning Time and Task Repetition

Two general implementation options—allowing planning time and task repetition assist in helping students produce more fluent language. Planning and preparation can be done individually, with the help of guide sheets or in groups. Before doing a pair-based information gap activity for example, the students who are 'A' get together and work on what they will say, and the students who are 'B' do the same. After this has been done the 'A's pair up with the 'B's to do the activity. Crookes (1989) investigated students who were given 10 minutes to plan what words, phrases and ideas that they would use in their explanation of how to build a LEGO® model or complete a map. He found that, compared to students who were not given time to plan, the students who planned produced longer utterances, and produced more grammatically complex speech. Depending on how students allocate their planning time, it can result in more complex, more accurate and/or more fluent performance (Pang & Skehan, 2014). But whichever of these outcomes is achieved, speaking performance is likely to reach a higher level than it would without preparation.

Task repetition is a sure way of developing fluency with the particular items and sequences used in the activity. It is necessary to change the audience when designing repetition into meaning-focused speaking so that the message is still of interest to the listener and so that the speaker doesn't feel the need to substantially change the message to keep the listeners interest, and thus undermine the fluency practice opportunities inherent in repetition.

Let's now look at how the three fluency conditions and opportunities for planning and repetition are built into two fluency activities, the 4–3–2 activity and poster carousal activity.

The 4–3–2 Activity

In this activity, students work in pairs with one acting as the speaker and the other as listener. The speaker talks for four minutes on a topic while the other student listens. Then the pairs change with each speaker giving the same information to a new partner in three minutes, followed by a further change and a two-minute talk. Roles are then reversed and the listeners become the speakers for a second 4–3–2 round. The donut arrangement described earlier in the chapter is ideal for managing this activity.

How are the three fluency conditions met in this activity? First, the changing audience ensures a fresh pair of ears for each repeat of the talk and thus a focus on the message. This condition is undermined if the teacher sets the same topic for all the class and if this topic allows little individual variation. For example, asking all the class to prepare a talk summarizing the plot of a book or movie studied by the class is not likely to motivate students to attend to each other's talks. On the other hand, asking all the students to prepare a talk on their favorite movie, favorite place, or favorite family memory is more likely to motivate both speakers and listeners. For academic purposes, different texts on a topic can be distributed and used as the basis for ensuring that listeners and speakers are bringing fresh information or perspectives to the task.

The second condition (limited demands) is met because the speaker chooses the ideas and language items, and plans the way of organizing the talk. The 4- and 3-minute deliveries allow the speaker to bring these aspects well under control, so that fluency can become the learning goal of the activity. For many students, talking for four minutes is a big challenge. To address this, the teacher can invest a little more time and support in the planning phase. For example, the teacher can provide a structured outline or set of prompt questions to guide the students to flesh out their talk. If the 4–3–2 activity is used towards the end of a learning cycle or unit of work this additional support may not be needed since the activity is functioning as a form of revision of learned content and language.

Third, the student is helped to reach a high level of performance by having the opportunity to repeat and by the challenge of decreasing time to convey the same message. It is also worth noting that the activity engages students in a large quantity of speaking practice through the three deliveries of the talk.

But what happens to accuracy and errors under the pressure to speak in less and less time? Boers (2014) looked at this question. He found that the ten adult ESL students in his study improved their fluency across the iterations of the talk but that a high number of errors were also repeated from the first to the third talk. He argues that this is an unintended by-product of the performance pressure created by reduced time for each talk. This pressure forces students to fall back on verbatim duplication rather than attending to the accuracy or complexity of their utterances. To counter this risk of errors being reinforced, Boers suggests relatively simple pedagogic interventions such as providing guided planning time, allowing the first iteration of the talk to be interactive, and/or allowing time for corrective feedback after the first talk.

Task 13.1

Consider ways to enhance 4–3–2 activities in a class by answering the following questions:

1. What topics might suit this activity?
2. How much time would you give for planning?
3. How could you model giving a short talk?
4. How could you increase the level of guidance or experience for lower proficiency students who find this activity too challenging?
5. How could you incorporate feedback into the process?
6. How will you manage the physical arrangement of this activity in your particular teaching space?
7. What will you do with an uneven number of students?

The Poster Carousel Task

The poster carousel task is a good example of incorporating meaningful repetition into an activity. In this activity, pairs or groups of students prepare posters on different topics which they prepare to present to other students. A particularly useful aspect of this task is that it mirrors the presentation of posters seen at many academic conferences, and so gives students a taste of this experience. Once the posters are ready, a student from each pair/group acts as the host for their poster, introducing it and answering questions. The other students circulate around the other posters, usually with a set time allocated to each poster visit. Once a full circuit has been completed by all the circulating students, roles are reversed with the host student now visiting the other posters (See Rossiter et al., 2010, p. 596)

ACCESS

Gatbonton and Segalowitz (2005) developed an approach to developing fluency called 'ACCESS'—*Automatization in Communicative Contexts of Essential Speech Elements*. ACCESS consists of three steps, each involving authentic communicative practice.

Step 1: *Creative automatization.* Essential speech segments are elicited and practiced in communication tasks.
Step 2: *Language consolidation.* Students engage in language-focused activities which draw their attention to important grammatical features of the utterances they have been using.
Step 3: *Free communication.* Students use the 'essential speech elements' from the previous phases in additional, more challenging, communication tasks.

The authors provide an example of a task cycle for beginner students they refer to as 'FAMILY'. In simplified terms, this task involves the following steps. Step 1 begins with a simple communication task in which the teacher elicits or introduces 'essential speech segments' such as the vocabulary for describing families and simple phrases such as "____ is my brother". Then the students, working in groups, create an imaginary family, adopting whatever roles they agree on as a group. They then interview another group about that group's family structure and report what they found out to the class. In step 2, the teacher sets language focused exercises to draw students' attention to key structures used in phase 1. In step 3, they participate in a more wide ranging comparison of the family structures the groups created, thus putting the essential speech elements to extended use.

Student Mini-Podcasts[3]

This activity is useful for encouraging speaking fluency practice beyond the classroom on issues that require academic vocabulary and critical thinking. It involves the following steps:

1. The teacher and class decide on a range of issues related to a topic the class has studied (e.g., on the topic of work–life balance, issues might include workload, gender differences, a minimum wage, etc.). The teacher may want to provide guidelines to help students structure their talk (e.g., agree/disagree plus two reasons).

2. Each student, in their own time, uses their cell phone to rehearse and record a brief talk giving an opinion on the topic.
3. They upload their talks to a shared platform such as Google Docs®.
4. Students listen to and comment on each other's talks.
5. The teacher also listens and comments or gives feedback.

Monitoring and Assessing Speaking

An important distinction can be made between assessment *of* learning (i.e., assessing what students have achieved) and assessment *for* learning (i.e., assessing to help students learn). [See Grabe & Stoller, Chapter 3, this volume, for a discussion of this distinction]. The terms summative and formative assessment refer to these respective approaches to assessment.

For formative assessment purposes, effective speaking teachers will pay careful attention to students' performance in speaking activities so they can provide useful feedback and keep track of student progress. Teachers can use simple systems for tracking progress to obtain useful and reliable information such as the following:

1. Use simple observation checklists when students are performing speaking activities.
2. Get students to regularly self-assess their progress. One option is to ask students to develop their own self-assessment criteria.
3. Tick items on a syllabus list when satisfied that the students are able to cope with that part of the syllabus.
4. Students build up a portfolio of completed activities and a record of feedback they have received and how they have acted on it.

For both formative and summative assessment purposes, teachers can choose from a range of types of speaking tests such as recording a short talk based on a prompt, individual interviews, and group discussions. Choosing a speaking test involves careful consideration of validity (how well a test measures what it sets out to measure), reliability (how stable the results of a test are) and practicality (the time, money and effort involved in conducting a test). For example, using student recordings of short rehearsed monologues is of questionable validity if the goal is communicative proficiency, although it might be more reliably graded compared to other less controlled forms of speaking test. On the other hand, individual interviews might have better validity but are impractical where large classes are involved.

For individual interviews the interviewer should follow a set series of questions for at least part of the interview but with some opportunity for freer conversation included as well. The IELTS speaking interview is a good example of how to balance scripted questions with more open discussion. Role plays can also be used. For example[4], the student is given a card which describes this situation:

You want to join an English course but you want to find out several things about the course before you make your final decision. Some of the things you want to know are the cost, the hours, the size of the groups. You are rather worried about being put in a large group where you will not get much individual attention. You also want to work a part time job in the late afternoons.

The examiner also has a role to play:

You are the course director. The six week course costs $3000. There are usually around 14 people in a class. Classes are held from 9 to 3 each week day with an hour for lunch. You expect anyone who does the course to attend regularly.

For group speaking tests, the students can be divided into groups of three to five people. Each student is given a card with the topic and a few questions about it. After a short time for reading the card and thinking about the topic, the group discusses the topic. Group discussions have strong validity for assessing academic speaking because they entail academic uses of language such as presenting a reasoned argument and negotiating different points of view. Group tests can also be based on role plays, partly scripted dialogues, or partly improvized plays, but these options have less validity for assessing readiness for academic study in English.

A Case Study of Speaking Assessment: Assessing Spoken Presentation Skills

A program of academic seminars by students in an EAP course at Victoria University of Wellington[5] illustrates how assessment can be integrated into an instructional package so as to provide both assessment *of* and *for* their learning. The goal of the program is for students to present a 10-minute seminar on a topic of their choosing for summative assessment purposes. This is a high-stakes assessment since, in this course, the grades contribute to determining whether students are accepted into university programs. To prepare students for this assessment, the following steps are involved:

1. Teachers provide instruction and models on how to prepare an academic seminar. A seminar booklet is provided for this purpose. Course learning objectives (CLOs) which focus on qualities such as awareness of genre features, critical thinking and fluency are presented and discussed.
2. Students engage in a cycle of five-minute seminars to prepare for the final 10-minute seminar. For these short seminars, the class is divided into small groups of listeners with each group given responsibility to provide feedback in relation to one of the CLOs. These CLOs are circulated amongst the groups so that, over the seminar practice cycle,

each group has the opportunity to give feedback on the full range of CLOs. The teacher also provides comments on each CLO.
3. Each speaker watches a video of their presentation and completes a self-evaluation form which they hand to the teacher for further comment.

We can see how assessment *for* learning in this instructional cycle provides students with rich opportunities to develop their formal presentation skills. In doing so, the seminar program reflects the following three aspects of assessment for learning identified by Chappuis and Stiggins (2002):

1. Student-involved assessment.
2. Effective teacher feedback.
3. The skills of self-assessment.

Assessing Speaking and the CEFR

Finally, the Common European Framework of Reference for Languages (CEFR) offers a useful source of information on assessing speaking (as well as the other skills), as well as a readily available, comprehensive set of scales of language proficiency which are widely used world-wide (outside of the North American context where ACTFL[6] Proficiency Guidelines[7] are more commonly used). In simple terms, the CEFR framework provides detailed descriptors of spoken second language proficiency on a six level scale, from A1 (Basic user) to C2 (Proficient user). The scale (including various sub-scales) and the assessment tools available online for CEFR users are useful both for testing and for diagnostic analysis of students' communicative proficiency. Also available online, and without cost, is a CEFR self-assessment grid[8] which has been developed to help students identify what they 'can do' based on these scales.

Chapter Summary

Speech is ubiquitous in language classrooms, although, as Hughes (2011) notes, "there may be a great deal of speaking going on in classrooms, [but] this may be different from the effective teaching of speaking as holistic skill" (p. 7). The activities described in this chapter seek to address this gap. They illustrate instructional options for meeting five speaking skill goals, those of developing: (1) clarity in spoken communication; (2) communicative and conversational ease; (3) dialogic reasoning skills and negotiating points of view; (4) fluency; and (5) formal speaking skills. Of course, the rich learning affordances provided by many of these activities means that any one activity can meet multiple goals. However, the fact that they can doesn't mean that they always should. EAP students will benefit from being able to focus on particular speaking sub-skills when they engage in a communicative activity, and teachers should be aware of the particular affordances of different types of activities so that they can align instructional activities to learning needs in a principled manner.

The reader will notice that the chapter has focused on not just stand alone activities, but general types of activities such as information gap tasks, role play, and problem-solving tasks. Familiarity with the essential features of 'task types' and not just stand-alone tasks can equip teachers to be more principled and creative in ways to adapt textbook tasks and create their own tasks.

Finally, as discussed in the previous chapter, speaking activities should be embedded in coherent activity cycles involving, for example, goal setting, planning activities, task repetition, language-focused exercises, feedback, and metacognitive reflection. Taking this approach, an activity becomes the jumping off point for a broader suite of language and skill development opportunities which goes well beyond simply accomplishing the task. In other words, effective language instruction is not only about choosing the right activity. It is much more about having the skills to implement the activity in ways which create a rich and balanced range of relevant learning opportunities. Thus, the seven guidelines presented in the previous chapter are an essential component for framing the use of the activities discussed above.

Discussion Questions and Tasks

1. Choose any activity from this chapter and sketch out a list of ideas for what a teacher might do before and after the task to enrich learning opportunities from the task (refer to the framework of seven learning opportunities in Figure 12.4 (Guideline 7) in Chapter 12 for ideas).
2. Identify the speaking activities included in a unit of work in a published ESL/EFL textbook. What types of tasks are these (e.g., information gap, problem-solving, etc.)? For each activity, what learning goals are explicitly stated or implied?
3. As discussed in the fluency section above, task repetition is important for fluency development. Aside from the tasks described in the fluency section, what repetition/rehearsal opportunities are built into other tasks discussed in this chapter? You might be surprised.
4. How, if at all, are the speaking skills of students formally assessed in your teaching context? For what purpose are they assessed? What impact, if any, does this assessment have on teaching?

Further Reading

Walsh, J. A., & Sattes, B. D. (2015). *Questioning for classroom discussion: Purposeful speaking, engaged listening, deep thinking.* Alexandria, VA: ASCD.

This book, while not specifically EAP-focused, provides a wealth of practical ideas for stimulating questioning and discussion in the EAP classroom. The authors emphasize the importance of well-structured discussion for engaging high level thinking and learning, academic achievement, and active citizenship in a democratic society.

Taylor, L. (Ed.) (2011). *Examining Speaking: Research and practice in assessing second language speaking (Vol. 30)*. Cambridge, UK: Cambridge University Press.

This edited volume provides a detailed up-to-date review of the research literature on assessing speaking (although its main focus is on Cambridge speaking exams).

Notes

1   Common European Framework of Reference
2   www.ted.com/.
3   My thanks to Alison Hamilton-Jenkins and Ha Hoang, teachers in the Victoria University of Wellington English Proficiency Programme, for sharing this idea.
4   This example is adapted from Nation and Newton (2009).
5   My thanks to Jill Musgrave, a teacher in the Victoria University of Wellington English Proficiency Programme, for sharing this material.
6   American Council on the Teaching of Foreign Languages
7   www.actfl.org/publications/guidelines-and-manuals/actfl-proficiency-guidelines-2012/english/speaking.
8   http://europass.cedefop.europa.eu/resources/european-language-levels-cefr.

14 Language Skill Development and EAP

A Reflection on Seven Key Themes

Jonathan M. Newton, William Grabe, and Fredricka L. Stoller

This volume has sought to provide a principled, theoretical account of language skill development to guide teachers in their pedagogic decision making. Each of the four skills presents unique teaching and learning challenges in addition to opportunities that teachers need to understand to teach effectively. It follows that teachers with a firm understanding of the nature of each of the skills, and principles for teaching and learning them, are likely to be more effective practitioners. This is true for teachers who use published English language textbooks as well as for teachers who have the freedom to construct their own curriculum and classroom content.

In the first chapter, we outlined four overarching assumptions which, we argue, lay the foundation for effective skills-based instruction in EAP contexts. These assumptions are summarized as follows:

1. Successful skill development requires explicit teacher effort to build student motivation for learning.
2. Opportunities for meaningful language use, and especially academic uses of language, should be at the core of EAP instruction.
3. Knowledge of the language system (vocabulary and grammar) should be systematically developed alongside *and* through skills-based development.
4. Metacognitive awareness training needs to be an integral part of skills-based teaching. Such training has the goal of helping students to develop learning expertize and, as a result, to become active managers of their learning in and beyond the EAP classroom.

These four assumptions have been touched on throughout this volume in pedagogic principles, curriculum guidelines, instructional activities, and assessment guidance. In this final chapter, we move beyond these assumptions and the specific subject matter of each section, and synthesize a number of common themes that we have addressed explicitly in each of the respective skill sections of this book. In presenting these themes, we seek to provide the reader with a coherent overview of common learning and teaching concepts and to bring the book to a unified conclusion. The themes have a second purpose. They reveal the common ground across skills-based language teaching, on the one hand, and evidence for effective pedagogy drawn from broader educational research traditions beyond EAP, on the other. The chapter thus seeks to make connections by reflecting *back* over the contents of the book and *outwards* to wider educational scholarship.

Theme 1: Incorporating Integrated Skills Teaching

A two-pronged principle that we consider to be central to effective skills teaching is that (a) skills development for academic purposes is best approached through integrated-skills activities and tasks, and (b) integrated skills development best reinforces the specific language skills we have addressed. A justification for this principle is that EAP students need to develop expertize in orchestrating skill use because this is a fundamental characteristic of academic study.

Content- and task–based curricula are both a natural medium for integrated skills teaching. This point is illustrated in the list of integrated skills activities in Figure 14.1. These activities are part of a theme-based[1] unit on the topic of population growth developed by teaching staff and used in a pre-sessional English proficiency program. In its full form (only a part of the unit is displayed here), the unit was designed for two weeks of full time study. The target task in the unit was for each student to write a 1,000-word report/essay on an aspect of population growth. The unit illustrates how the four skills can be interwoven into a sequence of linked activities, and how specific language skills such as paraphrasing and summarizing (e.g., Activity 7 in Figure 14.1) are addressed as *natural* consequences of a content focus and of specifying a meaningful purpose/outcome (writing an essay in this case).

Task 14.1

Teaching skills in integrated sequences

1. Which of the activities listed in Figure 14.1 involve expressing opinions or positions on the topic, and/or encountering arguments for different positions on the topic?
2. What conclusions about integrated skills teaching does your answer to (1) suggest?
3. What explicit course learning objectives might you incorporate in this unit as a result?
4. What deliberate instruction options might be needed to meet these objectives?

Figure 14.1 An example of integrated skills teaching

Theme Unit: World Population Growth

INTRODUCTION TO THE UNIT

Activity 1 *Agenda setting.* Discussion on population growth—What do
you know? What are the issues? What measures should be
taken? What questions would we like answered as we study
this unit?

Activity 2 *Vocabulary study.* Focus on: (a) Previewing vocabulary from
the Academic Word List that will appear in this unit; (b)
Reviewing vocabulary learning strategies.

Activity 3 *Setting learning goals.* Focus on: (a) Previewing learning
objectives; (b) Identifying personal learning priorities; (c) Setting
assignment writing topics and planning for the writing process.

POPULATION STATISTICS

Activity 4 *Reading* ('Global Swarming'). Focus on: (a) Text organization;
(b) Giving group presentations.

Activity 5 *Listening* ('European Numbers'). Focus on listening for details.

Activity 6 *Reading* ('Estimations of the Ethnic Composition of the New
Zealand Population by 2021'). Focus on exploring different
approaches to note-taking from a reading text.

Activity 7 *Reading* ('Population Projections in New Zealand'). Focus on:
(a) Reading to understand the main ideas; (b) Paraphrasing
and writing summaries.

Activity 8 *Listening* (Guest lecture 'Demography'). Focus on learning from
lectures.

Activity 9 *Independent research & short oral reports.* Content focus:
Population projections in different parts of the world

POPULATION GROWTH AND CONTROL

Activity 10 *Listening* ('Quinacrine and Birth Control'). Focus on listening
for main ideas.

Activity 11 *Reading* ('Era of Forced Sterilizations / It's Ok for Women
Not to Have Children'). Focus on: (a) Synthesizing information;
(b) Reading critically and identifying an author's stance.

Activity 12 *Group discussion.* Topic—Issues in the Control of World
Population Growth.

Activity 13 *Group ranking task.* Topic—Ways of Dealing with Increasing
World Population.

Activity 14 *Concept mapping* ('Arguments Against Population Control').

Activity 15 *Assignment writing.* Focus on: (a) Reviewing progress; (b)
Planning for peer feedback on drafts.

Content/theme-based curricula such as this highlight a transition from learning the language to *using language to learn*. An emphasis on content learning plays a number of important roles. It provides a connection to real-world issues, a focus for student engagement (in part motivated by the topicality of the content), greater lesson and curricular coherence, and a basis for sequenced learning activities. Principled sequencing decisions ensure that activities involving any of the four skills will be mutually supportive of activities involving the other skills. The intended consequence of this approach is that students will be better equipped to successfully perform more complex tasks as they progress through a study unit than would be the case if the skills were taught without integration.

Theme 2: Providing Practice

Throughout the four sections of this book, there is discussion of the importance of practice as a key factor for building procedural and automatic language skills in the L2. Language skill development requires many opportunities for practice, that is, for systematic and deliberate rehearsal with the goal of mastering specific knowledge and skills. However, the role of practice in language learning has been a contentious issue in ELT. It has suffered from association with behaviorist theories of learning and from its link to the largely discredited assumption that language is best acquired through careful, sequential practice of rule-based structures (Doughty, 2008). The well-known presentation–practice–production (PPP) approach has been criticized for similar reasons. Nevertheless, theorists such as DeKeyser (2009, 2014) argue persuasively for a reconsideration of the role of deliberate practice in ELT (see also Ericsson & Pool, 2016), especially, but not exclusively, practice that is purposeful, goal directed, and communicative. In literacy domains, it is well documented that students become better readers by reading a lot (Grabe, 2009) and the same could be said for writing (Ferris, 2015).These reading and writing perspectives also apply to speaking and listening.

Underlying the renewed interest in practice is the work of Anders Ericsson, the leading psychologist on the development of expertize across many domains of skilled performance (Ericsson, 2006; 2009). Developing advanced L2 abilities in academic contexts certainly qualifies as skilled performance that requires multiple forms of expertize (see also Kellogg, 2006, on writing expertize). In a book intended for a wider audience, Ericsson and Pool (2016) examine the nature of expertize and deliberate learning across many performance domains. Their scholarship provides us with some answers to the question of what makes for successful (deliberate) practice. While deliberate practice is only a part of the complex business of teaching and learning a second language, these answers provide intriguing starting points for reflecting on how we understand and implement 'practice' in language learning contexts. Following are eight key features of effective deliberate practice across many performance domains proposed by Ericsson and Pool:

1. Deliberate practice is both purposeful and informed: There is an understanding of what expert performers have done and do to excel. Deliberate practice is purposeful practice that knows where it is going and how to get there.
2. Deliberate practice develops skills based on expert coaches/teachers who know how best to develop these abilities.
3. Deliberate practice takes place outside of one's comfort zone (cf. Vygotsky's Zone of Proximal Development or ZPD).
4. Deliberate practice involves well-defined specific goals for improving aspects of target performance. Goals can be broken down to sub-goals and more specific sub-routines that develop the larger skill. Staged and sequenced learning tasks and goals are essential.
5. Deliberate practice requires learners' full attention. The student must concentrate as much as possible.
6. Deliberate practice requires feedback and modification of effort in response to that feedback. Self-monitoring requires effective mental representations that the learner develops. Improving performance goes hand in hand with improving mental representations of task performance, skills, and goals.
7. Deliberate practice nearly always involves building or modifying previously acquired skills and working to improve them specifically.
8. Deliberate practice requires a *lot* of practice; learner motivation is needed to engage in that practice.

More advanced second language learning, especially for academic purposes, involves the development over time of language use expertize. (After all, and for example, seeking a degree at an English medium university, when one is a non-native speaker of English, does require a level of expertize for the students.) Ericsson's central argument, and one that we can probably all agree with, is that the teacher, course goals, and day-to-day instruction are crucial factors contributing to effective practice. However, Ericsson argues that practice (generally speaking) is not the goal, but "deliberate practice" is the desired process whereby skilled people develop true expertize. Not only does deliberate practice develop automaticity but it builds better and more mental representations for the skills that people are learning (with the help of master coaches and teachers). So practice not only builds specific skills but also supports accelerated learning. The intriguing questions for us are two-fold: (1) How can we adapt student learning practice so that it is more like deliberate practice? And (2) how can we adapt instruction so that it promotes deliberate practice for our students?

Theme 3: Developing Fluency

Fluency is a key aspect of teaching and learning for each of the four skills, with fluency development identified as a key goal of instruction throughout the volume. Fluency is an outcome of extensive practice and is supported

Task 14.2

The practice of practice

1. As teachers, how would we answer the two questions (that conclude the Theme 2 section) in relation to our own students and teaching contexts?
2. Consider, also, the following questions related to practice:

   a. How do we as teachers provide feedback?
      Do students understand why teachers provide feedback?
      Do students value these teacher goals?
   b. Do students try again after receiving feedback?
   c. Do students have opportunities for multiple cycles of meaningful feedback?
   d. Do students actively look for additional feedback?
   e. Do students incorporate feedback into subsequent performance that shows new adaptations?

either by specific instructional activities or through effective feedback directed to more fluent performance. Fluency can be understood as a combination of (a) appropriate rate of language comprehension or performance, (b) accuracy (for comprehension) or non-hesitancy (for performance), and (c) appropriate break points in language comprehension or performance (automatically recognizing phrasal, clausal, or intonational boundaries in the language). Fluency typically involves performing under some degree of time pressure. The development of fluency emerges from extensive practice over time, and it is an expectation for advanced EAP skills. At the same time, the concept of language fluency is clearly not the same for each language skill.

In this volume, we all talk about fluency in one way or another, from quick writes, to reading, to re-listening, to practice cycles for speaking preparation. But fluency does seem to refer to somewhat different traits for each skill. Fluency implies both automaticity and accuracy for reading comprehension, but it can be a conflicting force for the other three skills (the fluency/accuracy debate). If someone is a fluent reader, this usually means that they understood what they read. But for speaking, the degrees of observable fluency can be due to smaller hesitancies involving a vocabulary item or a grammatical structure which do not necessarily make the communicative act incomprehensible. From another perspective, speaking and listening deal with the more ephemeral spoken mode while reading and writing are anchored in more permanent written language. Another distinction is that reading and writing differ in the ultimate goal; in reading, the goal is not to attend to the language of the text (unless for literary analyses) but to the underlying information. However, in writing, a goal is to attend to more finely calibrated language choices that the written language itself might convey (or not). What do these distinctions mean for assessing fluency and fluency development? It is worth thinking about distinctions such as these (as well as commonalities) across all four language skills.

Task 14.3

Teaching for fluency development

Take any two language skills discussed in this volume. List features of fluency or fluency instruction that are similar and distinct from each other.

1. What does your list say about the role of fluency in EAP language development?
2. In what ways are the conditions for fluency development complementary across language skill areas?
3. How might integrated skills instruction help develop a more complex approach to fluency development?
4. How can fluency instruction be added to or incorporated within a language learning curriculum when it is not emphasized in the existing curriculum plan?
5. Finally, how much practice is needed for fluency development?

Theme 4: Building a Collaborative Learning Environment

Each of the language skills sections in this volume addresses the importance of pair and group work, of multiple forms of peer feedback, and of the support and assistance that students can receive from peers when carrying out various language learning tasks. It is an understatement to say that effective instruction, motivation development, and a trusting classroom environment can only come about through an investment in building a classroom community focused on learning and helping others to learn. To illustrate the point, Figure 14.2 lists some of the main benefits of group work. The reader may be able to add others.

Drawing on ideas from this volume, a number of specific grouping and collaborative practices can be identified. In general terms, these involve two broad types of group work. The first is small group discussion. Group discussions involve learners sharing opinions and/or knowledge of a topic set by the teacher and/or the class. These discussions fulfil a range of purposes, but generally their purpose is to encourage learners to actively engage with the learning content. As discussed in the volume, group discussions can be

Figure 14.2 The benefits of group work (adapted from Killen, 2016, p. 187)

1. Group work builds a sense of classroom community by providing a safe learning environment for students to explore ideas and take risks as they perform classroom tasks.
2. Group work encourages students to take a more active role in learning.
3. Group work encourages learners to verbalize their thinking, which, in turn, deepens understanding.
4. Group work provides many more opportunities for students to use English for meaningful communication than is possible in whole-class discussions.
5. Through sharing ideas with others and observing others, group work encourages self- and metacognitive awareness.
6. Group work helps students to become aware of the diversity of perspectives on a topic and so to 'de-center' from their own perspective.
7. Through group work, students are often able to perform more demanding tasks than they are capable of performing independently.
8. Group work allows the teacher to differentiate instruction and to spend time with small groups of students.
9. Group work allows the teacher to monitor the understanding and performance of students without undue pressure.
10. Group work allows students to take on a wider range of roles (e.g., leader, questioner, initiator) and forms of discourse related to these roles (e.g., negotiating agreement, questioning, suggesting, proposing).

used to generate ideas in preparation for writing, to activate content schemata (i.e., prior knowledge) in pre-reading/listening phases of a lesson, and to share understandings derived from input in post-reading/listening phases.

The second type of group work we have explored in this volume is more focused on producing a defined outcome such as proposing a solution to a problem, preparing a report, or creating an artifact or performance of some kind, such as a poster, website, role-play, or jointly written text. Jigsaw reading/listening is an example of this type of outcomes-focused group work. Jigsaw activities involve groups preparing written or oral summaries of different but linked written/spoken input on a common topic, with different groups receiving different input to summarize. The groups then share their summaries so that, at the conclusion of the activity, all groups have encountered ideas from the different input sources. [See Newton, Chapter 13, this volume.]

What is not always as clear is how to ensure that collaborative and group learning is operationalized most effectively. Managing group work requires considerable teaching skill and an awareness of the principles of learning in groups. One general guideline is "think, pair, share." Before any group or pair task-based discussion, each student should commit to some ideas or answers individually, usually by writing down a few notes, a few phrases, or answering some task prompt. This individual commitment gives everyone something to share with others, and it allows group members to ask others what they were thinking or how they are responding to a task.

A second general guideline is to encourage others to share so that all students learn to become comfortable with peers and not feel threatened. A third guideline is to encourage students to find something positive to say about the contributions of others or ask a question about an answer rather than to disagree directly.

One of the best formal approaches to building collaborative communities is through the learning approach known as Cooperative Learning. This approach involves a number of guidelines for organizing discussion and feedback among peers. For example, "grades" are often given to all group members equally to ensure that everyone is trying. There is a considerable amount of well-designed research to support language learning (and all learning) within Cooperative Learning environments (see Johnson and Johnson n.d.; Li, n.d.; Slavin, 2013, 2014). [See Newton, Chapter 12 for a fuller description of cooperative learning.]

Finally, collaboration has been widely recognized as a core 21st-century competency (National Research Council, 2012; Voogt et al., 2013). For these reasons, EAP teachers would do well to ensure not only that group work is a core component of their pedagogy, but also that they are conversant with the evidence-based principles for implementing effective group work and cooperative learning.

Task 14.4

Reflecting on the experience of group work

Reflect on a recent group-work experience that you have had.

1. Overall, was the experience positive or negative?
2. What factors do you think contributed to your evaluation of the experience?
3. What can you draw from this experience to inform your professional practice as an EAP teacher?

Theme 5: Developing the Strategic Language User

Each section of this volume addresses the need for students to become more strategic language learners. This goal for EAP learners is critical because in academic contexts, L2 students will be asked to carry out more complex and more difficult tasks. They will need to be strategic in how they approach these more challenging language activities so that they can persist and succeed academically.

The idea of becoming strategic is very different from being taught language learning strategies one at a time out of a textbook. Strategic learners develop much greater metacognitive self-awareness as well as clear goals for successfully completing academically oriented language tasks. Strategic learners develop a repertoire of strategies that are proven to help them carry out challenging tasks. They use strategies in combinations that lead to successful outcomes. They engage in discussions with other students about how to complete tasks and what strategies have been helpful. They are skilled at monitoring their relative success with academic tasks and seek out ways to address difficulties. When faced with difficulties, they apply new strategies and gradually build additional effective repertoires.

Helping students become more strategic language learners is a major challenge. For students to build appropriate self-awareness of goals and specific learning strategies takes a fairly long period of time. Similarly, building strategy repertoires that are most effective combinations for task success is an incremental process. In response to these challenges, the training of strategic learners is important in EAP contexts. This theme is stressed in each section of the book because it is a core ability that, while difficult, nonetheless must be mastered.

Task 14.5

Strategic learners across language skills

1. What major language learning and language use strategies are common to reading and writing and why might these similarities exist?
2. How does face to face oral interaction lead to different ways for learners to build strategic repertoires?
3. Why might the fairly automatic application of effective sets of strategies in response to challenging tasks take a long time to develop?

Theme 6: Providing Effective Assessment and Feedback

In Chapter 3, Grabe and Stoller discuss the important distinction between assessment *of* learning and assessment *for* learning. They emphasize the point that assessment is an essential part of teaching, curriculum development, and student learning rather than an addendum to the teaching and learning process.

Naturally, when we consider how assessment contributes to learning, we are drawn to the role of feedback, a topic discussed extensively by Ferris in Chapter 7 with respect to writing, and Newton in Chapters 11 and 12 with respect to speaking. Drawing on a meta-analysis of over 1,000 research studies on factors that influence student learning, Hattie (2009) shows that feedback is not only among the highest of any single factor that influences learning, but it underpins many of the other powerful influences as well.

It is all too easy to think of giving feedback as providing information about what is wrong, what we might think of as the 'low hanging fruit' of feedback. It is, though, much more than this. As Boud and Molley (2013) argue, feedback is not an act that occurs at a single point in time, but is a learning process:

> Whereby learners obtain information about their work in order to appreciate the similarities and differences between the appropriate standards for any given work, and the qualities of the work itself, in order to generate improved work.
>
> (p. 6)

Two additional points emerge from this definition of feedback. The first is that for an activity to be considered as feedback, it must involve a feedback loop whereby the feedback is understood and it results in some kind of impact on learning (Boud, 2015). The second point is that feedback is a responsive process involving two-way interactions in which the learner is an "active agent" (Boud, 2015, p. 4) who seeks and chooses how to use information obtained through feedback. A further implication is that teachers need to work with students to develop (a) an appropriate disposition towards the feedback process, and (b) the skills to take on an effective agentive role in this process. These skills involve, for example, knowing what the appropriate standards are, being able to analyse one's work in comparison with these standards, and

---

Task 14.6

Making connections

1. How can assessment and feedback contribute to deliberate practice?
2. What types of feedback and assessment would help students develop greater fluency?
3. How does feedback relate to the development of a community of collaborative learners?
4. How is strategy learning dependent on feedback and assessment?

knowing how to close the gap between the two (Sadler, 1989, as cited in Boud, 2015, p. 6). We can see here a strong connection between effective feedback processes and developing strategic language users (Theme 5).

Theme 7: Incorporating Technology

Each section of the volume discusses the impact of technology on language learning and language use. At the same time, there is less consensus on what sorts of technologies and learning software will be most useful for EAP students. There are technology-driven language teaching resources, language learning support resources, social media platforms, auxiliary resources for student learning, and standard general tools such as word processing, spell checkers, and e-dictionaries. There is also an almost inexhaustible store of information sources available in many presentation formats. The myriad of sometimes contradictory discussions around technologies for language learning most likely reflects the seeming lack of coherence among technology developers, curriculum developers, and teachers themselves. But, ultimately, the discussion is not about whether technology-oriented instruction will produce greater language learning gains: This is not a question that can be answered. Rather the issue is how students can best use technologies to help them carry out language-use tasks more effectively.

For teachers, the key issue is determining which technologies will be useful for which learners, when, and for what purposes. Technology is here to stay in a bewildering array of formats, applications, and instructional programs. For both teachers and students, this raises the challenge of how to incorporate required technologies into instruction and learning without getting overwhelmed by choice or seduced by superficial visual or interactive features. Finding the most effective, technologically enhanced, language-learning and language-use pathways for EAP contexts is a challenge for the future, but that future includes tomorrow.

Task 14.6

The teacher as resource curator

In Chapter 13, Newton suggested that the growth in resources for technology-enhanced language teaching and learning requires the teacher to, more than ever, take on the role of *resource curator.*

1. Putting on your curator hat, what technology resource categories initially come to mind? For example, should resources be categorized by language skill, primary user (teacher or student), and/or interactive features?
2. How would you share a list of resources with students? How would you provide opportunities for student input?

3. What criteria would you use to evaluate the value of items in the list and to justify inclusion in the list?
4. How could you build student engagement with this list into classroom instruction?

Chapter Summary

In this last chapter, we have highlighted seven themes that emerged across all four sections of the volume. While there may be other common themes, these seven stood out for us as we read through the whole volume:

1. incorporating integrated skills teaching;
2. providing practice;
3. developing student fluency;
4. building a collaborative learning environment;
5. developing the strategic language user;
6. providing effective assessment and feedback;
7. incorporating technology.

At this point, we can combine these seven themes with the four assumptions about language teaching introduced in the first chapter to provide a fuller picture of the foundational principles on which we have written this volume:

1. promoting motivation;
2. structuring lessons for meaningful language use;
3. developing language knowledge and skills;
4. raising metacognitive awareness.

This combined list of 11 themes (and assumptions) provides the EAP teacher with a useful checklist for reviewing the quality of instruction they provide. To do this, a teacher could embed each theme in the question, "How am I . . .?", as in, for example, "How am I promoting motivation?". Not all themes will be equally pertinent in all EAP instructional contexts, and so a further job for the reader/EAP teacher is to contextualize and prioritize each theme with regard to specific contexts of instruction.

These themes support the more detailed presentations of the four skill areas in Chapters 2–13. It is our hope that teachers use the information and resources provided in the volume to help their EAP students achieve academic success.

Notes

1   Theme-based curricula represent a form of content-based instruction (CBI).

Author Biographies

Ferris, Dana R.

Dana R. Ferris is Professor of Writing at University of California, Davis, where she directs the second language writing program. She is interested in second language writing, reading, response to student writing, and language development in the context of writing. Her most recent books include *Language Power* (Bedford St. Martin's, 2014), *Teaching L2 Composition* (3rd ed., with John Hedgcock, Routledge, 2014), and *Written Corrective Feedback in Second Language Acquisition and Writing* (with John Bitchener, Routledge, 2012). She was the founding editor-in-chief of the *Journal of Response to Writing* and is currently co-editor of the *Journal of Second Language Writing*.

Goh, Christine C. M.

Christine Goh is Professor of Linguistics and Language Education at Singapore's National Institute of Education of the Nanyang Technological University. She is a qualified English language teacher with nearly 30 years of experience in language teaching and teacher education in various contexts. She is interested in second language speaking and listening and the role of metacognition in language learning. She has many international refereed publications in the form of books and journal articles. Her recent books are *Teaching Speaking: A Holistic Approach* (with Anne Burns, 2012, Cambridge University Press) and *Teaching and Learning Second Language Listening: Metacognition in Action* (with Larry Vandergrift, 2012, Routledge). *Teaching Listening in the Language Classroom* (2002, RELC) has been translated into Chinese and Portuguese. She also co-edited *Language Learning in New English Contexts: Studies of Acquisition and Development* (2009, Continuum/ Bloomsbury), and was the guest editor for three journal special issues on listening.

Grabe, William

William Grabe is Regents' Professor of Applied Linguistics at Northern Arizona University. He is interested in reading, writing, literacy, written discourse analysis, and content based L2 instruction. He has lectured and given teaching training workshops in over 30 countries around the world. His most recent books are *Teaching and Researching Reading* (with F. Stoller, 2nd ed., Routledge, 2011) and *Reading in a Second Language: Moving from theory to practice* (Cambridge University Press, 2009). He has also co-authored *Theory and Practice of Writing* (with R. B. Kaplan; Longman, 1996) and co-edited *Directions in Applied Linguistics* (Multilingual Matters, 2005). He is a past President of the American Association for Applied Linguistics (2001–2002). He received the 2005 Distinguished Scholarship and Service Award from the American Association for Applied Linguistics.

Newton, Jonathan M.

Jonathan Newton is Associate Professor and Director of the MA TESOL program at Victoria University of Wellington, New Zealand. He has worked in language teaching and teacher education for 30 years, both in New Zealand and in China where he began his teaching career. His research interests include teaching and learning vocabulary in a second language, task-based instruction, intercultural language teaching, and language/communication training and materials design for the multicultural workplace. He has published more than 50 chapters and articles and has co-authored two books, one with Paul Nation, *Teaching ESL/EFL Listening and Speaking* (2009), and a second with Nicky Riddiford, *Workplace talk in action: An ESOL resource* (2010).

Stoller, Fredricka L.

Fredricka L. Stoller is Professor of English at Northern Arizona University, where she teaches in the MA-TESL and Ph.D. in Applied Linguistics programs. She is co-author of *Teaching and Researching Reading* (2nd ed., 2011, Routledge); co-editor of *A Handbook for Language Program Administrators* (2nd ed., 2012, Alta English Publishers); and co-author of *Write Like a Chemist* (2008, Oxford University Press). She has published in *English for Specific Purposes, English Teaching Forum, Journal of English for Academic Purposes,* and *Reading in a Foreign Language.* Her professional areas of interest include L2 reading, content-based instruction, project-based learning, and disciplinary writing. She was a Fulbright scholar in Turkey (2002–2003), Timor Leste (2014), and Vietnam (2018) and has trained EFL teachers, teacher trainers, and language program administrators in 30 other countries.

Vandergrift, Larry

Larry Vandergrift was Professor Emeritus from the Official Languages and Bilingualism Institute at the University of Ottawa. He published widely on listening, particularly the role of metacognition in successful L2 listening. His book, with Christine Goh, *Teaching and Learning Second Language*

Listening: Metacognition in Action, was published in 2012. In 2009, the Canadian Association of Second Language Teachers honored him with the Robert Roy Award for his teaching, research, writing and dedication to the improvement of L2 teaching and learning in Canada. He was also a co-editor of the *Canadian Modern Language Review*, and after Larry's passing in 2015, the journal named their annual award for best Graduate Student Paper in his honor.

References

Adler-Kassner, L., & Wardle, E. (2015). *Naming what we know: Threshold concepts in writing studies.* Boulder, CO: University Press of Colorado.

Alexander, R. (2012). Improving oracy and classroom talk in English schools: Achievements and challenges. Retrieved from www.robinalexander.org.uk/wp-content/uploads/2012/06/DfE-oracy-120220-Alexander-FINAL.pdf.Anderson, A., & Lynch, T. (1988). *Listening.* Oxford, UK: Oxford University Press.

Anderson, J. R. (1995). *Cognitive psychology and its implications* (4th ed.). New York, NY: Freeman.

Anderson, N. J. (2009). ACTIVE reading: The research base for a pedagogical approach in the reading classroom. In Z. H. Han & N. J. Anderson (Eds.), *Second language reading research and instruction: Crossing the boundaries* (pp. 117–143). Ann Arbor, MI: The University of Michigan Press.

Anderson, N. J. (2014). Developing engaged second language readers. In M. Celce-Murcia, D. M. Brinton, & M. A. Snow (Eds.), *Teaching English as a second or foreign language* (4th ed., pp. 170–188). Boston, MA: Cengage/National Geographic Learning.

Anderson, N. J. (2015). Academic reading expectations and challenges. In N. W. Evans, N. J. Anderson, & W. G. Eggington (Eds.), *ESL readers and writers in higher education: Understanding challenges, providing support* (pp. 95–109). New York, NY: Routledge.

Andrade, M. S., & Evans, N. W. (2013). *Principles and practices for response in second language writing: Developing self-regulated learners.* New York, NY: Routledge.

Andrade, M. S., Evans, N. W., & Hartshorn, K. J. (2015). Perceptions and realities of ESL students in higher education: An overview of institutional practices. In N. W. Evans, N. J. Anderson, & W. G. Eggington (Eds.), *ESL readers and writers in higher education: Understanding challenges, providing support* (pp. 18–35). New York, NY: Routledge.

Andringa, S., Olsthoorn, N., van Beuningen, C., Schoonen, R., & Hulstijn, J. (2012). Determinants of success in native and non-native listening comprehension: An individual differences approach. *Language Learning, 62*(2), 49–78.

Atkinson, D., & Ramanathan, V. (1995). Cultures of writing: An ethnographic comparison of L1 and L2 university writing/language programs. *TESOL Quarterly, 29*, 539–568.

Aubrey, S. (2017). Inter-cultural contact and flow in a task-based Japanese EFL classroom. *Language Teaching Research, 21*(6), 717–734. doi: 13621688166 83563.

Baddeley, A. (2000). The episodic buffer: A new component of working memory? *Trends in Cognitive Sciences, 4*(11), 417–423.

Baddeley, A. (2003). Working memory and language: An overview. *Journal of Communication Disorders, 36*(3), 189–208.

Bandura, A. (1993). Perceived self-efficacy in cognitive development and functioning. *Educational Psychologist, 28*(2), 117–148.

Bauerlein, M. (2015). The resistance to 21st-century reading. In R. J. Spiro, M. DeSchryver, M. Schira Hagerman, P. M. Morsink, & P. Thompson (Eds.) *Reading at a crossroads? Disjunctures and continuities in current conceptions and practices* (pp. 26–34). New York, NY: Routledge.

Birch, B. M. (2007). *English L2 reading: Getting to the bottom* (2nd ed.). Mahwah, NJ: Erlbaum.

Blachowicz, C., & Ogle, D. (2008). *Reading comprehension: Strategies for independent learners* (2nd ed). New York, NY: Guilford Press.

Boers, F. (2014). A reappraisal of the 4/3/2 activity. *RELC Journal, 45*(3), 221–235.

Bonk, W. J. (2000). Second language lexical knowledge and listening comprehension. *International Journal of Listening, 14*(1), 14–31.

Boud, D. (2015). Feedback: ensuring that it leads to enhanced learning. *The clinical teacher, 12*(1), 3–7.

Boud, D., & Molloy, E. (Eds.). (2013). *Feedback in higher and professional education: Understanding it and doing it well.* New York, NY: Routledge.

Braidi, S. M. (2002). Reexamining the role of recasts in native-speaker/ nonnative-speaker interactions. *Language Learning, 52*(1), 1–42.

Brice, A., & Montgomery, J. (1996). Adolescent pragmatic skills: A comparison of Latino students in English as a second language and speech and language programs. *Language, Speech, and Hearing Services in Schools, 27*(1), 68–81.

Broersma, M., & Cutler, A. (2011). Competition dynamics of second-language listening. *The Quarterly Journal of Experimental Psychology, 64*(1), 74–95.

Brown, G. (1987). Twenty-five years of teaching listening comprehension. *English Teaching Forum, 25*(4), 11–15.

Brown, G. (1990). *Listening to spoken English* (2nd ed.). London, UK: Longman.

Brumfit, C. (2001). *Individual freedom in language teaching: language education and applied linguistics.* Oxford, UK: Oxford University Press.

Buck, G. (2001). *Assessing listening.* Cambridge, UK: Cambridge University Press.

Cain, K., & Oakhill, J. (2012). Reading comprehension development from seven to fourteen years: Implications for assessment. In J. P. Sabatini, E. A. Albro, & T. O'Reilly (Eds.), *Measuring up: Advances in how to assess reading ability* (pp. 59–76). Lanham, MD: Rowman & Littlefield Education.

Canagarajah, S. (2011). Codemeshing in academic writing: Identifying teachable strategies of translanguaging. *The Modern Language Journal, 95*(3), 401–417.

Carlson, R. A. (1997). *Experienced cognition.* Hove, UK: Psychology Press.

Carson, J. E., & Nelson, G. L. (1994). Writing groups: Cross-cultural issues. *Journal of Second Language Writing, 3,* 17–30.

Carver, R. (1992). Reading rate: Theory, research, and practical implications. *Journal of Reading, 36*, 84–95.

Chamot, A. U. (1995). Learning strategies and listening comprehension. In D. Mendelsohn & J. Rubin (Eds.), *A guide for the teaching of second language listening* (pp. 13–30). San Diego, CA: Dominie Press.

Chamot, A. U., & O'Malley, J. M. (1994). *The CALLA handbook: Implementing the cognitive academic language learning approach*. Reading, MA: Addison Wesley.

Chandler, J. (2003). The efficacy of various kinds of error feedback for improvement in the accuracy and fluency of L2 student writing. *Journal of Second Language Writing, 12*, 267–296.

Chappuis, S., & Stiggins, R. J. (2002). Classroom assessment for learning. *Educational Leadership, 60*(1), 40–44.

Chen, X., Dronjic, V., & Helms-Park, R. (Eds.). (2016). *Reading in a second language: Cognitive and psycholinguistic issues*. New York, NY: Routledge.

Chiang, C. S., & Dunkel, P. (1992). The effect of speech modification, prior knowledge, and listening proficiency on EFL lecture learning. *TESOL Quarterly, 26*(2), 345–374.

Chiang, Y.-S., & Schmida, M. (1999). Language identity and language ownership: Linguistic conflicts of first-year university writing students. In L. Harklau, K. M. Losey, & M. Siegal (Eds.), *Generation 1.5 meets college composition*. (pp. 81–96). Mahwah, NJ: Erlbaum.

Cho, B. Y., & Afflerbach, P. (2017). An evolving perspective of constructively responsive reading comprehension strategies in multi-layered digital text environments. In S. E. Israel (Ed.), *Handbook of research on reading comprehension* (2nd ed., pp. 109–134). New York, NY: Guilford Press.

Chopin, K. (1894). The story of an hour. Originally published in *Vogue*, December 6, 1894, retrieved from www.vcu.edu/engweb/webtexts/hour/.

Cobb, T. (n.d.) *The compleat lexical tutor*. www.lextutor.ca/.

Cohen, J. (2011). Building fluency through the repeated reading method. *English Teaching Forum, 49*(3), 20–27.

Coiro, J. (2015). Purposeful, critical, and flexible: Vital dimensions of online reading and learning. In R. Spiro, M. DeSchryver, M. Hagerman, P. Morsink, & P. Thompson (Eds.), *Reading at a crossroads? Disjunctures and continuities in current conceptions and practices* (pp. 53–64). New York, NY: Routledge.

Conference on College Composition and Communication (CCCC) (2014). *Statement on second language writing and second language writers*. Retrieved from www.ncte.org/cccc/resources/positions/secondlangwriting.

Connor, U. (2011). *Intercultural rhetoric in the writing classroom*. Ann Arbor, MI: University of Michigan Press.

Conrad, S. M., & Goldstein, L. M. (1999). ESL student revision after teacher written comments: Text, contexts, and individuals. *Journal of Second Language Writing, 8*, 147–180.

Coxhead, A. (2000). A new academic word list. *TESOL Quarterly, 34*, 213–238.

Crabbe, D. (2007). Learning opportunities: Adding learning value to tasks. *ELT Journal, 61*(2), 117–125.

Crawford, M. (2005). Adding variety to word recognition exercises. *English Teaching Forum, 43*(2), 36–41.

Crookes, G. (1989). Planning and interlanguage variation. *Studies in Second Language Acquisition, 11*(4), 367–383.

Cross, J. (2009). Diagnosing the process, text, and intrusion problems responsible for L2 listeners' decoding errors. *Asian EFL Journal, 11*(2), 31–53.

Cross, J. (2010). Raising L2 listeners' metacognitive awareness: A sociocultural theory perspective. *Language Awareness, 19*(4), 281–297.

Cross, J. (2016). Podcasts and autonomous L2 listening: Pedagogical insights and research direction. *The European Journal of Applied Linguistics and TEFL, 5*(2), 59–72.

Crusan, D. (2010). *Assessment in the second language writing classroom.* Ann Arbor, MI: University of Michigan Press.

Cutler, A. (2012). *Native listening: Language experience and the recognition of spoken words.* London, UK: MIT Press.

de Guerrero, M. C., & Commander, M. (2013). Shadow-reading: Affordances for imitation in the language classroom. *Language Teaching Research, 17*(4), 433–453. doi: 10.1177/1362168813494125.

Dehaene, S. (2009). *Reading in the brain: The science and evolution of a human invention.* New York, NY: Viking.

DeKeyser, R. M. (1998). Beyond focus on form: Cognitive perspectives on learning and practising second language grammar. In C. Doughty & J. Williams (Eds.), *Focus on form in classroom second language acquisition* (pp. 42–63). Cambridge, UK: Cambridge University Press.

DeKeyser, R. M. (2007). *Practice in a second language: Perspectives from applied linguistics and cognitive psychology.* Cambridge, UK: Cambridge University Press.

DeKeyser, R. M. (2009). Cognitive-psychological processes in second language learning. In M. Long & C. Doughty (Eds.), *Handbook of language teaching* (pp. 119–138). Malden, MA: Wiley-Blackwell.

DeKeyser, R. M. (2014). Skill Acquisition Theory. In B. VanPatten & J. Williams (Eds.), *Theories in second language acquisition: An introduction* (2nd ed., pp. 94–112). London, UK: Routledge.

Derwing, T. M., & Munro, M. J. (2015). *Pronunciation fundamentals: Evidence-based perspectives for L2 teaching and research* (Vol. 42). Amsterdam, The Netherlands: John Benjamins.

Ding, Y. (2007). Text memorization and imitation: The practices of successful Chinese learners of English. *System, 35*(2), 271–280. doi: 10.1016/j.system. 2006.12.005.

Dobler, E., & Eagleton, M. B. (2015). *Reading the Web: Strategies for Internet inquiry* (2nd ed.). New York, NY: Guilford Press.

Dörnyei, Z., Henry, A., & MacIntyre, P. D. (2014). *Motivational dynamics in language learning* (Vol. 81). Bristol, UK: Multilingual Matters.

Doughty, C. J. (2008). Instructed SLA: Constraints, compensation, and enhancement. In C. Doughty & M. H. Long (Eds.), *The handbook of second language acquisition* (Vol. 27, pp. 256–310). Malden, MA: Blackwell.

Douglas, S. R., & Kim, M. (2015). Task-based language teaching and English for academic purposes: An investigation into instructor perceptions and practice in the Canadian context. *TESL Canada Journal, 31*, 1. doi: 10.18806/tesl.v31i0.1184.

Downs, D., & Wardle, E. (2007). Teaching about writing, righting misconceptions: (Re)envisioning "First-Year Composition" as "Introduction to Writing Studies." *College Composition and Communication, 58*, 552–584.

Dressler, C., & Kamil, M. (2006). First- and second-language literacy. In D. August & T. Shanahan (Eds.), *Developing literacy in second-language learners* (pp. 197–241). Mahwah, NJ: Erlbaum.

Dronjic, V., & Bitan, T. (2016). Reading, brain, and cognition. In X. Chen, V. Dronjic & R. Helms-Park (Eds.), *Reading in a second language: Cognitive and psycholinguistic issues* (pp. 32–69). New York, NY: Routledge.

Dudley-Evans, T. (1994). Variations in the discourse patterns favoured by different disciplines and their pedagogical implications. In J. Flowerdew (Ed.), *Academic listening: Research perspectives* (pp. 146–158). Cambridge, UK: Cambridge University Press.

Dunkel, P. (1991). Listening in the native and second/foreign language: Toward an integration of research and practice. *TESOL Quarterly, 25*(3), 431–457.

Dunn, L. M., & Dunn, D. M. (2007). *Peabody picture vocabulary test.* New York, NY: Pearson Education.

Dunn, L. M., Dunn, L. M., & Thériault-Whalen, C. M. (1993). *Échelle de vocabulaire en images Peabody: série de planches.* Toronto, Canada: Psycan.

Eggington, W. G. (2015). When everything's right, but it's still wrong. In N. W. Evans, N.J. Anderson, & W.G. Eggington (Eds.), *ESL readers and writers in higher education: Understanding challenges, providing support* (pp. 198–208). New York, NY: Routledge.

Elbow, P. (1973). *Writing without teachers.* Oxford, UK: Oxford University Press.

Elk, C. K. (2014). Beyond mere listening comprehension: Using TED Talks and metacognitive activities to encourage awareness of errors. *International Journal of Innovation in English Language Teaching and Research, 3*(2), 215–246.

Elkhafaifi, H. (2005). Listening comprehension and anxiety in the Arabic language classroom. *The Modern Language Journal, 89*(2), 206–220.

Ellis, R. (2003). *Task-based language learning and teaching.* Oxford, UK: Oxford University Press.

Ellis, R. (2005). *Planning and task performance in a second language* (Vol. 11). Amsterdam, The Netherlands: John Benjamins.

Ellis, R., & Shintani, N. (2013). *Exploring language pedagogy through second language acquisition research.* New York, NY: Routledge.

Ericsson, A. (Ed.). (2006). *Development of professional expertize.* New York, NY: Cambridge University Press.

Ericsson, A. (2009). The influence of experience and deliberate practice on the development of superior expert performance. In A. Ericsson, N. Charness, P. Feltovich & R. Hoffman (Eds.), *The Cambridge handbook of expertise and expert performance* (pp. 683–703). New York, NY: Cambridge University Press.

Ericsson, A., & Pool, R. (2016). *Peak: Secrets from the new science of expertize.* Boston, MA: Houghton Mifflin Harcourt.

Eskey, D. E. (1983). Meanwhile, back in the real world . . . Accuracy and fluency in second language teaching. *TESOL Quarterly, 17*, 315–323.

Evans, N. W., Anderson, N. J., & Eggington, W. G. (Eds.) (2015). *ESL readers and writers in higher education: Understanding challenges, providing support.* New York, NY: Routledge.

Eyraud, K., Giles, G., Koenig, S., & Stoller, F. L. (2000). The word wall approach: Promoting L2 vocabulary learning. *English Teaching Forum, 38*(3), 2–11.

Fathman, A., & Whalley, E. (1990). Teacher response to student writing: Focus on form versus content. In B. Kroll (Ed.), *Second language writing: Research insights for the classroom* (pp. 178–190). Cambridge, UK: Cambridge University Press.

Ferris, D. (2015). Supporting multilingual writers through the challenges of academic literacy: Principles for English for academic purposes and composition instruction. In N. W. Evans, N. J. Anderson, W. G. Eggington (Eds.), *ESL readers and writers in higher education: Understanding challenges, providing support* (pp. 147–163). New York, NY: Routledge.

Ferris, D. R. (1995). Student reactions to teacher response in multiple-draft composition classrooms. *TESOL Quarterly, 29*, 33–53.

Ferris, D. R. (1997). The influence of teacher commentary on student revision. *TESOL Quarterly, 31*, 315–339.

Ferris, D. R. (2003). *Response to student writing: Research implications for second language students.* Mahwah, NJ: Lawrence Erlbaum.

Ferris, D. R. (2009). *Teaching college writing to diverse student populations.* Ann Arbor, MI: University of Michigan Press.

Ferris, D. R. (2011). *Treatment of error in second language student writing* (2nd ed.). Ann Arbor, MI: University of Michigan Press.

Ferris, D. R. (2015a). Inclusivity through community: Designing response systems for "mixed" academic writing courses. In M. Roberge, K. M. Losey, & M. Wald (Eds.), *Teaching U.S-Educated multilingual writers: Practices from and for the classroom* (pp. 11–46). Ann Arbor, MI: University of Michigan Press.

Ferris, D. R. (2015b). Supporting multilingual writers through the challenges of academic literacy: Principles of English for academic purposes and composition instruction. In N. W. Evans, N. J. Anderson & W. G. Eggington (Eds.), *ESL readers and writers in higher education: Understanding challenges, providing support* (pp. 147–163). New York, NY: Routledge.

Ferris, D. R. (2016). Promoting grammar and language development in the writing class: Why, what, how, and when. In E. Hinkel (Ed.), *Teaching English grammar to speakers of other languages* (pp. 222–245). New York, NY: Routledge.

Ferris, D. R., & Hedgcock, J. S. (2014). *Teaching L2 composition: Purpose, process, and practice* (3rd ed.). New York, NY: Routledge.

Ferris, D. R., Liu, H., & Rabie, B. (2011). "The job of teaching writing": Teacher views of responding to writing. *Writing and Pedagogy, 3*, 39–77.

Field, J. (1998). Skills and strategies: Towards a new methodology for listening. *ELT Journal, 52*(2), 110–118.

Field, J. (2008). *Listening in the language classroom.* Cambridge, UK: Cambridge University Press.

Flavell, J. H. (1979). Metacognition and cognitive monitoring: A new area of cognitive-developmental inquiry. *American Psychologist, 34*(10), 906–911.

Flowerdew, J. (1994). Research of relevance to second language lecture comprehension: An overview. In J. Flowerdew (Ed.), *Academic listening: Research perspectives* (pp. 7–29). Cambridge, UK: Cambridge University Press.

Flowerdew, J., & Miller, L. (2005). *Second language listening: Theory and practice*. New York, NY: Cambridge University Press.

Foster, P., & Ohta, A. S. (2005). Negotiation for meaning and peer assistance in second language classrooms. *Applied Linguistics*, *26*(3), 402–430. doi: 10.1093/applin/ami014.

Gatbonton, E., & Segalowitz, N. (2005). Rethinking communicative language teaching: A focus on access to fluency. *Canadian Modern Language Review*, *61*(3), 325–353, doi: 10.3138/cmlr.61.3.325..

Geva, E,. & Ramírez, G. (2015). *Focus on reading*. New York, NY: Cambridge University Press.

Godwin-Jones, R. (2012). Emerging technologies for language learning. In C. Chapelle (Ed.), *The encyclopedia of applied linguistics* (pp. 1882–1886). London: Blackwell.

Goh, C. (1997). Metacognitive awareness and second language listeners. *ELT Journal*, *51*(4), 361–369.

Goh, C. (2008). Metacognitive instruction for second language listening development: Theory, practice and research implications. *RELC Journal*, *39*(2), 188–213.

Goh, C. (2010). Listening as process: Learning activities for self-appraisal and self-regulation. In N. Harwood (Ed.), *Materials in ELT: Theory and practice* (pp. 179–206). New York, NY: Cambridge University Press.

Goh, C. C. M. (2000). A cognitive perspective on language learners' listening comprehension problems. *System*, *28*(1), 55–75.

Goh, C. C. M. (2002). Exploring listening comprehension tactics and their interaction patterns. *System*, *30*(2), 185–206.

Goh, C. C. M., & Wallace, M. (2017, forthcoming). Lexical segmentation. In J. I. Liontas (Ed.), *The TESOL encyclopedia of English language teaching*, Chichester, UK: Wiley-Blackwell.

Goh, C., & Taib, Y. (2006). Metacognitive instruction in listening for young learners. *ELT Journal*, *60*(3), 222–232.

Goldstein, L. (2005). *Teacher written commentary in second language writing classrooms*. Ann Arbor, MI: University of Michigan Press.

Grabe, W. (2009). *Reading in a second language: Moving from theory to practice*. New York, NY: Cambridge University Press.

Grabe, W., & Stoller, F. L. (2011). *Teaching and researching reading* (2nd ed.). New York, NY: Routledge.

Grabe, W., & Zhang, C. (2013). Reading and writing together: A critical component of English for academic purposes teaching and learning. *TESOL Journal*, *4*(1), 9–24.

Graham, S. (2006). A study of students' metacognitive beliefs about foreign language study and their impact on learning. *Foreign Language Annals*, *39*(2), 296–309.

Graham, S., & Macaro, E. (2008). Strategy instruction in listening for lower-intermediate learners of French. *Language Learning*, *58*(4), 747–783.

Hairston, M. (1986). On not being a composition slave. In C. W. Bridges (Ed.), *Training the new teacher of college composition* (pp. 117–124). Urbana, IL: NCTE.

Hamada, Y. (2016). Shadowing: Who benefits and how? Uncovering a booming EFL teaching technique for listening comprehension. *Language Teaching Research*, *20*(1), 35–52.

Hamrick, P., & Pandza, N. B. (2014). Competitive lexical activation during ESL spoken word recognition. *International Journal of Innovation in English Language Teaching and Research, 3*(2), 159–247.

Harklau, L., Losey, K. M., & Siegal, M. (Eds.). (1999). *Generation 1.5 meets college composition.* Mahwah, NJ: Erlbaum.

Hatch, E. (1978). Discourse analysis and second language acquisition. In E. Hatch (Ed.), *Second language acquisition: A book of readings* (pp. 401–435). Rowley, MA: Newbury House.

Hattie, J. (2009). The black box of tertiary assessment: An impending revolution. In L. H. Meyer, S. Davidson, H. Anderson, R. Fletcher, P. M. Johnston, & M. Rees (Eds.), *Tertiary assessment & higher education student outcomes: Policy, practice & research* (pp. 259–275). Wellington, NZ: Ako Aotearoa.

Hedgcock, J. S., & Ferris, D. R. (2009). *Teaching readers of English: Students, texts, and contexts.* New York, NY: Routledge.

Helder, A., van den Broek, P., Van Leijenhorst, L., & Beker, K. (2013). Sources of comprehension problems during reading. In B. Miller, L. Cutting, & P. McCardle (Eds.), *Unraveling reading comprehension: Behavioural, neuro-biological, and genetic components* (pp. 43–53). Baltimore, MD: Paul H. Brookes.

Hinds, J. (1987). Reader vs. writer responsibility: A new typology. In U. Connor & R. B. Kaplan (Eds.), *Writing across languages: Analysis of L2 text* (pp. 141–152). Reading, MA: Addison-Wesley.

Hinkel, E. (2002). *Second language writers' text: Linguistic and rhetorical features.* Mahwah, NJ: Erlbaum.

Hinkel, E. (Ed.) (2016). *Teaching English grammar to speakers of other languages.* New York, NY: Routledge.

Hirvela, A. R. (2016). *Connecting reading and writing in second language writing instruction* (2nd ed.). Ann Arbor, MI: University of Michigan Press.

Holmes, J. (2005). When small talk is a big deal: Sociolinguistic challenges in the workplace. In M. H. Long (Ed.), *Second language needs analysis* (pp. 344–372). Cambridge, UK: Cambridge University Press.

Horowitz, D. (1986). Process, not product: Less than meets the eye. *TESOL Quarterly, 20,* 141–144.

Horwitz, E. K. (2010). Foreign and second language anxiety. *Language Teaching, 43*(2), 154–167.

Howard, R. M. (2001). Collaborative pedagogy. In G. Tate, A. Rupiper, & K. Schick (Eds.), *A guide to composition pedagogies* (pp. 54–70). Oxford, UK: Oxford University Press.

Hughes, R. (2011). *Teaching and researching speaking.* (2nd ed.). Harlow, UK: Longman/Pearson.

Jenkins, J. (2002). A sociolinguistically based, empirically researched pronunciation syllabus for english as an international language. *Applied Linguistics, 23*(1), 83–103. doi:10.1093/applin/23.1.83

Jiang, X. (2012). Effects of discourse structure graphic organizers on EFL reading comprehension. *Reading in a Foreign Language, 24*(1), 84–105.

Jiang, X., & Grabe, W. (2007). Graphic organizers in reading instruction: Research findings and issues. *Reading in a Foreign Language, 19*(1), 34–55.

Jiang, X., & Grabe, W. (2009). Building reading abilities with graphic organizers. In R. Cohen (Ed.), *Explorations in second language reading* (pp. 25–42). Alexandria, VA: TESOL.

Johns, A. M. (1997). *Text, role, and context: Developing academic literacies.* New York, NY: Cambridge University Press.

Johns, A. M. (1999). Opening our doors: Applying socioliterate approaches to language minority classrooms. In L. Harklau, K. M. Losey, & M. Siegal (Eds.), *Generation 1.5 meets college composition: Issues in the teaching of writing to U.S.-educated learners of ESL* (pp. 191–209). Mahwah, NJ: Lawrence Erlbaum.

Johnson, D., & Johnson, R. (n.d.) Cooperative learning, values, and culturally plural classrooms. http://civil.utm.my/undergraduate-office/files/2014/01/Cooperative-Learning-Jonson-Jonson.pdf (retrieved September 3, 2017).

Jung, E. H. S. (2003). The role of discourse signaling cues in second language listening comprehension. *The Modern Language Journal, 87*(4), 562–577.

Kagan, S. (1994). *Cooperative learning.* San Clemente, CA: Kagan Publishing.

Kamil, M. L. (2015). Past, present, and future conditions and practices of reading. In R. J. Spiro, M. DeSchryver, M. Schira Hagerman, P. M. Morsink, & P. Thompson (Eds.), *Reading at a crossroads? Disjunctures and continuities in current conceptions and practices* (pp. 139–147). New York, NY: Routledge.

Kaplan, R. B. (1966). Cultural thought patterns in intercultural education. *Language Learning, 16,* 1–20.

Kellogg (2006). Professional writing expertize. In A. Ericsson, N. Charness, P. Feltovich, & R. Hoffman (Eds.), *The Cambridge handbook of expertise and expert performance* (pp. 389–402). New York, NY: Cambridge University Press.

Kennedy, K., & Howard, R. M. (2013). Collaborative writing. In G. Tate, A. R. Taggart, K. Schick, & H. B. Hessler (Eds.), *A guide to composition pedagogies* (2nd ed.) (pp. 37–54). Oxford, UK: Oxford University Press.

Killen, R. (2016). *Effective teaching strategies: Lessons from research and practice* (7th ed.). Melbourne: Cengage Learning Australia.

Kim, Y., & Payant, C. (2014). A pedagogical proposal for task sequencing: An exploration of task repetition and task complexity on learning opportunities. In M. Baralt, R. Gilabert, & P. Robinson (Eds.), *Task sequencing and instructed second language learning* (pp. 151-177). New York, NY: Bloomsbury.

Kintsch, W. (2012). Psychological models of reading comprehension and their implications for assessment. In J. P. Sabatini, E. A. Albro, & T. O'Reilly (Eds.), *Measuring up: Advances in how to assess reading ability* (pp. 21–38). Lanham, MD: Rowman & Littlefield Education.

Klauda, S. L., & Guthrie, J. T. (2008). Relationships of three components of reading fluency to reading comprehension. *Journal of Educational Psychology, 100,* 310–321.

Kobayashi, H., & Rinnert, C. (1992). Effects of first language on second language writing: Translation versus direct composition. *Language Learning, 42*(2), 183–215.

Koda, K. (2016). Development of word recognition in a second language. In X. Chen, V. Dronjic, & R. Helms-Park (Eds.), *Reading in a second language: Cognitive and psycholinguistic issues* (pp. 70–98). New York, NY: Routledge.

Komiyama, R. (2009). CAR: A means for motivating students to read. *English Teaching Forum, 47*(3), 32–37.

Kormos, J. (2014). *Speech production and second language acquisition.* New York, NY: Routledge.

Kormos, J., & Sáfár, A. (2008). Phonological short-term memory, working memory and foreign language performance in intensive language learning. *Bilingualism: Language and Cognition, 11*(2), 261–271.

Kramsch, C. (1993). *Context and culture in language teaching.* Oxford, UK: Oxford University Press.

Krashen, S. D. (1984). *Writing: Research, theory, and application.* Oxford, UK: Oxford University Press

Laufer, B., & Girsai, N. (2008). Form-focused instruction in second language vocabulary learning: A case for contrastive analysis and translation. *Applied Linguistics, 29*(4), 694–716. doi: 10.1093/applin/amn018.

Leki, I. (2009). Before the conversation: A sketch of some possible backgrounds, experiences, and attitudes among ESL students visiting a writing center. In S. Bruce & B. Rafoth (Eds.), *ESL writers: A guide for writing center tutors* (2nd Ed., pp. 1–17). Portsmouth, NH: Heinemann Boynton/Cook.

Leki, I., Cumming, A., & Silva, T. (2008). *A synthesis of research on second language writing in English.* New York, NY: Routledge.

Levelt, W. J. (1989). *Speaking: From intention to articulation.* Cambridge, MA: MIT Press.

Li, (n.d.). *Cooperative learning.* www.eduhk.hk/aclass/Theories/cooperative-learningcoursewriting_LBH%2024June.pdf (Retrieved September, 3, 2017).

Liu, J., & Hansen, J. G. (2002). *Peer response in second language writing classrooms.* Ann Arbor, MI: University of Michigan Press.

Liu, X., & Goh, C. (2006). Improving second language listening: Awareness and involvement. In T. S. C. Farrell (Ed.), *Language teacher research in Asia* (pp. 91–106). Alexandria, VA: TESOL.

Long, D. R. (1990). What you don't know can't help you. *Studies in Second Language Acquisition, 12*(1), 65–80.

Long, M. H. (1996). The role of the linguistics environment in second language acquisition. In W. C. Ritchie & T. K. Bhatia (Eds.), *Handbook of second language acquisition* (pp. 413–468). New York, NY: Academic Press.

Long, M. H. (2015). *Second language acquisition and task-based language teaching.* Oxford, UK: Wiley-Blackwell.

Lyster, R., & Ranta, L. (1997). Corrective feedback and learner uptake. *Studies in Second Language Acquisition, 19*(1), 37–66.

Lyster, R., Saito, K., & Sato, M. (2013). Oral corrective feedback in second language classrooms. *Language Teaching, 46*(01), 1–40. doi: 10.1017/S026 1444812000365.

Macaro, E., Graham, S., & Vanderplank, R. N. (2007). A review of listening strategies: Focus on sources of knowledge and on success. In A. Cohen & E. Macaro (Eds.), *Language learner strategies: Thirty years of research and practice* (pp. 165–185). Oxford, UK: Oxford University Press.

Macaro, E., Vanderplank, R., & Graham, S. (2005). *A systematic review of the role of prior knowledge in unidirectional listening comprehension.* Retrieved from http://eppi.ioe.ac.uk/cms/Portals/0/PDF%20reviews%20and%20summaries/ MFL_rv2.pdf?ver=2006-03-02-125000-953

McCardle, P., Chhabra, V., & Kapinus, B. (2008). *Reading research in action: A teacher's guide for student success.* Baltimore, MD: Paul H. Brookes.

McKay, S. L., & Brown, J. D. (2015). *Teaching and assessing EIL in local contexts around the world.* New York, NY: Routledge.

Mackey, A., & Philp, J. (1998). Conversational interaction and second language development: Recasts, responses, and red herrings? *The Modern Language Journal, 82*(3), 338–356.

Manchón, R. M., Roca de Larios, J., & Murphy, L. (2007). A review of writing strategies: Focus on conceptualizations and impact of first language. In A. D. Cohen & E. Macaro (Eds.), *Language learner strategies* (pp. 229–250). Oxford, UK: Oxford University Press.

Manning, S. J. (2017). Supporting state-approved materials with the values clarification task. *RELC Journal*, 0033688216684284.

Mareschal, C. (2007). *Student perceptions of a self-regulatory approach to second language listening comprehension development* (Unpublished doctoral dissertation). University of Ottawa, Canada: Ottawa University Press

Matsuda, A. (2017). *Preparing teachers to teach English as an international language* (Vol. 53). Clevedon, UK: Multilingual Matters.

Matsuda, P. K. (2003). Second language writing in the twentieth century: A situated historical perspective. In B. Kroll (Ed.), *Exploring the dynamics of second language writing* (pp. 15–34). Cambridge, UK: Cambridge University Press.

Matsuda, P. K. (2008). Myth 8: International and U.S. resident ESL writers cannot be taught in the same class. In J. M. Reid (Ed.), *Writing myths: Applying second language research to classroom teaching* (pp. 159–176). Ann Arbor, MI: University of Michigan Press.

Matsuda, P. K. (2012). Let's face it: Language issues and the writing program administrator. *Writing Program Administration, 36*, 141–163.

Mecartty, F. H. (2000). Lexical and grammatical knowledge in reading and listening comprehension by foreign language learners of Spanish. *Applied Language Learning, 11*(2), 323–348.

Mendelsohn, D. (1995). Applying learning strategies in the second/foreign language listening comprehension lesson. In D. Mendelsohn & J. Rubin (Eds.), *A guide for the teaching of second language listening* (pp. 132–150). San Diego, CA: Dominie Press.

Mendelsohn, D. J. (1994). *Learning to listening: A strategy-based approach to the second-language learner.* San Diego, CA: Dominie Press.

Mendelsohn, D. J. (1998). Teaching listening. *Annual Review of Applied Linguistics, 18*, 81–101.

Mikulecky, B., & Jeffries, L. (2007). *Advanced reading power: Extensive reading, vocabulary building, comprehension skills, reading faster.* New York, NY: Pearson.

Mills, N., Pajares, F., & Herron, C. (2006). A reevaluation of the role of anxiety: Self-efficacy, anxiety, and their relation to reading and listening proficiency. *Foreign Language Annals, 39*(2), 276–295.

Milton, J. (2012). Second language acquisition via Second Life. In C. Chapelle (Ed.), *The Encyclopedia of Applied Linguistics* (pp. 1–7). London, UK: Blackwell. doi: 10.1002/9781405198431.wbeal1318.

Mokhtari, K., & Sheorey, R. (Eds). (2008). *Reading strategies of first- and second-language learners: See how they read.* Norwood, MA: Christopher-Gordon.

Munby, J. (1978). *Communicative syllabus design: A sociolinguistic model for defining the content of purpose-specific language programmes.* Cambridge, UK: Cambridge University Press.

Murphy, L., & Roca de Larios, J. (2010). Searching for words: One strategic use of the mother tongue by advanced Spanish EFL writers. *Journal of Second Language Writing, 19*(2), 61–81.

Myles, J. (2009). Oral competency of ESL technical students in workplace internships. *TESL-EJ, 13*(1). Retrieved from https://eric.ed.gov/?id=EJ898196.

Nagy, W., & Townsend, D. (2012). Words as tools: Learning academic vocabulary as language acquisition. *Reading Research Quarterly, 47*(1), 91–108.

Nakahama, Y., Tyler, A., & van Lier, L. (2001). Negotiation of meaning in conversational and information gap activities: A comparative discourse analysis. *TESOL Quarterly, 35*(3), 377–405.

Nassaji, H., & Fotos, S. S. (2011). *Teaching grammar in second language classrooms: Integrating form-focused instruction in communicative context.* New York, NY: Routledge.

National Research Council. (2012). *Education for Life and Work: Developing Transferable Knowledge and Skills in the 21st Century.* Washington, DC: The National Academies Press.

Nation, I. S. P. (2009). *Teaching ESL/EFL reading and writing.* New York, NY: Routledge.

Nation, I. S. P. (2013). *Learning vocabulary in another language.* Cambridge, UK: Cambridge University Press.

Nation, I. S. P., & Newton, J. (2009). *Teaching ESL/EFL listening and speaking.* New York, NY: Routledge.

Newkirk, T. (1995). The writing conference as performance. *Research in the Teaching of English, 29*, 193–215.

Newton, J. (2013). Incidental vocabulary learning in classroom communication tasks. *Language Teaching Research, 17*(2), 164–187.

Newton, J. (2016). Cultivating intercultural competence in tertiary EFL programs. In *Proceedings from the 11th Conference on Crossing Borders in Language Teaching and Business Communication* (pp. 1–22). Taiwan: Chaoyang University of Technology.

Newton, J., & Kennedy, G. (1996). Effects of communication tasks on the marking of grammatical relations by second language learners. *System, 24*(3), 159–177.

Newton, J., Milligan, A., Yates, E., & Meyer, L. (2010). Global-mindedness and intercultural competence: Two responses to the challenge of educating for a linguistically and culturally diverse world. In V. Green & S. Cherrington (Eds.), *Delving into diversity: An international exploration of issues of diversity in education* (pp. 287–299). Hauppauge, NY: Nova Science Publishers.

Nguyen, T. B. T. (2013). *Tasks in action in Vietnamese EFL high school classrooms: The role of rehearsal and performance in teaching and learning through tasks.* (PhD), Victoria University of Wellington, Wellington: University Press.

O'Malley, J. M., & Chamot, A. U. (1990). *Learning strategies in second language acquisition.* Cambridge, UK: Cambridge University Press.

O'Malley, J. M., Chamot, A. U., & Küpper, L. (1989). Listening comprehension strategies in second language acquisition. *Applied Linguistics, 10*(4), 418–437.

Ortmeier-Hooper, C. (2008). English may be my second language—but I'm not "ESL." *College Composition and Communication, 59*(3), 389–419.

Oxford, R. (1990). *Language learning strategies: What every teacher should know.* Rowley, MA: Newbury House.

Pang, F., & Skehan, P. (2014). Self-reported planning behaviour and second language performance in narrative retelling. In P. Skehan (Ed.), *Processing perspectives on task performance* (pp. 95–127). Amsterdam, The Netherlands: John Benjamins.

Patthey-Chavez, G. G., & Ferris, D. R. (1997). Writing conferences and the weaving of multi-voiced texts in college composition. *Research in the Teaching of English, 31*, 51–90.

Perfetti, C., & Adlof, S. M. (2012). Reading comprehension: A conceptual framework from word meaning to text meaning. In J. P. Sabatini, E. A. Albro, & T. O'Reilly (Eds.), *Measuring up: Advances in how to assess reading ability* (pp. 3–20). Lanham, MD: Rowman & Littlefield Education.

Pica, T., Kanagy, R., & Falodun, J. (1993). Choosing and using communication tasks in language teaching and research. In G. Crookes & S. Gass (Eds.), *Tasks and language learning: Integrating theory and practice* (pp. 9–34). Philadelphia, PA: Multilingual Matters.

Pimsleur, P., Reed, D., & Stansfield, C. (2004). *Pimsleur Language Aptitude Battery*. Bethesda, MD: Second Language Testing Foundation.

Raimes, A. (1985). What unskilled ESL students do as they write: A classroom study of composing. *TESOL Quarterly, 19*, 229–258.

Raimes, A. (1991). Out of the woods: Emerging traditions in the teaching of writing. *TESOL Quarterly, 25*, 407–430.

Rayner, K., Pollatsek, A., Ashby, J., & Clifton Jr., C. (2012). *Psychology of reading* (2nd ed.). New York, NY: Psychology Press.

Reichelt, M. (2011). Foreign language writing: An overview. In T. Cimasko & M. Reichelt (Eds.), *Foreign language writing instruction: Principles & Practices* (pp. 3–21). Anderson, SC: Parlor Press.

Reznitskaya, A. (2012). Dialogic teaching: Rethinking language use during literature discussions. *The Reading Teacher, 65*(7), 446–456.

Richards, J. C. (1983). Listening comprehension: Approach, design, procedure. *TESOL Quarterly, 17*(2), 219–240.

Riddiford, N., & Newton, J. (2010). *Workplace talk in action: An ESOL resource*: School of Linguistics and Applied Language Studies, Victoria University of Wellington.

Roberge, M., Losey, K. M., & Wald, M. (Eds.) (2015). *Teaching U.S.-educated multilingual writers: Pedagogical practices from and for the classroom*. Ann Arbor, MI: University of Michigan Press.

Roberge, M. M. (2009). A teacher's perspective on Generation 1.5. In M. M. Roberge, M. Siegal, & L. Harklau (Eds.), *Generation 1.5 in college composition* (pp. 3–24). New York, NY: Routledge.

Rossiter, M. J., Derwing, T. M., Manimtim, L. G., & Thomson, R. I. (2010). Oral fluency: The neglected component in the communicative language classroom. *Canadian Modern Language Review, 66*(4), 583–606.

Rost, M. (1990). *Listening in language learning*. London, UK: Longman.

Rost, M. (2013). *Teaching and researching: Listening*. New York, NY: Routledge.

Rost, M., & Wilson, J. J. (2013). *Active listening*. Harlow, UK: Pearson Education Limited.

Rubin, J. (1994). A review of second language listening comprehension research. *The Modern Language Journal, 78*(2), 199–221.

Rumbaut, R. G. & Ima, K. (1988). *The adaptation of Southeast Asian refugee youth: A comparative study.* Final Report to the U.S. Department of Health and Human Services, Office of Refugee Resettlement, Washington, DC: U.S. Department of Health and Human Services. San Diego, CA: San Diego State University. (ERIC Document Reproduction Service ED 299 372).

Rumelhart, D. E. (1980). Schemata: the building blocks of language. In R. J. Spiro, B. Bruce, & W. Brewer (Eds.), *Theoretical issues in reading comprehension* (pp. 33–58). Hillsdale, NJ: Erlbaum.

Savage, A. (2010). Chapter 5: An ocean of plastic. In *Read this! 3: Fascinating stories from the content areas* (pp. 33–39). New York, NY: Cambridge University Press.

Schmitt, N., Jiang, X., & Grabe, W. (2011). The percentage of words known in a text and reading comprehension. *Modern Language Journal, 95*(1), 26–43.

Schoonen, R., Hulstijn, J., & Bossers, B. (1998). Metacognitive and language-specific knowledge in native and foreign language reading comprehension: An empirical study among Dutch students in grades 6, 8 and 10. *Language Learning, 48*(1), 71–106.

Seidenberg, M. (2017). *Reading at the speed of sight.* New York, NY: Basic Books.

Sheerin, S. (1987). Listening comprehension: Teaching or testing? *ELT Journal, 41*(2), 126–131.

Silva, T. (1990). Second language composition instruction: Developments, issues, and directions in ESL. In B. Kroll (Ed.), *Second language writing: Research insights for the classroom* (pp. 11–23). Cambridge, UK: Cambridge University Press.

Silva, T. (1993). Toward an understanding of the distinct nature of L2 writing: The ESL research and its implications. *TESOL Quarterly, 27*, 657–677.

Skehan, P. (2015). Limited attention capacity and cognition: Two hypotheses regarding second language performance on tasks. In M. Bygate (Ed.), *Domains and directions in the development of TBLT: A decade of plenaries from the international conference* (pp. 123–156). Amsterdam, the Netherlands: John Benjamins.

Skehan, P., Xiaoyue, B., Qian, L., & Wang, Z. (2012). The task is not enough: Processing approaches to task-based performance. *Language Teaching Research, 16*(2), 170–187.

Slavin, R. (2013).Coopertaive learning and achievement: Theory and research. In W. Reynolds, G. Miller, & I. Weiner (Eds.), *Handbok of psychology* (2nd ed., Vol. 7, pp. 199–212). Hoboken, NJ: Wiley.

Slavin, R. (2014). Cooperative learning and academic achievement: Why does groupwork work? *Anales de psicologia, 30*(3), 785–791. http://revistas.um.es/analesps/article/view/analesps.30.3.201201/164871.

Snow, M. A., & Brinton, D. M. (Eds.). (2017). *The content-based classroom: New perspectives on integrating language and content* (2nd ed.). Ann Arbor, MI: University of Michigan Press.

Sommers, N. (1982). Responding to student writing. *College Composition and Communication, 33*, 148–156.

Spack, R. (1988). Initiating ESL students into the academic discourse community: How far should we go? *TESOL Quarterly, 22*(1), 29–51.

Stæhr, L. S. (2009). Vocabulary knowledge and advanced listening comprehension in English as a foreign language. *Studies in Second Language Acquisition, 31*(4), 577–607.

Stoller, F. L. (2012). Developing word and phrase recognition exercises. In R. R. Day (Ed.), *New ways in teaching reading* (revised version, pp. 254–257). Alexandria, VA: TESOL.

Stoller, F. L., & Robinson, M. S. (2016). Assisting ESP students in reading and writing disciplinary genres. In N. W. Evans, N. J. Anderson, & W. G. Eggington (Eds.), *ESL readers and writers in higher education: Understanding challenges, providing support* (pp. 164 –179). New York, NY: Routledge.

Stoller, F. L., Anderson, N., Grabe, W., & Komiyama, R. (2013). Instructional enhancements to improve students' reading abilities. *English Teaching Forum*, *51*(1), 2–11, 33.

Storch, N. (2008). Metatalk in a pair work activity: Level of engagement and implications for language development. *Language Awareness*, *17*(2), 95–114. doi: 10.1177/1362168810375362.

Swain, M. (1985). Communicative competence: Some roles of comprehensible input and comprehensible output in its development. In S. Gass & C. Madden (Eds.), *Input in second language acquisition* (pp. 165–179). Rowley, MA: Newbury House.

Swain, M., & Lapkin, S. (1995). Problems in output and the cognitive processes they generate: A step towards second language learning. *Applied Linguistics*, *16*(3), 371–391. doi: 10.1093/applin/16.3.371.

Swales, J. M. (1990). *Genre analysis: English in academic and research settings.* Cambridge, UK: Cambridge University Press.

Swan, E. A. (2003) *Concept-oriented reading instruction: Engaging classrooms, lifelong learners.* New York, NY: Guilford Press.

Taguchi, N. (2008). The effect of working memory, semantic access, and listening abilities on the comprehension of conversational implicatures in L2 English. *Pragmatics & Cognition*, *16*(3), 517–539.

Tannen, D. (2007). *Talking voices: Repetition, dialogue, and imagery in conversational discourse* (Vol. 26). Cambridge, UK: Cambridge University Press.

Tardy, C. M. (2009). *Building genre knowledge.* West Lafayette, IN: Parlor Press.

Tate, G., Taggart, A. R., Schick, K., & Hessler, H. B. (Eds.) (2013). *A guide to composition pedagogies* (2nd ed.). Oxford, UK: Oxford University Press.

Thaiss, C., Bräuer, G., Carlino, P., Ganobcsik-Williams, L, & Sinha, A. (Eds.) (2012). *Writing programs worldwide: Profiles of academic writing in many places.* Fort Collins, CO: The WAC Clearinghouse and Parlor Press.

Tsao, F. M., Liu, H. M., & Kuhl, P. K. (2004). Speech perception in infancy predicts language development in the second year of life: A longitudinal study. *Child development*, *75*(4), 1067–1084.

Tsui, A. B. M., & Fullilove, J. (1998). Bottom-up or top-down processing as a discriminator of L2 listening performance. *Applied Linguistics*, *19*(4), 432–451.

Underwood, M. (1989). *Teaching listening.* Harlow, UK: Longman.

Ur, P. (1984). *Teaching listening comprehension.* New York, NY: Cambridge University Press.

Van der Branden, K., Bygate, M., & Norris, J. M. (2009). *Task-based language teaching: a reader.* Amsterdam, The Netherlands: John Benjamins.

van den Broek, P. (2012). Individual and developmental differences in reading comprehension: Assessing cognitive processes and outcomes. In J. Sabatini, E. Albro, & T. O'Reilly (Eds.), *Measuring up: Advances in how to assess reading ability* (pp. 39–58). New York, NY: Rowman & Littlefield Education.

van den Broek, P., & Kendeou, P. (2015). Building coherence in web-based and other non-traditional reading environments: Cognitive opportunities and challenges. In R. J. Spiro, M. DeSchryver, M. Schira Hagerman, P. M. Morsink, & P. Thompson (Eds.), *Reading at a crossroads? Disjunctures and continuities in current conceptions and practices* (pp. 104–114). New York, NY: Routledge.

van Zeeland, H., & Schmitt, N. (2013). Incidental vocabulary acquisition through L2 listening: A dimensions approach. *System, 41*(3), 609–624.

Vandergrift, L. (2003a). From prediction through reflection: Guiding students through the process of L2 listening. *Canadian Modern Language Review, 59*(3), 425–440.

Vandergrift, L. (2003b). Orchestrating strategy use: Toward a model of the skilled second language listener. *Language Learning, 53*(3), 463–496.

Vandergrift, L. (2004). Listening to learn or learning to listen? *Annual Review of Applied Linguistics, 24*, 3–25.

Vandergrift, L. (2005). Relationships among motivation orientations, metacognitive awareness and proficiency in L2 listening. *Applied Linguistics, 26*(1), 70–89.

Vandergrift, L. (2006). Second language listening: Listening ability or language proficiency? *The Modern Language Journal, 90*(1), 6–18.

Vandergrift, L. (2007). Recent developments in second and foreign language listening comprehension research. *Language Teaching, 40*(3), 191–210.

Vandergrift, L., & Baker, S. (2015). Learner variables in second language listening comprehension: An exploratory path analysis. *Language Learning, 65*(2), 390–416.

Vandergrift, L., & Baker, S. C. (accepted). Learner variables important for success in L2 listening comprehension in French immersion classrooms. *Canadian Modern Language Review.*

Vandergrift, L., & Goh, C. (2012). *Teaching and learning second language listening: Metacognition in action.* New York, NY: Routledge.

Vandergrift, L., & Tafaghodtari, M. H. (2010). Teaching L2 learners how to listen does make a difference: An empirical study. *Language Learning, 60*(2), 470–497.

Vandergrift, L., Goh, C. C. M., Mareschal, C. J., & Tafaghodtari, M. H. (2006). The metacognitive awareness listening questionnaire: Development and validation. *Language Learning, 56*(3), 431–462.

Vogely, A. (1999). Addressing listening comprehension anxiety. In D. J. Yong (Ed.), *Affect in foreign language and second language learning: A practical guide to creating a low-anxiety classroom atmosphere* (pp. 106–123). Boston, MA: McGraw Hill.

Voogt, J., Erstad, O., Dede, C., & Mishra, P. (2013). Challenges to learning and schooling in the digital networked world of the 21st century. *Journal of Computer Assisted Learning, 29*(5), 403–413.

Wang, L. (2003). Switching to first language among writers with differing second-language proficiency. *Journal of Second Language Writing, 12*(4), 347–375.

Wang, W., & Wen, Q. (2002). L1 use in the L2 composing process: An exploratory study of 16 Chinese EFL writers. *Journal of Second Language Writing, 11*, 225–246.

Wenden, A. (1998). Metacognitive knowledge and language learning. *Applied Linguistics, 19*(4), 515–537.

Wiliam, D. (2011). *Embedded formative assessment*. Bloomington, IN: Solution Tree Press.

Wiliam, D., & Leahy, S. (2015). *Embedding formative assessment: Practical techniques for K–12 classrooms*. West Palm Beach, FL: Learning Sciences International.

Willis, D., & Willis, J. (2007). *Doing task-based teaching* (Vol. Oxford handbooks for language teachers). Oxford, UK: Oxford University Press.

Willis, J. (1996). *A framework for task-based learning*. Harlow, UK: Longman.

Wilson, I., Kaneko, E., Lyddon, P., Okamoto, K., & Ginsburg, J. (2011, August). *Nonsense-syllable sound discrimination ability correlates with second language (L2) proficiency*. Paper presented at the 17th International Congress of Phonetic Sciences (ICPhS XVII), Hong Kong. Retrieved from http://web-ext.u-aizu.ac.jp/~wilson/WilsonEtAl2011ICPhS.pdf.

Wilson, M. (2003). Discovery listening—improving perceptual processing. *ELT Journal, 57*(4), 335–343.

Wong, W., & VanPatten, B. (2003). The evidence is IN: Drills are OUT. *Foreign Language Annals, 36*(3), 403–423.

Wood, D. (2009). Preparing ESP learners for workplace placement. *ELT Journal, 63*(4), 323–331. doi: 10.1093/elt/ccp005.

Yancey, K. B., Robertson, L., & Tacsak, K. (Eds.) (2014). *Writing across contexts: Transfer, composition, and cultures of writing*. Logan, UT: Utah State University Press.

Young, L. (1994). University lectures—macro-structure and micro-features. In J. Flowerdew (Ed.), *Academic listening: Research perspectives* (pp. 159–176). Cambridge, UK: Cambridge University Press.

Zamel, V. (1982). Writing: The process of discovering meaning. *TESOL Quarterly, 16*, 195–209.

Zamel, V. (1985). Responding to student writing. *TESOL Quarterly, 19*, 79–102.

Zeng, Y. (2012). *Metacognition and self-regulated learning (SRL) for Chinese EFL listening development* (Unpublished doctoral dissertation). National Institute of Education, Nanyang Technological University, Singapore: University Press.

Zeng, Y. (2014). Investigating the effects of metacognitive instruction on Chinese EFL learners' listening performance. *International Journal of Innovation in English Language Teaching and Research, 3*(2), 139.

Zeng, Y., & Goh, C. C. M. (2017, in-press). A self-regulated learning approach to extensive listening and its impact on listening achievement and metacognition awareness. *Studies in Second Language Learning and Teaching, 7*(2).

Zhang, S. (1995). Reexamining the affective advantage of peer feedback in the ESL writing class. *Journal of Second Language Writing, 4*, 209–222.

Zimmerman, C. B. (2009). *Word knowledge: A vocabulary teacher's handbook*. New York, NY: Oxford University Press.

Index

writing in a second language 75–87; contexts and characteristics of L2 writing/writers 81–86; differences between L2 and L1 writing 76–77; experiences/backgrounds of L2 writers 78–80; foreign language (FL) contexts 81; language acquisition of L2 writers 80; language knowledge of L2 writers 77–78; role of the L1 when writing in L2 78; second language (SL) contexts 81; subgroup characteristics 84; summary 86–87
writing systems, differences across 77–78

Xiaoyue, B. 197

Young, L. 136

Zhang, C. 38